KNOW YOUR BROTHER

Other books in the Creative Machine Arts Series, available from Chilton:

Claire Shaeffer's Fabric Sewing Guide
The Complete Book of Machine Embroidery, by Robbie and Tony Fanning
Creative Nurseries Illustrated, by Debra Terry and Juli Plooster
Creative Serging Illustrated, by Pati Palmer, Gail Brown and Sue Green
The Expectant Mother's Wardrobe Planner, by Rebecca Dumlao
The Fabric Lover's Scrapbook, by Margaret Dittman
Friendship Quilts by Hand and Machine, by Carolyn Vosburg Hall
Innovative Serging and Innovative Sewing, by Gail Brown and Tammy Young
Know Your Bernina, 2nd ed., by Jackie Dodson
Know Your Brother, by Jackie Dodson with Jane Warnick
Know Your Elna, by Jackie Dodson with Carol Ahles
Know Your New Home, by Jackie Dodson with Audrey Griese
Know Your Pfaff, by Jackie Dodson with Audrey Griese
Know Your Sewing Machine, by Jackie Dodson
Know Your Simplicity, by Jackie Dodson with Jane Warnick
Know Your Singer, by Jackie Dodson
Know Your Viking, by Jackie Dodson with Jan Saunders
Know Your White, by Jackie Dodson with Jan Saunders
Owner's Guide to Sewing Machines, Sergers, and Knitting Machines, by Gale Grigg Hazen
Petite Pizzazz, by Barb Griffin
Sew, Serge, Press, by Jan Saunders
Sewing and Collecting Vintage Fashions, by Eileen MacIntosh

KNOW YOUR BROTHER

JACKIE DODSON
with *Jane Warnick*

Creative Machine Arts Series
CHILTON BOOK COMPANY
RADNOR, PENNSYLVANIA

Copyright © 1990 by Jackie Dodson and Jane Warnick
All Rights Reserved

Published in Radnor, Pennsylvania 19089, by Chilton Book Company

No part of this book may be reproduced, transmitted or stored
in any form or by any means, electronic or mechanical,
without prior written permission from the publisher

Designed by William E. Lickfield
Manufactured in the United States of America

Library of Congress Cataloging in Publication Data
  Know your Brother/Jackie Dodson with Jane Warnick
  p.cm. — (Creative machine arts series)
  Includes bibliographical references
  Includes index.
  ISBN 0-8019-7987-0
  1. Machine sewing. 2. Sewing machines. I. Warnick, Jane.
II. Title. III. Series.
TT713.D6314 1990
646.2'044 — 89-42848

2 3 4 5 6 7 8 9 0   9 8 7 6 5 4 3 2 1

Contents

Foreword ix   **Preface** xi   **Acknowledgments** xii

Chapter 1 Getting Started   1
     Love your Brother   3
     Presser feet   4
     Accessories   6
     Supplies   8
     Helpful hints for sewing   13

Chapter 2 Adding Stitches to Your Fabric   14
     Lesson 1. Using built-in stitches   14
     Lesson 2. Using free machining: darning, whipping, feather stitching   16
         Project: Buttons and Pendants   21

Chapter 3 Adding Texture to Your Fabric   26
     Lesson 3. Building up sewing stitches   26
     Lesson 4. Applying thick threads from the top and bobbin   31
         Applying thick thread through the needle   31
         Couching thread down on top of fabric   31
             Project: Greeting Card   31
         Attaching cord with the cording foot   35
         Using thick thread in the bobbin   35
             Project: Tote Bag Square (Cabling)   38
     Lesson 5. Fringing yarn and fabric   40
         Project: Fringed Denim Rug   41
     Lesson 6. Adding buttons, beads, shisha   44
         Attaching buttons   44
         Attaching beads and baubles   44
         Attaching shisha mirrors   47
             Project: Bird Collage   49
     Lesson 7. Smocking and gathering   53
         Smocking   53
             Simple gathered smocking   53
             Smocking with cordonnet   53
             Embroidering with thick thread in the bobbin   54
             Smocking with elastic   55
         Gathering   55
             Using cord   55

                    Using elastic   56
                    Using a gathering foot   56
          Lesson 8. Pulling threads together   57

Chapter 4   Adding Fabric to Fabric: Appliqué   **59**
          Lesson 9. Methods of applying appliqués   59
          Lesson 10. Appliquéing with feed dogs up   62
                    Satin stitches three ways   62
                              Standard method   62
                              Stained-glass method   62
                              Reverse appliqué   62
                                        Project: Tote Bag Square (Modified Reverse Appliqué)   63
                    Blind hemming   63
                    Straight stitching   65
                              Project: Tote Bag Square (Edge-Stitch Appliqué)   65
                              Project: Tote Bag Square (Straight Stitch)   65
                    Cording edges   67
          Lesson 11. Appliquéing with feed dogs lowered   69
                    Blurring   69
                              Project: Flower of Sheers and Overlays   69
                    Scribbling   71
                    Stitching Carrickmacross   73
                              Project: Carrickmacross Doily   73
                    Layering transparent fabrics   75
                              Project: Shadow Work Picture   75
                              Project: Stitching Three-dimensional Appliqués   78
                    Helpful hints for appliqué   79

Chapter 5   Stitching Across Open Spaces   **81**
          Lesson 12. Cutwork and eyelets   81
                    Cutwork   81
                              Project: Cutwork Needlecase   82
                    Eyelets   84
          Lesson 13. Free-machined needlelace   84
                              Project: Earrings   86
          Lesson 14. Battenberg lace   90
                              Project: Bird-Shaped Lace   90
          Lesson 15. Hemstitching   94
                              Project: Infant's Bonnet   94
          Lesson 16. Stitching in rings   99
                              Project: Christmas Ornaments   99
          Lesson 17. Making Alençon lace   100
                              Project: Alençon Pincushion   101

Chapter 6   Drawing Threads Out of Your Fabric   **104**
          Lesson 18. Needleweaving   104
                              Project: Openwork on Sleeves   104

Chapter 7 Layering Fabrics: Quilting   **107**
    Lesson 19. Quilting with feed dogs up 107
            Project: Tote Bag Square (Appliqué and Quilting) 108
    Lesson 20. Quilting with feed dogs lowered 110
    Lesson 21. Trapunto 111
    Lesson 22. Italian cording 111
            Project: Tote Bag Square (Italian Cording) 111

Chapter 8 Adding Interesting Seams to Your Fabric   **114**
    Lesson 23. Heirloom sewing by machine 114
        Sewing French seams 115
        Stitching rolled and whipped edges 115
        Gathering rolled and whipped edges 117
        Applying insertion 117
        Joining scalloped lace 117
        Using entredeux 118
        Gathering lace edging 119
        Attaching straight-edged lace to rolled and whipped edges 119
        Attaching entredeux to lace insertion 119
        Sewing lace to lace 120
        Fagoting 120
            Project: Wedding Handkerchief 121
    Lesson 24. Seaming with feed dogs up and lowered 124
        Sewing a fake lapped hem 124
        Seaming with the side cutter 125
        Stitching over thread on knits 125
        Imitating hand-piecing on quilts 126
        English piecing by machine 126
        Joining veiling with a scallop stitch 127
        Using built-in stitches 127
        Creating seams with feed dogs lowered 127

Chapter 9 Adding Hems and Edges   **129**
    Lesson 25. Turning hems once 129
        Using double needles on knits 129
        Hemming with a double needle on sheers 130
        Hemming with built-in stitches on front 130
        Quilting a hem 130
    Lesson 26. Blind hemming 131
    Lesson 27. Sewing narrow hems 132
        Straight stitching 132
        Sewing on lace 133
        Attaching scalloped lace 134
        Stitching shell edging 134
        Roll and shell hemming 134
    Lesson 28. Using bias tape 135
    Lesson 29. Zigzagging a narrow edge 136

Lesson 30. Covering wire for shaped edges   136
Lesson 31. Cording edges   137
    Covering cords   137
    Creating crocheted edges   139
    Reshaping knits with elastic   139
Lesson 32. Making thread fringe   139
Lesson 33. Piping edges   141
Lesson 34. Topstitching   141

Chapter 10 Machine Tricks: Adding Threads to Threads   142

Lesson 35. Making cord   142
    Twisting monk's cord   142
    Stitching belt and button loops   144
Lesson 36. Making tassels   144
      Project: Tassel Collar   144
      Project: Covered Wire Tassel   146
      Project: Doll Tassel   147
      Project: Making Two Tassel Tops by Machine   147

Chapter 11 Decorative Stitches   150

    Learning about line   151
      Project: Tote Bag Square   154
Lesson 37. Highlighting structural details   156
      Project: Shadow Appliqué Collar   157
      Project: Belt Ornament   164
Lesson 38. Coordinating separate elements   167
      Project: Scarf   170
      Project: Shoe Ornament   173
Lesson 39. Guiding the eye   175
      Project: Purse   175

Chapter 12 Making the Tote Bag   181

Finishing the squares   181
Tote bag construction   182
Afterword   187

A Brief History of Brother International   188

Sources of Supply   190   Bibliography   194   Index   195

Foreword

In 1987 we published a book by Jackie Dodson called Know Your Bernina. *Jackie and I had met more than ten years ago by accident on a tour bus in Chicago. Since then she has showered me with wacky, inspiring letters. This is a woman who is brimming with laughter and ideas, sharing both freely. Most of the letters arrived with swatches of machine-embroidered fabric pinned to them. "Have you tried this?" she'd ask, again and again.*

When it came time to revise my machine-embroidery book, I knew who to ask for help as a designer and critic: Jackie. Next I asked her to write a book about her teaching methods; the result was the Bernina book.

Chilton and I knew Know Your Bernina *was a good book, but even we were surprised at the enthusiastic response: for example, we had to reprint it four times in the first six months. We also received letters and calls from storeowners and home sewers saying, "I bought the book, even though I don't have a Bernina—but I wish you'd publish one for my brand."*

So we did. In Spring 1988, we published a generic version called Know Your Sewing Machine. *Having taught on all major brands, Jackie adapted her techniques to include all of them. She kept the same lesson format, but changed all the tote-bag squares and some of the projects, added a chapter on using decorative stitches, and showed some of the projects on color pages, along with inspiring artists' work.*

But as the second book developed, Jackie and I realized we could barely touch on the unique features of each brand. Like cars or computers, sewing machines are not all alike. They each have special features, stitches, feet, capabilities: that's why Jackie and I own so many machines. (We've been known to buy a brand-new computer sewing-machine that does everything but your income taxes . . . and to hold on to four old machines "because I love the feather stitch on this one and the buttonhole on this one and I'm keeping this one in case my daughter wants it and this one in case all the others fail.")

So Know Your Brother *was born and I knew exactly who to ask to be co-author. I've known Jane Warnick for about 15 years and have admired her creativity for as long. She has one of the most playful minds I know. She's also* been a staunch Brother fan for years. Whenever a new model of a pricey European brand came out, touting a special feature, she'd say "Oh, my Brother could do that years ago." Obviously, Jane was the perfect co-author for this book.

Jane stitched her way through the entire manuscript, making changes appropriate to Brother machines. Again, Jackie changed all the tote-bag squares and many of the project designs. Then Jane wrote two special chapters—Getting Started" (Chapter 1) and "Using Decorative Stitches" (Chapter 11). The latter shows you how to guide the eye with your use of decorative stitches, a principle very important to embellishing your clothing.

We are also publishing versions for other brands—Elna, New Home, Pfaff, Singer, Brother, Necchi and a revised Bernina book, so far—in which knowledgeable co-authors have adapted the book to their brand and have contributed a unique chapter on decorative stitches. All of the Chapter 11s are completely different, as are all the tote-bag squares, so even if you don't own that brand, be sure to read the book. Your head will be filled with enough ideas to make clever gifts, garments, and accessories for many years to come.

And best of all, after stitching your way through the book(s), you will truly know your sewing machine.

Robbie Fanning

Series Editor, Creative Machine Arts, and co-author
The Complete Book of Machine Embroidery

Are you interested in a quarterly magazine about creative uses of the sewing machine? Robbie Fanning and Jackie Dodson are planning to start one. For more information, write:

The Creative Machine
PO Box 2634
Menlo Park, CA 94026

Preface

When our children were small, we took long car trips. I remember one that took longer than planned. We all grumbled about being lost, but one of our boys said, "It's just one of Dad's long-cuts."

We loved that new word, so we came up with dictionary meanings.

Long-cut (noun): When it takes longer, but Dad convinces everyone he wanted it that way. A "little something extra." An adventure. An educational side-trip. You are happier when you finally reach your destination. And so on.

What does this have to do with the sewing machine? This book contains long-cuts, those adventurous techniques that help you and your sewing machine create something special, something out of the ordinary.

Most of us learned basic techniques of sewing when we bought our machines—how to thread it, wind a bobbin, make a buttonhole, sew a straight seam. We were shown each presser foot and how to use it. . . and, I'll bet, except for the zipper and buttonhole feet, you haven't looked at those other feet again.

But there's so much more to learn. Join me on an educational side-trip. By the time you're done with this book, you'll truly know your machine.

Let's begin by exploring how we can change a piece of fabric: we can add texture to it, appliqué it, quilt it, stitch across holes in it, draw thread out of it, gather it up and decorate it. We can stitch in space with our sewing machines, make cording–but, more importantly, once we understand the machine, it makes all our stitching easier.

As we explore all these effects, which are presented in 39 lessons, we'll make small samples for a notebook; make finished 6" squares to fit on a totebag, displaying what we've learned; and make 23 other projects. In the process of stitching the samples and projects in the book, you'll take an educational side-trip as well. You'll learn to adjust and manipulate your sewing machine until you can use it to its full potential.

This workbook of ideas does not take the place of your basic manuals. Instead, it is to be used as a reinforcement and supplement to what you already know. By working through the lessons, you will come to know your machine better.

Yes, there is much more to sewing than straight stitching. And wouldn't you rather go that long-cut route–to make your stitching more interesting and original?

In my classes I often hear this progression: "I can't do that" to "Can I really do that?" to "I can do that!" I hope this book is the next best thing to having me prompting, prodding, patting you on the back in person.

Jackie Dodson
LaGrange Park, Illinois

Acknowledgments

Thank You:

To Brother International Corporation—and Donna Lombardo-Duffy in particular—for help throughout our writing this book.

To Caryl Rae Hancock, Nora Lou Kampe, Gail Kibiger, Pat Pasquini and Marcia Strickland for sharing ideas; Ladi Tisol who helped me before I had to ask; and Marilyn Tisol, critic, sounding-board, and special friend.

To Chuck, who took photos, and to the rest of my family, who accept chaos as normal and never complain.

To Robbie Fanning, for her optimism, encouragement, and endless support.

And especially to Jane Warnick. Jane is an incredible source of information on all the needle arts and loves sharing her own original, creative ideas. Added to that, for years she's told me how she loves her Brother sewing machine. You'll find this winning combination, along with her sense of fun, is evident throughout the book.

JD

Thank You:

To Brother International Corporation for its cooperation and for its commitment to building superior sewing machines at affordable prices.

To Donna Lombardo-Duffy of Brother International for supplying information whenever I asked.

To Robbie Fanning, friend and patient editor, whose faith in me has always been a source of wonder, for providing yet another opportunity to share my enthusiasm for the sewing machine.

To Jackie Dodson, who started it all, for her inspiration, expertise, designs, and good humor to the end.

To the late Jerry Zarbaugh for understanding and sharing my love of process rather than product.

And most especially to my children Shannon, Philip, Alyson and Mary for cheerfully growing up with the disorder, dust, and deadlines; for wearing my creations even when they didn't want to; and for their constant inspiration and support.

JW

KNOW YOUR BROTHER

CHAPTER 1

Getting Started

by JANE WARNICK

This book is organized by the changes you can make to a piece of fabric—add stitches, add texture, subtract threads, and so on. Following this introductory chapter, each chapter consists of several lessons, and some projects. Each lesson asks you to stitch up practice samples for a notebook or for finished projects. The largest project in the book is the tote bag (directions for making it are in Chapter 12). It was designed to show off interchangeable decorative squares, which you'll make as you proceed through the lessons.

For the practice samples, you will want to set up a three-ring notebook—the kind with the largest rings—to keep track of your stitching (Fig. 1.1). I created the notebook form shown in Fig. 1.2 that I use to record all the machine settings, thread used, feet, any pertinent notes, etc. I do my samples in a 4″ (10.2cm) spring hoop, trim them to fit the open area and stitch them in place. I put the completed forms in plastic protectors, but you could punch holes in them and put them directly into your notebook. Copy my form or make up one of

Fig. 1.1 A reference notebook, open to a page of stitch samples. Notations on the stitchery will help you reset the machine.

BROTHER SEWING MACHINE MODEL 870

STITCH/TECHNIQUE

THREAD: Top _____   STITCH: Straight   Zigzag
          Bobbin _____   Pattern No. _____

LENGTH: _____   WIDTH: _____

GROUND FABRIC: _____   STABILIZER: _____

ACCESSORIES: _____

NEEDLE: _____   Worked from Right/Wrong Side

TENSION: Top _____   FEED DOGS: Up   Down
           Bobbin   Loose   Tight   Normal   Bypass

FOOT: A   G   I   J   L   M   N   Free in Frame   Other _____

NOTES:
_____
_____
_____

From *Know Your Brother,* © 1988 Jane Warnick

Fig. 1.2 A notebook form for recording settings and mounting samples.

your own and have them printed on card stock paper at your local copy store.

Or buy plastic pockets and blank notebook paper (both available at office supply stores). Write the settings you've used directly on the stitched samples and slip them into the plastic pockets for future reference.

Clip pictures from magazines that trigger ideas. Ask yourself: Could I get that effect if I loosened the bobbin? Which presser foot would I use for that? Which thread would produce loops like that? Write notes to yourself with ideas to try and add these to the notebook along with the magazine pictures.

Love your Brother

When I finished high school, my father asked me what I wanted for a graduation present. I never hesitated a moment. "My very own zigzag sewing machine." Off to college, I could imagine leaving my family, my friends, my room, and my mother's car, but I could not conceive of being without a sewing machine. My father obliged, and I got my very first, very own machine. During the ensuing years I've had more than a few sewing machines of several different brands, but my Brother sewing machines are my favorites.

I bought my first Brother seven years ago at our county fair, a Pacesetter, model XL5001. I bought it for two reasons—it had a 7mm width zigzag stitch and it had the right price. I had other brands of sewing machines at home—even a commercial one that sewed 6,000 stitches a minute—but I wanted that wide zigzag.

At first I used the Pacesetter mostly for fill-in work and satin stitch blocks. Then one day I decided to explore it. I discovered a feature I've never seen on another machine and that I still value today: a portion of the needle plate moves and there is a *single* hole for straight stitching rather than the elliptical hole found on other zigzag machines. When I change back to zigzag, the plate on the Brother automatically moves so that I don't break a needle.

Of course, you can purchase a single-hole plate for most machines, but you must first physically remove the zigzag plate and replace it with the other one. If you forget you have the single-hole plate on the machine, your needle will immediately break when you switch to any other stitch.

Not only that, but the Pacesetter has a chain stitch, something I only had once before on an old Singer Touch-and-Sew. No, I don't use it very much, but it's nice to know it's there.

I started using the machine more and more for my everyday work, and my other machines less and less.

The next year I again stopped at the Brother booth at the fair and took a closer look at the Brother Galaxie. Within minutes I had convinced myself that I needed the programming capability and the alphabet to write out wondrous quotes and profound thoughts. I quickly decided that I would welcome a machine that talks to me when I mess up ("Please lower presser foot lever") but one that doesn't call me "dummy." My banker greatly appreciated the fact that the price did not rival the national debt. And so I made a deal and brought home my second Brother sewing machine. When I moved several years later and knew that I wouldn't have room for all my machines, I got rid of most of them, but I kept the two Brothers.

I love many features on the Galaxie: my rayon threads feed without breaking or needing special holders; the speed can be set anywhere from fast to slow, from turtle to rabbit, with all the other animals in between; my fifty-year-plus eyes appreciate the automatic needle threader. The Galaxie makes four different kinds of one-step buttonholes with an attachment that holds the button and makes the proper size buttonhole as many times as necessary. I can use a foot controller or I can disconnect it and start and stop the machine with a button positioned right above the presser foot (great for long lines of decorative stitching or when I want to twist a monk's cord that's 10' long). I can direct the machine to stop with the needle *either* up or down. I can program my own stitches. I can bypass the bobbin tension and fill the bobbin with thick threads, yarn and ribbons. When I do this, the bobbin tension is really loose (which it isn't on all makes of machines) — necessary for making craters or sewing shisha directly to the cloth. I can put on the side-cutter and beautifully finish seams and samples. I can sew through many layers of denim or on one layer of the finest silk.

I also love the Brother 950. For several hundred dollars, I have a machine with three needle positions, built-in stretch stitches, satin stitches, free machine embroidery, a one-step buttonhole, fagoting stitch, several decorative stitches, and two blind stitch hems. It also has an electronic display that provides instructions and signals errors. I think it's important to have versatile, trustworthy sewing machines that most people can afford without hocking the family jewels.

Today, Brother International is selling several models at discount stores, on teleshopping channels, and through some department stores, such as Macy's New York. And if I have any questions, all I have to do is call their hotline, 1-800-284-HELP.

What else do I love about my Brothers? They have always done what I asked of them, despite having survived a year in a storage shed in California, the ubiquitous dust in my studio, and a 2500-mile move across country. Through all the use and abuse, they keep right on ticking.

So let's begin. Get out the dusty box of attachments and presser feet that came with your machine, as well as the basic manual of instructions. If you can't find the manual, call 1-800-284-HELP and arrange to purchase another.

While Brother International is selling only two machines under its own name at the present time — the 950 and the 940 — some sewing/vacuum stores still have the computerized model, the Galaxie, for sale. And if you're ever at any of the California county fairs, look for my old friend. He always has some on hand.

No matter which Brother you have, with its zigzag and blind-hem stitches you can stitch up the projects and complete the lessons in this book, except for some in Chapter 11. Your machine includes many other built-in stitches that are not neglected here either.

Presser feet

But built-in stitches are only part of this book. Presser feet are also a part of it — an important part. When you purchased your machine, you probably asked what built-in stitches were included, but didn't think of asking about the presser feet. Most sewers don't look beyond the standard zigzag, zipper, and buttonhole feet, even though presser feet expand the capabilities of the machine.

Your Brother machine has a low-shank, side-screw fitting for the presser feet. It also has a snap-on presser foot holder, unless it is a very old machine. While Brother only makes available the presser feet which come with the machine (even if you call their HELP line), you are in no way limited to these.

I have found that snap-on New Home feet work very well on the Galaxie and the Pacesetter, which both have the 7mm zigzag. You must be careful when working a wide zigzag with these, in case the opening is not large enough. I bought an Elna snap-on cording foot, and while it snapped on both the Galaxie and the 950 without a problem, the hole for the needle was too close to the shank to work. My old Viking feet would not snap on. When you go presser foot shopping, take along your presser-foot holder and foot J (zigzag). Make sure that the new feet will snap on and that the openings match. If you have the 940/950 machine, you will definitely need a transparent zigzag embroidery foot.

Check the Sources of Supply at the end of the book for mail-order catalogues where you can purchase generic presser feet—available for almost every machine. I've also discovered that sewing machine repairmen and some mail-order houses will modify presser feet to fit your machine if you can't find exactly what you need.

Take out your manual and your presser feet and match each foot to its picture. Turn each over and look at the bottom: it's the most important part. If it's the buttonhole foot A, it will be long and have two deep grooves to keep the fabric moving freely and in line as the beads of satin stitches are being stitched. The movable area at the back is where the button is placed so that all buttonholes will fit the button and be the same size. I use this foot without a button to make slightly elongated eyelets. The foot is also used to make bar-tacks.

The transparent zigzag foot N has a wide groove cut out and is flared in front to allow the fabric not only to feed more freely as the decorative stitches are sewn in place, but to allow corners to be easily turned. The front opening is wide and transparent to allow you to see the edge at all times. The standard all-purpose foot J (zigzag) is solid on the bottom to allow the foot to hold the fabric securely against the feed dogs. The overlock stitch foot G has a narrow metal bar across the opening that keeps the fabric from curling under and allows the thread to lay gently over the edge without pulling. The blind-stitch foot L has an adjusting screw which allows you to set the foot guide so the needle will barely bite the fold, thereby showing almost no thread on the front. This foot also is great as an edge guide for topstitching. The zipper foot I use is adjustable so that you can sew on both sides of the zipper. The button foot M that comes with the Galaxie has a sliding bar that allows you to create a thread shank when sewing on the button, while the button foot supplied with the 950 has a slot which holds a pin, needle or toothpick to accomplish the same task. The 950 also comes with a straight stitch foot, but be careful when using it that you only sew with a straight stitch in the center position or you'll break your needle. The 950 also has a seam guide and a darning plate to cover the feed dogs.

Do a sample for each foot, write on the fabric which foot you've used, and file it in your notebook. Though I'll include some of the basics in this book, you'll learn new ways to use them as well. You can't use your machine to its full potential until you understand what the presser feet can do and then take advantage of that knowledge.

New presser feet are introduced often. Use Chart 1.1 to keep a record of the ones you have. When you come to know your sewing machine well, you will quickly realize that a jeans foot is not only for jeans, a braiding foot is not only for soutache, and many feet can do the same job.

I love to sew on my Brother! One of the reasons my enthusiasm never wanes is because I have a group of friends who also love their machines. We exchange sewing advice, pass on our creative discoveries, recommend books to each other, and sometimes meet to try new ideas. If you don't have such friends already, you'll find them in classes at your fabric or sewing machine store where new ideas are taught regularly.

While at the store, check out the books and magazines there. Many of the advanced manuals and leaflets for other

**Chart 1.1
Presser Feet Included with Brother Machines**

	Galaxie	*940/950*
Blind stitch	x	
Button sewing	x	x
Buttonhole	x	x
Overedge	x	
Side-cutter	x	
Straight stitch		x
Zigzag		
general purpose	x	x
transparent	x	
Zipper	x	x

brands will have ideas that you can use on your Brother machine when you become more familiar with its features. And don't pass up the other books in this series merely because they're for a different machine. Each book has a different focus in Chapter 11, and you might find exactly what you're looking for in one of them.

What else can you use to make your sewing easier? Following is a list and description of useful accessories from other brands that fit the Brother.

Accessories

Bias binder

There is a low-shank bias binder that fits the Brother machines. The one I have is a generic, with no brand name anywhere. It has an adjustable screw so you can place the stitching as near the edge as you wish. There is also an elliptical opening that enables you to attach bias with decorative stitches, but do watch the width. Will the needle hit the opening? I always turn one rotation by hand to check out the needle's swing before I start running the machine. If you're wondering what all the holes are for down the side of the scroll, they're for different widths of bias. You can also apply fold-over military braid and ribbon.

An interesting effect that I found in a 1924 Singer Sewing Manual is to apply the bias directly to the background instead of the edge. Place the ground fabric under the foot rather than in the slot. This creates a folded trim that is attached along one side.

This attachment works best on straight edges and attaches binding in one operation, instead of the usual two steps.

Circle maker

The Galaxie does not have a hole on the bed to allow attachment of a circle maker, but the 950 does. I have an old Greist circle maker from the 50s that works beautifully on the 950. Before you go circle-maker shopping, make a rubbing of the bed of your machine by placing a piece of tracing paper over the bed and rubbing all over with a soft pencil. Take this rubbing to the store with you and the clerks can tell you if they have something that will fit.

If you don't have a circle maker, you can make your own by using transparent tape, a thumb tack and a hoop. Determine the radius of the circle you wish to stitch. Measure that distance from the needle to a place at the left of it on the machine bed. Place a tack there, point up. Hold the tack in place by pushing the tape over the point and sticking it onto the machine (Fig. 1.3).

Then stretch your fabric into the hoop and place the center of the circle over the tack. Push a small cork or eraser over the point. When you rotate the hoop and stitch, you'll create a perfect circle.

Side cutter

This accessory is like a serger, but not as fast, and is supplied with the Galaxie, along with its own foot. A portion of the needle plate raises and drops down into the machine to allow the side-cutter to be clamped into place. I have not found a generic side-cutter for the 950, but there may well be one available that will work (see Sources of Supply). The side-cutter cuts, sews, and neatens edges of fabric in a single operation. Use it for stay-stitching, overcasting raw edges, for French seams, and to replace ribbed bands on sweaters or T-shirts. Be sure to clean out the bobbin area immediately after using the cutter.

Eyelet maker

You can buy a Japanese flower-maker that fits on the 950 and makes eyelets, as well as flower petals around the eyelet. It also fits my older Brother, the Pacesetter. While these do make eyelets, they also make interesting circular flowers in three sizes. The designs are created through the choice of decorative or utility stitches. Unless I need a perfectly round eyelet, I make slightly elongated ones using the buttonhole foot.

Ruffler

While I have three low-shank ruffler attachments of varying ages, not one will fit any of my Brother machines. Don't purchase one unless you have your machine with you and can try it out. If that isn't possible, be sure the dealer will let you return the foot if it doesn't fit. Should you find a ruffler that works, the attachment will both ruffle and pleat fabric.

Gathering foot

What I do have that I love is a New Home gathering foot. It works on all three of my machines—the Pacesetter, the Galaxie and the 950. Lengthen your stitch and tighten the upper tension to create the most gathers. This foot works best with soft materials and can be used to make rows of soft shirring. Try it also with a short stitch length for stitching the ease on set-in sleeves.

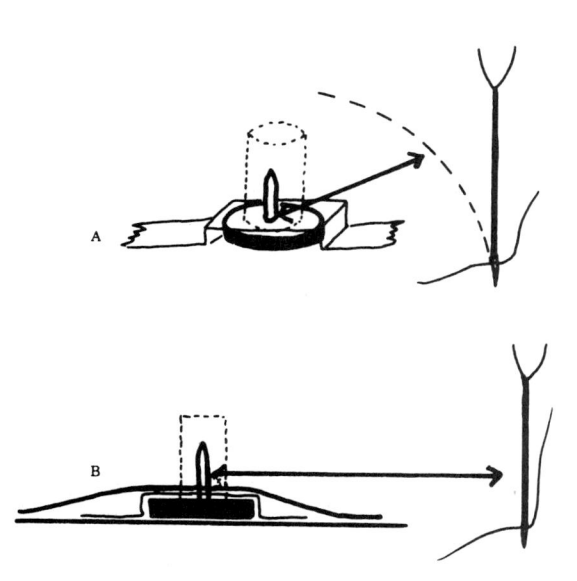

Fig. 1.3 A. Make your own circle maker by taping a thumbtack upside-down on the bed of the machine a radius away from the needle. Tape it in place. B. Place material in a hoop and stick the fabric onto the thumbtack wherever you want the center of the circle to be. Secure the fabric with a cork. Keep the fabric taut between the thumbtack and the needle as you sew a circular design.

Walking foot

There is a generic, low-shank walking foot—also referred to as an even-feed attachment or a plaid matcher—that will work on the Brother machines. I prefer, however, to use one of the silicone lubricants such as Tri-Flow sold by Clotilde when sewing Ultrasuede, plastics, or other hard-to-handle fabrics.

Darning foot or spring

If you are working on a piece that is too large to fit in a hoop or are worried about working freely without a presser foot, you can purchase a darning foot that puts pressure on the fabric as the needle penetrates it. Look for a darning foot that has either an elliptical or large round opening to accommodate a zigzag stitch. A darning spring also works beautifully. It slips over the needle and clips to the needle-holding screw. You must set the machine for darning when working with either of these attachments. On the Galaxie this means setting the stitch at zigzag, activating the width adjustment and setting it all the way to the left, then releasing the pressure adjusting lever, and dropping the feed dogs. If you don't take all of these steps, the computer will give you the error message, "Please change position of red knob to raise feed dog," and will not let you proceed. After you have taken all of these steps, you can change the width of the zigzag as much as you want, but the red light must stay lit, which simply means the width adjustment is activated. On the 950, you cover the feed dogs with the darning plate and release the pressure adjuster at the top of the machine.

Supplies

In addition to your sewing machine and a good supply of threads, here's a shopping list of what you'll need for the lessons. (Each lesson will give you a detailed materials list). You probably have many of the supplies in your sewing room.

1. Scissors and shears: sharp embroidery scissors, plus shears for cutting fabric and paper-cutting scissors.
2. Water-erasable markers for light fabrics; white opaque permanent marker for water-soluble stabilizer; slivers of soap or light-colored chalk pencils for dark fabrics.
3. Dressmaker's carbon. At one time we worried whether dressmaker's carbon would wash out or remain permanently on our garments. Today there are several excellent choices. One, Saral, advertises itself as the carbonless carbon. It's wax-free, and the tracing lines can be easily sponged out of fabric. The lines produced by another product, Dritz Trace-B-Gone Tracing paper, will also wash out in water. Dritz Mark-B-Gone Tracing paper is unique because the lines traced disappear after 24–72 hours, depending on fabric, temperature, and humidity. If you can't wait that long, they can also be sponged off with water. (Although both of these products are named "tracing paper," they are both dressmaker's carbons. Don't get them confused with see-through tracing paper I refer to often in the lessons.) Clo-Chalk by Clotilde looks like ordinary tailor's chalk but has the same properties as Dritz Mark-B-Gone Tracing paper (disappears in five days or immediately when washed or ironed). With it you can mark directly on the fabric without using a tracing wheel and paper.
4. T square or 6" × 24" (15.0cm × 61.0cm) plastic ruler; 6" (15.0cm) and 12" (30.5cm) see-through rulers are also helpful.
5. Wood and spring-type hoops in varied sizes, maximum 7" (17.8cm) for ease.

6. Rotary cutting wheel and cutting mat.
7. Optional extra bobbin case (available from Brother, 1-800-284-HELP).
8. Pressing pad. If I have one secret, it is my pressing pad. I took scraps of an open-weave 100% wool fabric and cut it into five 15" × 15" (38.1cm × 38.1cm) squares. Any size larger than 10" (25.4cm) would be sufficient. I stacked the layers together and sewed all around the edges. I can put anything I have embroidered wrong-side-up on top of this pad and press as hard as I possibly can without ever flattening the embroidery or damaging the thread. Any wrinkles can be pressed out—even on velveteen or corduroy—without harming the fabric. Several layers of a wool blanket would also work. The trick is to have a *porous wool surface*.

Have fabric ready for stitching samples. A handy size is a 9" (22.9cm) square. It will fit in the 7" (17.8cm) hoop and can be trimmed slightly for your notebook. Cut up a variety of fabrics from extra-lightweight types like organdy, lightweights like calicos, medium-weight poplins, and heavy-weight denim. Extra-heavy-weight canvas scraps will be left over from your tote bag and can be used for experiments.

In the projects, you'll also use felt, transparent fabrics, bridal veil, 1/8" (3.2mm) and 1/2" (12.7mm) satin double-faced ribbon, lace insertion, scalloped lace, lace beading, Battenberg tape, fleece, batting, stabilizers and fusibles. Now let's discuss your choices of threads needles, and other supplies.

Threads

One of the most useful charts I have in my notebook is a piece of doubled fabric with line after line of satin stitches on it. Each row is stitched using a different type of thread. I recommend that you make one, too. More important than telling you which thread to use, your chart will graphically convince you that what is called machine-embroidery cotton is usually more lustrous and covers an area more quickly and more beautifully than regular sewing thread. It's easy to compare differences among threads.

Generally, sewing threads are not used for machine embroidery. Ordinary sewing threads are usually thicker, stretch more (if polyester), and do not cover as well as machine embroidery threads. However, for durability or when you need a certain color, try using a high quality sewing thread. I never use thread from the sale bin—the ones that are three spools for 88 cents. This thread does not hold up to heavy use; it breaks, shrinks, knots, and, after all the time spent stitching with it, looks sloppy. If I am going to take the time to sew or embroider anything, then it deserves quality thread.

Machine embroidery rayons and cottons are more lustrous and have a softer twist than ordinary sewing thread. Rayon embroidery threads are silky and loosely twisted, but if you use a #90 needle and sew evenly and at a moderate speed, they are easy to use. If you are having trouble with rayon threads winding around the spool pin, try removing the round spool holder at the end. I find that this often alleviates the problem. Do be sure, however, that it is firmly in place when using thread on spools. If you find the thread breaking often, check to see that it is not wrapping around the first thread guide. I find this happens most often when I am stitching at an uneven speed. Don't use rayons or any other machine embroidery threads for clothing construction because they aren't strong enough.

Besides regular sewing threads and those used for machine embroidery, there are others to become acquainted with. The fine nylon used for lingerie and woolly overlock used for serging are just a couple of them. Another is darning thread: It's often used on the bobbin for machine embroidery because it's lightweight and you can get so much more of it wound on. It comes in only a few colors, so it cannot always be used should you want the bobbin thread to be seen on the surface.

Monofilament, another popular thread, comes in two shades. One blends into light-colored fabrics, the other darks. It is not the wild, fish-line type anymore, so don't be afraid of making it work. I use it on the top and bobbin constantly.

We now have wonderful metallic threads for the sewing machine. These come in gold, silver, copper, antique gold, many colors and all sorts of variegated assortments—from opalescent tints to rainbow colors to rich dark combinations. I use them on the top of the machine and use a monofilament or a rayon thread in the bobbin. There are also some super blending metallics available in knitting shops that work well in the bobbin.

Another new thread is called ribbon thread. It can be found on large expensive spools at Elna dealers or on smaller inexpensive spools through the mail or at a needlework shop. Ribbon floss, which resembles ribbon thread, is also available in small spools. Don't limit your search for unusual threads to sewing machine dealers or fabric stores. Try knitting shops, craft stores, wherever a fiber might be sold.

If you use silk and silk buttonhole twists as well as fine pearl cottons, crochet and cordonnet, the needle must be large enough to keep the threads from fraying against the fabric and the eye large enough to enable the thread to go through smoothly. Sometimes top-stitching needles are called for. Or you may have to use a needle larger than you normally would to do the embroidery.

Waxed or glacé finished quilting thread should never be used on your machine, as the finish wears off and does your machine no good.

Chart 1.2 is a handy guide, showing which needles and threads to use with which fabrics. More about where to purchase threads can be found in Sources of Supplies at the end of the book.

Chart 1.2
Needle and Thread Chart

Fabric	Thread	Needles
Very heavy (upholstery, canvas, denim)	Heavy-duty cotton; polyester; buttonhole twist; cordonnet	18 (110)
Heavy (sailcloth, heavy coating)	Heavy-duty cotton; polyester	16 (100)
Medium weight (wool, poplin, velvet)	Ordinary sewing cotton and polyester; machine-embroidery cotton and rayon	12, 14 (80, 90)
Lightweight (shirt cotton, dress fabrics, silk)	Extra-fine to ordinary sewing cotton and polyester	9, 11/12 (70, 80)
Very lightweight (lace, net, organdy, batiste)	Extra-fine sewing cotton and polyester	8, 9 (60, 70)

Needles

It is important to choose the right needle for the job. Match fabric weight, thread, and needle size, as well as type of material. The lighter the material, the smaller the needle and finer the thread should be. The heavier the fabric, the larger the needle should be.

Like presser feet, needles come in different sizes and shapes and produce different effects. I once had a student in quilting class who struggled to get a needle out of her machine—it was rusted in. "I don't do much sewing," she said. (Why didn't that surprise me?) No matter how mind-boggling this sounds, I know that few sewers change needles unless they break, even though a new needle keeps thread from fraying, fabric from being damaged, and your stitches from skipping. The correct size and shape enables you to stitch through the heaviest or the flimsiest materials with ease. Also, wing and double needles allow you to create unique, decorative work.

The only needle that I have not been able to use successfully on my Brother machines is the triple needle. The machines balk at having three threads pass through the tension wheels, though two threads and double needles work very well.

Needles are available in pierce point, used for woven fabrics; and ball point, used for knits to minimize cutting threads and causing runs in the fabric. The universal-point needle is all-purpose and can be used for knits, as well as woven fabrics. Instead of cutting through the fabric, the slightly rounded point deflects off the threads and slips between them. Because of its versatility, it is the needle in greatest use today.

Following is a list of needles and their uses:

Universal Needles: All-purpose sewing.
Fine Ballpoint Needles: Fine fabrics, including knits and wovens.
Medium Ballpoint Needles: Heavier knitted fabrics.
Medium Ballpoint Stretch Needles: Special needles for problem stretch fabrics.
Extra-Fine Point Needles: Used to pierce closely woven fabrics such as canvas or denim; often called jeans needles.
Topstitching Needles: Equipped with an eye and thread groove larger than a regular needle of the same size. Use buttonhole twist or double thread when topstitching. Use them for embroidery, too. These are my favorite needles in sizes 80 and 90 because I can switch back and forth from a light single thread, to two threads, to a heavy thread without having to change the needle each time.
Double Needles: Used for sewing with more than one thread on top. Double needles come in five sizes (1.6mm, 2mm, 2.4mm, 3mm, and 4mm). The size refers to the space between the two needles. If you set the machine for double needle, you can only use the needles up to 2mm in width, but you can do all the decorative stitches without worrying about setting the width or breaking a needle. If you use the larger widths (3mm and 4mm), you will need to confine yourself to straight stitching.
Wing (hemstitching) Needles: Double and single types are available, but the

Chart 1.3
Needle Size

	Very Fine	Fine	Med.	Strong	Large	Very Large
U.S.	8,9	10	11,12	14	16	18
Euro.	60,65	70	75,80	90	100	110

double needle consists of one wing needle and one regular needle, not two wing needles. I only use a #16 wing needle, as this gives me a nice big hole.

Leather Needles: Often called wedge needles because of their cutting points. Use them on real suede and leather. Or use a regular #110 needle in place of a leather needle.

To keep your machine running trouble-free, change the needle often. Be sure the needle is straight and has no burr on the point. Damaged needles damage fabric and machines.

If your machine is noisy and is skipping stitches, change the needle (assuming the machine is oiled and clean). Be sure you've used the correct needle system for your machine and be certain you've placed the needle in the machine correctly. Most of the time a damaged needle is the only problem—and an easy one to rectify.

To make it easier for you to prepare appropriate supplies before beginning the lessons, let's discuss items often called for and the terms I'll use.

Batting, fleece, and fiberfill

Batting, both cotton and polyester, is used between fabric layers for quilting. Different weights and sizes are available, as well as different qualities. For our use, most of the projects can be quilted with bonded batting, which holds together firmly, or with fleece, which is a filler that's thinner than bonded batting and about as thick as a heavy wool blanket. Alternative fillers can be flannel, when only a light garment is desired, or a wool blanket. Fiberfill is the shredded batting used to fill toys. Or stuff toys with batting.

Fusibles

Fusibles are used to hold appliqués to background fabrics so edges are held firmly for the final step of stitching them in place. Plastic sandwich bags or cleaner's garment bags can be used. Stitch Witchery, Fine Fuse, Magic Polyweb and Jiffy Fuse are commercial fusible webbings. To use, place them between two pieces of fabric and press with a hot iron until the webbing melts and holds the two fabrics together. Use a Teflon pressing sheet to protect your iron and also to allow you to press the fusible to one fabric at a time. The Applique Pressing Sheet or Teflon sheet has eliminated any problem with the fusible melting on your iron: it looks like opaque wax paper, is reusable, and comes in handy sizes.

A fusible webbing already backed by paper, which saves one step in application, is called Wonder-Under Transfer Fusing Web. Draw your design directly onto the paper and place it over the appliqué fabric. Press for a few seconds, which fuses the webbing to the fabric. Then cut out the pattern and pull the paper away from the webbing. Place the appliqué on the background fabric. Cover with a damp cloth and press (wool setting) for 10 seconds. Stitch in place.

Appliqué papers are paper-backed products that look very much like freezer wrap, but act like the transfer web. One side of the paper has a glue finish.

See Chapter 4 for more about fusibles.

Stabilizers

Stabilizers are used behind fabric to keep it from puckering when you embroider. At one time, we used typing paper, but today we have more choices of stabilizers, available at fabric and quilt shops and through mail-order (see Sources of Supplies).

The old standby, typing paper, still does the job. Or, use shelf paper when stitching large pictures and adding-machine tape for long strips of embroidery. A problem with paper is that it dulls machine needles faster than tear-away stabilizers do. It's also harder to remove from the back of the embroidery, although dampening the paper will help.

Another stabilizer you probably have in the cupboard is plastic-coated freezer wrap. I find I'm using it more and more. If I'm embroidering a fabric that could be damaged by the hoop, I back it instead with freezer wrap, which I iron to the back of the fabric. The freezer paper adheres to the fabric and stiffens it. When I finish my embroidery, I peel off the freezer paper. I like using it if I have a small piece of fabric to embroider. I iron the small piece to a larger, easier-to-manipulate piece of freezer paper.

Tear-away stabilizers come in crisp or soft finishes and some are iron-ons. When embroidering, place them between the fabric and machine. When the embroidery is completed, they tear away from the fabric easily.

Don't confuse stabilizers with interfacings. Interfacings are permanent and don't tear away. They can be used, of course, and so can fabrics like organdy, but they are usually used when you plan to leave the stabilizer on the back of the embroidery after it's completed.

One of the newest stabilizers is a thin film of plastic, available by the sheet or the yard, that will dissolve when wet. Clamp it into the hoop along with the fabric. It is transparent, and can be used on top of the embroidery, too. It can be marked on, but choose a water-erasable marker or permanent white opaque marker that will not leave ink on your embroidery when the plastic is dissolved. When your embroidery is completed, rinse out the stabilizer. It will become gooey, then disappear. I'll refer to it as water-soluble stabilizer.

Helpful hints for sewing

Before beginning to sew, check out the following general helpful hints:

1. Every machine has its own idiosyncracies, so the settings I recommend for each lesson are only suggestions; your machine may prefer different ones.

2. Take your sewing machine in for regular check-ups whether you think it needs it or not. Between checkups, keep it clean and oil it where shown in the manual. It should be oiled after every 10 or 12 hours of use. Or, if your machine starts clacking instead of humming, get out the oil can, but take it easy. There are more problems with over-oiling than with too little. To be sure the oil works its way through the areas that need lubricating, oil *before* sewing rather than when your sewing is completed. Check your manuals to learn all the spots on your machine that need oil.

3. No matter what machine you have, you must keep the inside free of lint and threads. Clean the bobbin area by first removing the bobbin, then wiping out all the lint. A Q-tip works well. Canned air sold in camera and some sewing machine shops contains freon and/or fluorocarbons, so I do not recommend using it. I sometimes vacuum out lint from inside the machine. Remember to clean the feed dogs whenever you finish sewing or during a long period of stitching nappy fabrics such as corduroy, fur, or velvets. Always clean during and after using a side-cutter accessory.

After the inside has been freed of lint, put a drop of oil in every spot that needs lubricating.

Now gather your supplies together and begin the adventure — to know your Brother.

13

CHAPTER 2

Adding Stitches to Your Fabric

- **Lesson 1. Using built-in stitches**
- **Lesson 2. Using free machining**

In this chapter you'll become acquainted with the range of stitches your Brother machine can produce. By the end of it, you'll easily switch back and forth from stitching with the feed dogs up to stitching with feed dogs down or covered. To demonstrate your new facility, you'll make beautiful small buttons and pendants.

Lesson 1. Using built-in stitches

The first thing I did when I bought my machine was to try all the built-in stitches. I wanted a reference, so I sewed stitches in rows at different widths and lengths and put them in a notebook, along with notations from the Basic Manual. I was determined to know my sewing machine, and this has been so helpful to me that I've made it your first lesson too.

To save you time, practical and decorative stitches have been built into sewing machines: I classify them as "closed" and "open." "Closed" refers to those where the beauty is in stitching it close together (wide stitch width, stitch length almost 0 to 1/2), like the satin stitch or scallop stitch. "Open" built-in stitches, like the serpentine stitch, blind hem, vari-overlock and gathering stitch, are usually sewn at a stitch length longer than 1/2.

To practice the built-in stitches and make a record of them, first set up your machine as indicated in the box at the beginning of the lesson.

Stitch width: varies
Stitch length: varies
Needle position: auto (center)
Needle: #90/14
Feed dogs: up
Presser foot: open embroidery foot
Tension: *top*, 3; *bobbin*, normal
Fabric suggestion: medium-weight striped cotton
Thread: machine-embroidery to contrast with fabric, different colors in top and bobbin
Accessories: fine-point marker
Stabilizer: tear-away or freezer paper

Stitch lines of the built-in stitches found on your machine (Fig. 2.1). The striped fabric will help you keep them straight. Start by using the settings suggested in the manual. Vary the settings as you stitch, making the stitches wider and narrower, longer and shorter. If there is a setting you find particularly useful, mark it right on the fabric with a marker to show where that setting begins.

This is a good time to determine the precise width and length settings for the best-looking closed, decorative stitches.

Using different colors of thread on top and bobbin will help you adjust the machine to find the perfect stitch. Adjust tension by loosening the top tension slightly

Fig. 2.1 Fabric is used to make a notebook cover that is a record of all the built-in stitches on my Brother Galaxie.

number, and begin stitching. The decorative stitch on the 950 will begin wherever the stitching stopped. You can analyze the pattern to find a middle thread (if one exists) and turn at this point or stop exactly on the ending thread, turn the fabric and start back. Since there is a large space between both the tulip and the swan motifs on the 940/950, you can put a swan between the tulips by stitching back on the same line; you can put in a different color tulip by changing the thread and stitching back, you can make two swans face each other by placing the mirror image on the same line, or you can have a white swan going in one direction and—by changing the thread and stitching back along the same line—have a black swan facing a white swan. When you're doing these samples, always ask yourself if there is something more you can do to it.

and leaving the bobbin tension normal. The top thread should be pulled down and show underneath the fabric and should mound slightly on top when making satin stitches.

Start by stitching the zigzag, with the widest stitch width, stitch length 2. Adjust the length as you stitch until the satin stitch is perfect. This will be somewhere between 0 and 1/2 length. Write the setting on the sample.

Now practice making mirror images. Since there is no automatic mirror imaging feature on the machines, you will have to perform this manually by turning the fabric and stitching back along the previous line. On the Galaxie you can accomplish this by determining the starting position of the motif you have used. Position the needle exactly opposite the end of the last motif in the line, re-enter the stitch

Fig. 2.2 Free-machine darning stitches were used to make a picture.

15

There are a number of variables with mirror images. Are you feeding the fabric through exactly? Don't pull on one side when the other has been fed through freely. Did you start the second row at exactly the right spot? Just one stitch off will make a difference. Do you have the same thickness of fabric under both sides of the design? If you're stitching on top of a seam allowance, the needle may go off the two layers.

As you sew line after line of practical and decorative stitches, imagine how they can be used. For example, the blind-hem stitch is used for blind hems and for the tricot scalloped hem. But it can also be an invisible way of stitching on a patch pocket or an appliqué, or the stitch to use when couching down heavy cords.

Lesson 2. Using free-machining: darning, whipping, feather stitching

In free machining, you — not the presser foot — control the movement of the fabric, which in turn determines the length of the stitch. With fabric stretched tightly in a hoop, it is easy to move your work forward, backward, in circles, whatever way you wish.

I suggest working with a wooden hoop when first learning machine stitchery. Choose one that has a smooth finish, and slips easily under the darning foot. But whatever wooden hoop you use, be sure it is the screw type, as that will hold the fabric tightly. To be sure that it does, the inside ring of the wooden hoop should be wound with narrow twill tape. This keeps the fabric from slipping. Take a few hand stitches at the end of the tape to hold it firmly.

If your needle will not clear the hoop you've chosen, turn the hoop on its side and slip it under the darning foot or put the hoop together and carve out a small wedge to make it easier. Then wrap the inside part with tape.

Fabric is placed in the hoop upside-down from the way you would put it in a hoop for hand embroidery (Fig. 2.3). Pull the cloth as tightly as you can. Tighten the screw; pull again; tighten. Tap on the fabric. If it sounds like a drum, it is tight enough. You may or may not want to use a stabilizer under a hoop, depending upon the effect you want and the weight of the fabric.

The lessons that follow throughout this book have been worked on the Brother Galaxie computer sewing machine and the VX-950. Any reference to the VX-950 is also true for the VX-940. There are other Brother machines which work pretty much along the lines of these machines — some do more and some do less, like my old Brother Pacesetter. You will, however, have no trouble using whichever machine you own. Simply start with the settings given here and make adjustments as necessary. No two machines ever perform exactly the same; they each have their own personality. (I once owned one that hated my children. I could stitch happily away for hours on it without incident, but if one of them walked into the room, the thread immediately broke.)

When I buy a new machine, I break in the motor much as I would a new car — I start slow with short trips before I ask it to climb Mt. Everest. I stitch straight stitches for about half an hour, gradually building

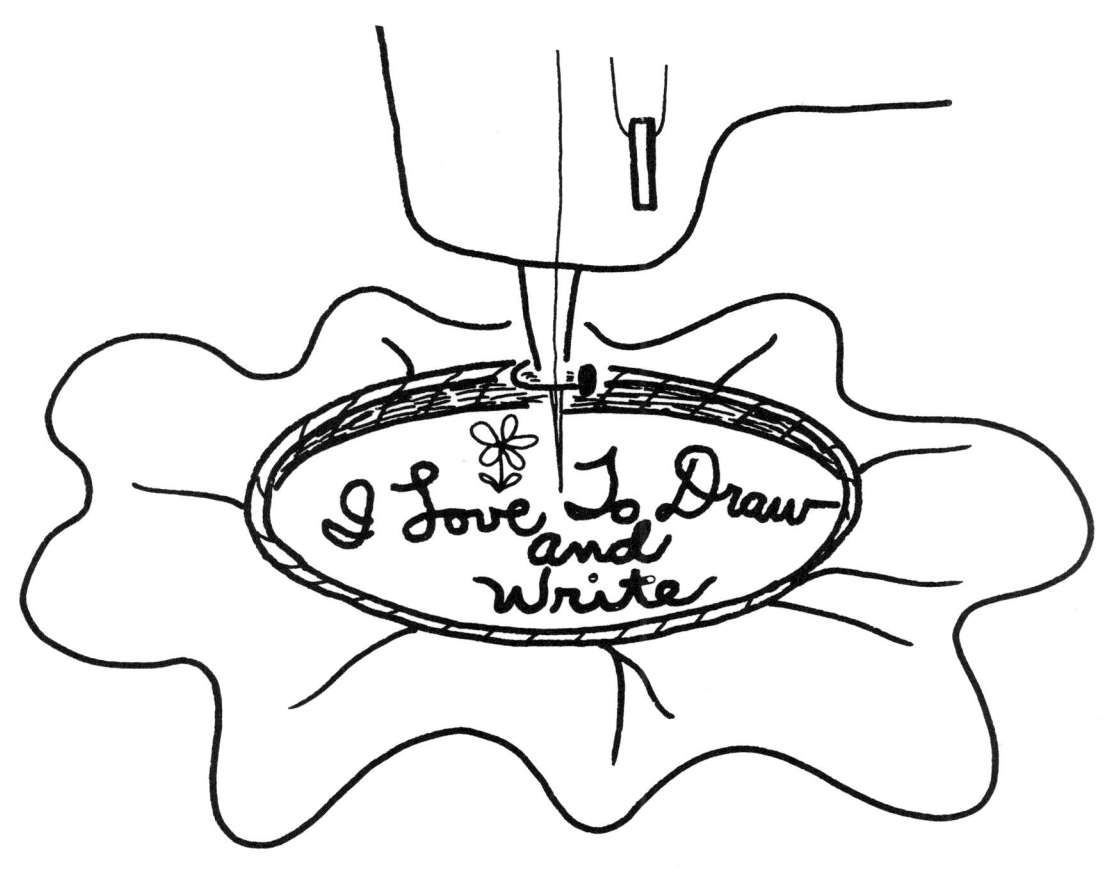

Fig. 2.3 Tighten fabric in a hoop. The fabric rests against the bed of the machine, with the material topside up for machine embroidery.

up speed, until I can sense the parts of the motor beginning to "sit in," a smoothing out of the sound. Then I proceed to put the machine through its paces, going page by page through the manual until I'm familiar with most of its idiosyncrasies.

In each lesson you will find settings for the machines—the settings are for the Galaxie with the ones for the 940/950 in parentheses if they differ. While the width and length settings are not calibrated on the Galaxie, note that there are seven stitches on the stitch length gauge. Counting from the left, put a little dot of nail polish above the 4th stitch for a reference point. This will make it easy to count, so if the directions indicate "4" you'll know where to place the slide; "0" will mean all the way to the left. You must first activate the slides by pushing the manual-stitch-width-release and/or the manual-stitch-length-release buttons to the left of the gauges. I have used N (narrow), M (medium) and W (wide) for the width settings.

The 950 has a left, right and center needle position, but a straight stitch on the Galaxie automatically places the needle in the left position. To obtain a straight stitch in the center position, set the machine at zigzag, activate the manual-stitch-width-release button and push it all the way to the left. The decorative stitches on the Galaxie automatically begin at the start of the motif. I have used "auto" where the settings for the Galaxie are not changed from those which are preset for each operation.

As stated in Chapter 1, you must cover the feed dogs on the 940 and 950 when doing free machine embroidery. If you don't want to bother or the cover gets in your way, then turn the stitch length to 0, and the feed dogs will be stationary. To set the Galaxie for free machine embroidery/darning turn the machine on and you will be at zigzag. Now lower the feed dogs by pushing the red knob beside the bobbin area to the left. Activate the manual-stitch-width-release button and move the slide to "0" (all the way to the left). After you have taken these steps, you may move the slide back and forth all you want. Failure to perform these steps will result in the error message, "Please change position of red knob to right to raise feed dogs," and you will not be able to proceed. Raise the pressure release lever even if you're not going to use a darning foot. Then you can switch back and forth from a darning foot or not, as you wish. I also lower my bobbin tension about 1/2 turn and lower my upper tension to 2. This allows me to freely move between whipping, satin and straight stitching without resetting anything except the top tension. All of the terms used are the same ones you will find in your manual, so keep it handy while working through the lessons and projects.

You can stitch with a darning foot on or without a presser foot (but keep your fingers a safe distance from the needle!).

It is possible to stitch freely without a hoop if you use your fingers to hold the fabric taut while stitching. If you don't use a hoop—or if you use a spring-type hoop—use a darning foot to prevent skipped stitches. It will hold the fabric down each time the machine makes a stitch so the threads interlock correctly underneath. Also, use a stabilizer under the fabric to keep the stitches from puckering.

> Stitch width: N–W (0–5)
> Stitch length: 0
> Needle position: auto (center)
> Needle: #80 and double needle
> Feed dogs: lowered or covered
> Presser foot: darning foot, spring, or none
> Tension: *top*, slightly loosened; *bobbin*, normal
> Fabric: light-colored, medium-weight fabric, such as poplin—scrap for practice; 18" x 18" (45.7cm x 45.7cm) square for your notebook
> Thread: one color for top, another for bobbin; both should contrast with fabric
> Accessories: wrapped wooden hoop no larger than 7" (17.8cm), fine-point marker
> Stabilizer: tear-away or freezer paper

The two samples in this lesson will give you practice in control and coordination. One sample will be for practice; the other, for your notebook. Keep a record of the new-found stitches you create with your machine and your imagination.

Free machining—darning, whipping and feather stitching—takes practice, but it is worth every minute. It opens up a new world of stitchery to you.

First, you are going to learn to draw, write, and sketch with your machine. It's called the darning stitch.

Set up your machine for darning. Always begin by dipping the needle into the fabric and bringing the bobbin thread to the top. Hold both threads to the side while stitching several stitches in one place to anchor the thread. Clip off the ends. When you begin your stitching, start slowly. Practice moving the hoop slowly, as well. You must coordinate the speed at which you move your hoop and your sewing speed. It is not necessary to stitch at top speed—moderate speed is fine. You'll soon learn how fast is right for you and for the particular stitching you are creating.

Move the hoop back and forth, then in circles — remember the old Palmer Method exercises for handwriting? Stitch faster; move your hoop faster. Then write your name, draw a picture of a tree, your dog, an old flame. It doesn't matter how well you draw; you are really practicing control.

Change to zigzag and try it all over again. Yes, it will take awhile to gain absolute control, but don't give up. Stitch tiny fill-in spirals, figure eights and jigsaw patterns.

Now stitch, hesitate, stitch. The bobbin color may come to the top. Good! That's what we want. To make sure it does, loosen or bypass the bobbin tension and tighten the top tension slowly. When you see the bobbin thread, note where the tension dial is set and write this on the sample. This type of stitchery is called whipping. If the hoop is moved slowly and the machine run very fast, a nubby, thickened line of bobbin thread will appear on the surface. If you match the top thread to your ground fabric or use monofilament and use a contrasting thread on the bobbin, you will

Fig. 2.4 Whipping and feather stitching.

only see the bobbin thread. This is a great technique for adding bits of color, such as flowers to a bush, without having a continuous line of color. It can be used in place of the darning stitch when embroidering — or used with it for variety. Whipping can be seen in the tiny circles of dark bobbin thread in Fig. 2.4.

With the top tension very tight and the bobbin tension loosened, stitch straight

Fig. 2.5 Draw 36 squares on a piece of fabric, then fill them in with the new stitches and techniques you've learned and will learn. Be sure to record machine settings.

lines, circles and spirals. Move the hoop quickly. The top thread is visible as a straight line on top of the fabric. Covering it are looping, feathery bobbin stitches. This is an exaggeration of whipping, which is called feather stitching. This can be seen in the hoop in some of the small circles as I went from tight to tighter top tension, and in the larger, spiky spirals (Fig. 2.4) that occurred when I loosened the bobbin tension until there was no resistance on the thread.

Also try this work with a zigzag stitch for a completely different look. If you have bypassed the tension and go around and around in the same area with a straight stitch, you will create craters or barnacles or filled-up holes. Turn the sample over and you will see mountains. I always use different colors in the bobbin and on top when whipping to add interest to the area.

Practice is the only way to learn control. When you feel you have accomplished co-ordination between moving the hoop and the speed of the machine, make the following record of what you've learned: On the 18" x 18" (45.7cm x 45.7cm) square of fabric, draw a grid of 3" (7.6cm) squares, six across, six down (Fig. 2.5). Then fill in your squares with examples of free machining—darning, whipping and feather stitching. Use both straight stitches and zigzag stitches in your squares. Try built-in stitches, too. You can stitch your own designs or use mine. But as you practice, write the machine settings on the fabric. Slip this into your notebook. Add new stitches as you discover them and refer to your notebook regularly for stitches you want to use on a project.

For variety, thread your needle with two colors, variegated thread, or try a double needle. But remember to activate the double needle button on the Galaxie or to check that your double needle will fall inside the hole of the plate on the 950 when setting it on zigzag.

Project Buttons and Pendants

The following one-of-a-kind projects include free machining and stitching with feed dogs up. Get to know your sewing machine by stitching up these small embroideries.

You have a choice of stitches on the designs and they can be finished as large buttons or as earrings (see color section). Buy button forms at fabric or needlecraft shops. I used a size 75, which is about 2" (5.1cm) in diameter. And I was inspired by Mary Ann Spawn of Tacoma, Washington, to finish some of them by attaching cords and tassels to make pendants (Fig. 2.9).

If you use the round design in Fig. 2.6, draw two circles with the same center point on your fabric. One is the area to be embroidered; the other circle, ½" (12.7mm) outside the first, is the cutting line. It's important to keep the area between the lines free from stitching. Use a

Fig. 2.6 Use button forms or cut shapes from heavy cardboard to make machine-embroidered pendants, pins or buttons. This pattern can be used for all three.

piece of fabric large enough to go into a spring hoop and place a piece of tear-away stabilizer underneath.

Embroider, using free machining such as whipping and darning, as well as satin stitches. Leave a ½" (12.7mm) margin on the other designs as well.

Stitch width: N–W (0–5)
Stitch length: 0–1/2
Needle position: auto (center)
Needle: #90/14 sharp
Feed dogs: up, lowered or covered
Presser foot: transparent zigzag foot N or darning foot
Tension: *top*, loosened; *bobbin*, normal
Fabric suggestion: medium-weight, tightly woven linen
Thread: variegated rayon embroidery and threads in many colors to match in cotton or silk
Accessories: wood or spring hoop, button forms or cardboard, batting, craft glue, cord, vanishing marker, small beads, three small pearl buttons, colored markers, tracing paper, dressmaker's carbon, empty ballpoint pen
Stabilizer: tear-away or iron-on freezer paper

On small embroidered pendants, I often use some of the decorative built-in stitches as a contrast to the more freely stitched areas. Often I imitate the decorative stitches as well, either shortening or elongating them, or making them wider or narrower to fit the space.

Satin stitches of different widths separate sections of the design or emphasize an area. Two built-in stitches I often use are the triple straight stitch (referred to as a stretch stitch) and the triple zigzag (rickrack stitch). If your machine doesn't have these stitches, then use two threads through your needle and use the regular straight or zigzag stitch. I use rickrack stitches on top of satin stitches, and stretch stitches next to them.

Before I begin any pendant, I plan my colors by drawing the design on a piece of paper and coloring it. Once I begin stitching, not only do I sometimes change my mind about the placement of some colors, but I may add others and combine some by sewing next to or on top of the first threads I've used.

First, find the colored threads you'll need and then wind bobbins for all the spools of colors you'll use when you add small beads to the pendants, keep them well within the outline.

General directions for making the pendants follow: Either back your fabric with iron-on freezer paper or place it tightly in a hoop and slip stabilizer under the hoop before you embroider. For each of these embroideries, I drew the design within the outline, using the vanishing or a water-erasable marker. You can either trace the design from the illustration, or sketch it on your fabric free-hand.

On all these pieces, I fill in the free-motion embroidery first. I use a scribbling that looks like small circles strung together, stitched layer upon layer, or in the case of variegated thread on the beaded pendant, I stitched in the center section by traveling from side to side as I moved from top to bottom of the area (Fig. 2.7). Knots and blobs of many different colors can also be used, as I did behind the beads on the pin (see Fig. 3.4). I also made sure I didn't cover the entire surface with stitches. Why cover a beautiful fabric completely? And also, I think that when fabric is completely hidden by machine embroidery, it looks too much like the appliqués you can pick up at the dime store.

The horizontal rectangular pendant in Fig. 2.8 uses decorative stitches along the bottom area and in the smaller rectangles at the sides. I did the stitching in the center in a free manner as a contrast to the exactness of the decorative stitching. The straight lines you see throughout are all triple stretch stitch. I removed the fabric from the hoop, reset the machine for regular sewing, added some more triple stretch

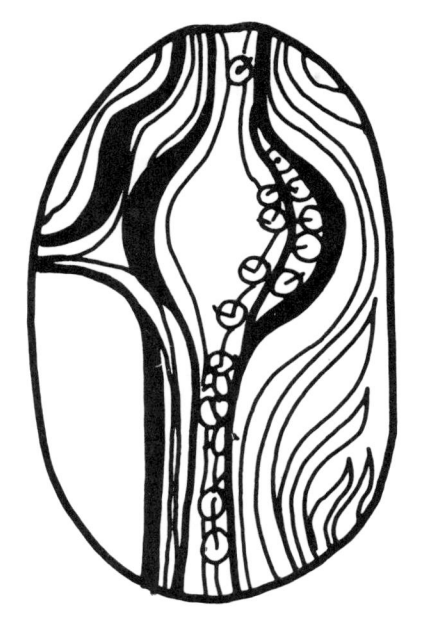

Fig. 2.7 Pattern for embroidered pin or pendant (see color section).

stitches to the center area and sewed on the small pearl buttons. Then I put a variegated (red, blue, yellow and green) thread, Natesh #512, on the top and outlined the areas using the widest zigzag. The tassels are made with embroidery floss in the same colors as the variegated thread.

To make the beige linen pin in Fig. 2.6, first stitch small knots of satin stitches in the center section (see Fig. 3.4) with variegated thread (I used one combining red, green, blue, lavender and yellow). Then change thread to one of those colors and begin stitching in the satin stitch curves. I used yellow first, then blue and lavender at the left side. Between the curves I straight stitched lines in green and yellow and sometimes used the triple stretch stitch for more emphasis. The curves at the top of the pin were stitched in with red satin stitches. Those curves are echoed by using red straight stitches.

The beads, which are the same colors as the threads, are sewn in the center area of the pin. Sew a large safety pin, or a jewelry

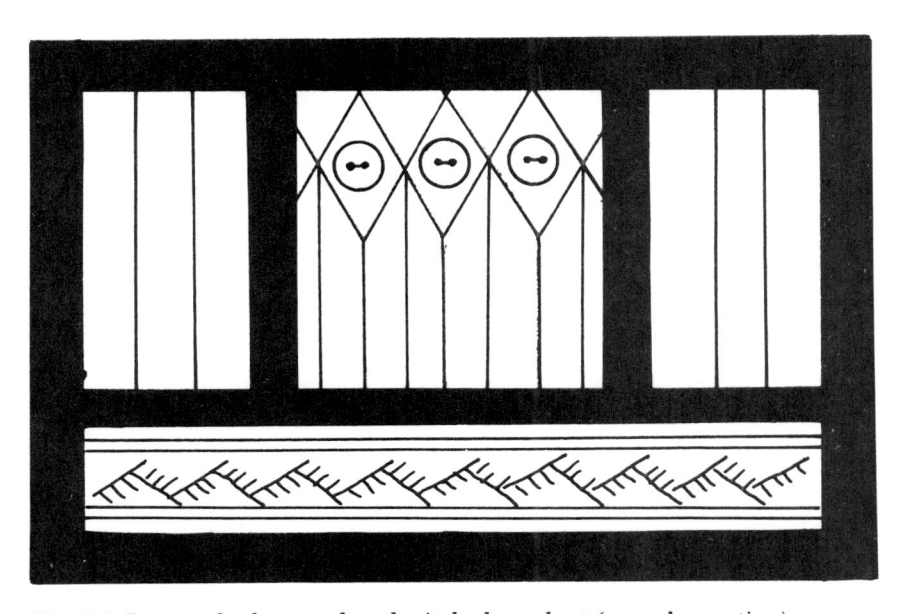

Fig. 2.8 Pattern for buttoned-and-stitched pendant (see color section).

pin (available at craft and fabric stores), to the back of the pin before you cover the cardboard with the fabric. Then finish the pin as described below.

The long, beaded pendant in Fig. 2.7 is sewn the same way. I chose the same variegated thread and matching colors, but changed the fabric to green linen. First I stitched freely in the center, then chose lavender thread to cover the two areas at the left with scribbling. Heavy blue satin stitches were added next (see color section), followed by lines of echo straight stitching in all the thread colors chosen.

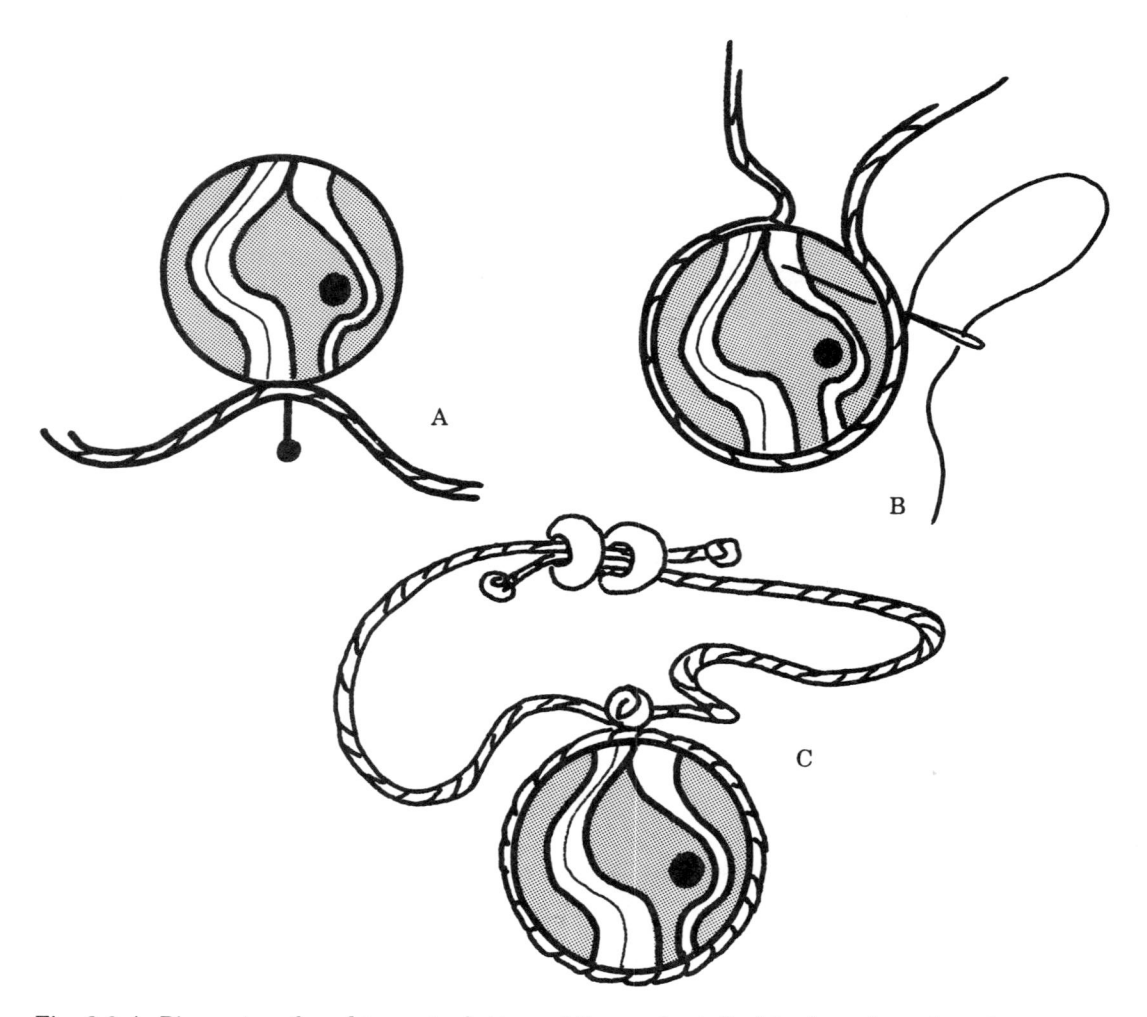

Fig. 2.9 A. Pin center of cord to center bottom of the pendant. B. Attach cord at edge of the pendant by hand, laying the thread in the twist of the cord as you stitch. C. Make an adjustable pendant cord by threading both cords through two beads in this manner.

Beads in the same colors were stitched on last and added to the tassel at the bottom of the pendant.

Pendants and buttons are small enough to do quickly and, if you make a mistake, they're easily disposable. There are no two alike. What a delightful way to spend an afternoon—stitching and getting to know your Brother sewing machine.

When you've finished embroidering, cut out the shapes. Use large button forms for the round ones, or cut cardboard shapes to fit your embroidery. Place a piece of batting between your embroidery and the cardboard. Take a piece of matching fabric for the back and write your name and the date on it, either freely with the 940/950 or using the alphabet and numbers on the Galaxie and use these to make an identical circle or rectangle, batting and cardboard the same way. Use a thick craft glue to glue the fabric edges over the cardboard pieces. Then join back-to-back by dabbing glue between and whipping around the edge by hand. Add tassels if you wish.

To attach the monk's cord (Chapter 10, Lesson 35) to the edge of the pendant by hand, lay the sewing thread in the twist of the cord, then poke the needle through both pendant edges (Fig. 2.9). This same cord can be extended to tie around your neck or can be made adjustable such as I have done. Pull both ends through two beads (the pony beads work great) in opposite directions and then knot the ends as shown in Fig. 2.9A or use a teasel brush to fluff out the edges as I have done. I like to make these cords fairly long and decorate the ends in some way to add interest to the back when they are being worn.

CHAPTER 3

Adding Texture to Your Fabric

- Lesson 3. Building up sewing stitches
- Lesson 4. Applying thick threads from top and bobbin
- Lesson 5. Fringing yarn and fabric
- Lesson 6. Adding buttons, beads, shisha
- Lesson 7. Smocking and gathering
- Lesson 8. Pulling threads together

Add to or create texture on fabrics by building up sewing stitches, using thick threads, attaching fringe or objects like buttons and beads, gathering fabric for smocking or for utilitarian purposes—to stitch elastic on sleeves or bodices, or to make ruffles for curtains.

You'll make samples for your notebook; stitch up a fabric greeting card; cable stitch a tote bag square; make fabric fringe for rugs and doll hair; and make a framed picture. Both projects and samples will suggest numerous other ways to use these stitches.

Lesson 3. Building up sewing stitches

One of the simplest ways to build up texture is to sew in one place many times. Sounds simple and it is. But you can do this in so many ways that even though it is simple, the results aren't. Texture can look studied and exact or free and wild.

I use the following techniques for landscapes, monograms, and flowers. Practice each one for your notebook, recording your machine settings and any notes on how you might use the stitches later.

Begin with my suggested settings, but change them if they are not correct for your machine or not to your liking.

Stitch width: W (5)
Stitch length: 0–1/2
Needle position: auto (left)

Needle: #90/12
Feed dogs: lowered (covered)
Presser foot: darning or transparent zigzag foot N
Tension: *top*, 3; *bottom*, normal
Fabric suggestion: experiment with varied weights, types, and colors
Thread: practice with any type, but use machine embroidery thread for smooth satin stitching; include several sizes of pearl cotton, cordonnet, yarns and 1/8" (3.2mm) ribbon
Accessories: 7" (17.8cm) spring hoop
Stabilizer: tear-away type

With the feed dogs up, and embroidery foot N, anchor the threads first; then use the widest satin stitch. Sew a block of 6 or

8 satin stitches. Anchor them by using 0 width again and stitch in place. Move the hoop and do another block of satin stitches. Keep them quite close together, but all at different angles (Fig. 3.1). Use these to fill in areas in designs.

The machine settings will remain the same for the next sample.

You can also do this with the feed dogs down. Stretch your fabric in the hoop and set your machine for darning. Use the darning foot if desired. Anchor the threads (use 0 width and stitch in place) and then use the widest satin stitch. Sew a block of six or eight or more satin stitches (I like to use as many stitches as necessary to make the blocks into squares). Move the hoop and do another block of satin stitches, again keeping them close together, but all at different angles (Fig. 3.1). After you've finished stitching the sample, study the results. If you used a rayon (very shiny) thread, you'll see different values of the same color depending on the way the light strikes the sample. Do this same exercise with one of the multicolored variegated threads, working each block in one color. When the color changes, do another block. Turn the stitches every which way and you'll have a multicolored area without changing thread. Use these to fill in areas in designs.

Anchor the threads by stitching in one place. Use the same wide zigzag, but sew in one place to build up 10 or 12 stitches.

Fig. 3.2 Blobs and loops.

Move to another spot close to the first blob of stitches and stitch again. If you wish to achieve the effect in Fig. 3.2, pull the threads into loops as you move from place to place and don't cut them off. You can make flower centers this way. Or finish by clipping between the satin stitches and then, using a different color on top, outlining with straight stitches (Fig. 3.3). Using variegated thread is especially effective.

In the next experiment, raise the feed dogs and set your machine for zigzag sewing. Put on the transparent embroidery foot N and set your machine for the widest satin stitch. Anchor the threads and sew a block of satin stitches at the left of the practice fabric. Pull the fabric down about three inches and over to the right slightly. Stitch another block of satin stitches. Pull

Fig. 3.1 Use satin stitches for flower centers or fill-in background stitches.

Fig. 3.3 Straight-stitching around blobs.

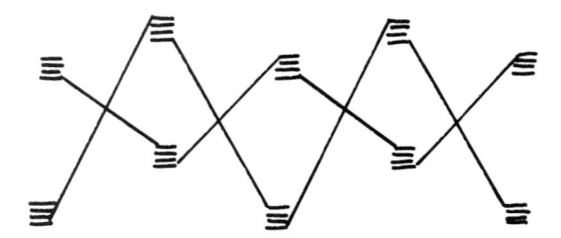

Fig. 3.4 Crossed threads and satin stitches.

Fig. 3.6 Zigzag star flowers.

up and over a bit to the right to stitch another block of satin stitches. Pull down and over for the third block. Continue across the fabric. Change threads and come back with another color. Cross the threads from the first pass as you do (Fig. 3.4). This is a good filler for garden pictures—the stitches become hedges of flowers—or use layers of these to crown trees (Fig. 3.5).

Speaking of flowers, try the ones in Fig. 3.6, with the machine set for darning and the needle position button set so the machine stops with the needle in the down position. Anchor the threads. Stitch one blob of about 10 or 12 satin stitches in one place and, ending on the left side, the needle still in the fabric, turn the hoop. Do another blob and end on the left side. Turn the hoop and do another and another. Lay in about five or six of these to create a satin-stitch flower. The satin stitches will all have that common center—at needle left.

Make the next satin stitch flower (Fig. 3.7) by first tracing around a drinking glass with a vanishing marker and making a dot in the center. Set your machine for darning, anchor the thread in the center, move to the outside without stitching and make a satin stitch blob perpendicular to the edge of the circle. Pull the thread to the center, anchor the thread, move across to the other side of the circle and make another blob. Return to the center and anchor the thread. Go to another place on, just within, or just without the circle and stitch another blob. *Pull the thread to the center and then over to the other side.

Fig. 3.5 This tree was stitched on cotton net. The trunk is encroaching zigzags, the crown of the tree is satin stitches and crossed threads.

Fig. 3.7 Create flowers using zigzag stitches and crossed threads.

Make another satin stitch blob. ** Repeat from * to ** until you have made a flower head.

Now you'll practice filling in shapes, another way to bring texture to your base fabric. Zigzagging is probably the most widely used method to fill in designs. You can use any stitch width, but the wider the setting, the looser the look. I feel I have more control if I use a 2 width — or better yet, I sew with straight stitches to fill in backgrounds. It is more like drawing with a pencil.

The drawback to straight-stitch filling is that the stitches are very tight to the fabric. On my 950 (remember, every machine has its own idiosyncracies), I can sew a loose zigzag if I *do not* lower the presser foot lever. I have had other machines that would do this. Experiment carefully with your machine, as the top thread will pile up in the bobbin if it is not going to work. On other machines if I sometimes want a lighter, loopier look, I may start with zigzagging to fill in a design and then draw on top of that with straight stitches to emphasize a color, to outline, or to add shading to my embroidery. So I've included three ways to add texture to fabric by filling in designs with zigzag stitches.

Method A

In this method you will follow the contour of your design with zigzag stitches, changing a flat circle into a ball shape.

Stitch width: W (5)
Stitch length: 0 (0)
Needle position: auto (center)
Needle: #90/14
Feed dogs: lowered (covered)
Presser foot: darning foot or spring, or use a wooden hoop with no foot
Tension: *top*, 3 (3); *bobbin*, normal
Fabric suggestion: medium-weight cotton
Thread: sewing thread for practice
Accessories: large hoop at least 7" (17.8cm); water-erasable marker

Using the marker, draw several circles on the fabric in the hoop (I drew around the base of a large spool of thread). Place stabilizer under the hoop. Zigzag the first circle into a ball shape by stitching in curved lines. To make it easier, first draw stitching guidelines inside the circle (Fig. 3.8, method A, *left*).

Start at the top of the circle, stitching and moving your hoop sideways and back while following the curves you've drawn (Fig. 3.8, method A, *right*). Move from top to bottom, creating the ball shape as you stitch. Don't build up stitches too fast in one place. Move the hoop evenly, slowly, and practice coordination.

Try other stitch widths on the other circles you've drawn. Put the samples in your notebook.

Method B

This has been described as the stair-step method. Designs can be filled in by zigzag stitching from lower-left corner to upper-right corner and back again (Fig. 3.8, method B). To practice this, set up your machine as you did in method A. Draw several 1½″ (3.8cm) squares on your fabric. Although you will start with the widest stitch, experiment with other widths as you did before. Each line of zigzags blends into the one before it. Add your experiments to your notebook.

Method C

Encroaching zigzag is another way to fill in a design (Fig. 3.8, method C). Set up your machine as follows:

Stitch width: W (5)
Stitch length: 0 (0)
Needle position: auto (center)
Needle: #90/14
Feed dogs: lowered (covered)
Presser foot: darning foot or spring or no foot
Tension: *top*, 3 (3); *bobbin*, normal
Fabric: medium-weight cotton
Thread: sewing thread for practice
Accessories: 7″ (17.8cm) hoop, tear-away stabilizer, vanishing marker

This time, draw only one 2″ (5.1cm) square on the fabric in the hoop, and place stabilizer under it. Keep the hoop in the same position in front of you; don't rotate it. Instead, move it backward and forward as you stitch. Start at the top of the right side of the square you've drawn and stitch down to the bottom, moving the hoop slowly to keep the stitches close together. Move the hoop to the left a bit and stitch back up to the top, overlapping the first stitching slightly. Continue until you have covered the square. Go back and stitch on top of stitches for more texture. Do a sample for your notebook.

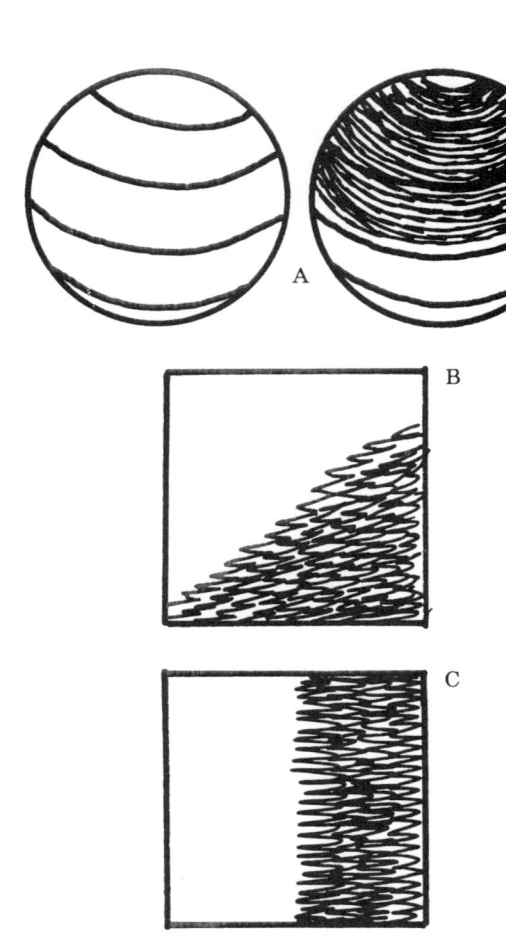

Fig. 3.8 Filling in designs with zigzag stitches. A. Draw guidelines in the circles, then move sideways and back, following the guidelines. B. Stair-step method. C. Encroaching zigzag.

Lesson 4. Applying thick threads from the top and bobbin

We created texture with regular sewing threads in Lesson 3, but in this lesson we'll change sewing and machine-embroidery threads for thicker threads, such as pearl cotton, cordonnet, and crocheted cotton. We'll explore four different ways to create texture by attaching these thick threads to fabric, including using them on the top spool, couched down on top of fabric, threaded up through the hole in the throat plate of the machine, and wound on the bobbin.

Adding texture adds interest to sewing and embroidery. Perhaps it's not essential—a dress is still a dress without textured decoration—but it is a long-cut, that something extra that takes your dress from ordinary to special. Adding cords, fringe, objects, and gathers to the background fabric are all easy techniques once you know your machine.

Applying thick thread through the needle

Thread as large as cordonnet can be sewn with a #110 needle. Topstitching needles also have eyes to accommodate double threads or thick threads like buttonhole twist, and are available in #80–#110 needles.

Whatever you use, the thread must slip through the needle easily and the needle must make a hole in the fabric large enough to keep the thread from fraying.

Couching thread down on top of fabric

If thread is too thick for the needle, try couching it down on top of the fabric using a cording foot. (The New Home snap-on cording foot works well.) Pull cord through the hole, front to back, and tie a knot at the back of your cord to keep from losing it before you begin. If you use a cording foot, as soon as you start stitching the thread will be fed through this hole with no help needed. It will stay exactly in place as you satin stitch over it with a zigzag or other decorative stitch. Cover the cord as closely or sparsely as you wish, using different stitch lengths.

You can substitute L, the blind hemming foot, or N, the transparent zigzag foot.

You may need to change needle position, depending upon which foot you use. Unlike the cording foot which feeds the thread automatically, you may have to guide the cord if you use one of the other feet mentioned.

Because of this, I feel that owning a cording foot is mandatory. I couldn't sew without it. Covering cord is just one use. I also use it without cord when I want to sew a perfectly straight line of stitches. The center hole is a perfect guide when I line it up with the stitching line on my fabric. Check the Sources of Supply list and order a generic cording foot if you can't find one locally.

Try multiple cords as well, using the transparent zigzag foot N.

Project Greeting Card

Practice applying thick threads on top of the fabric by making the greeting card shown in Fig. 3.9.

Stitch width: N–W (0–5)
Stitch length: 1/2–2 (0–2)
Needle position: auto (center)

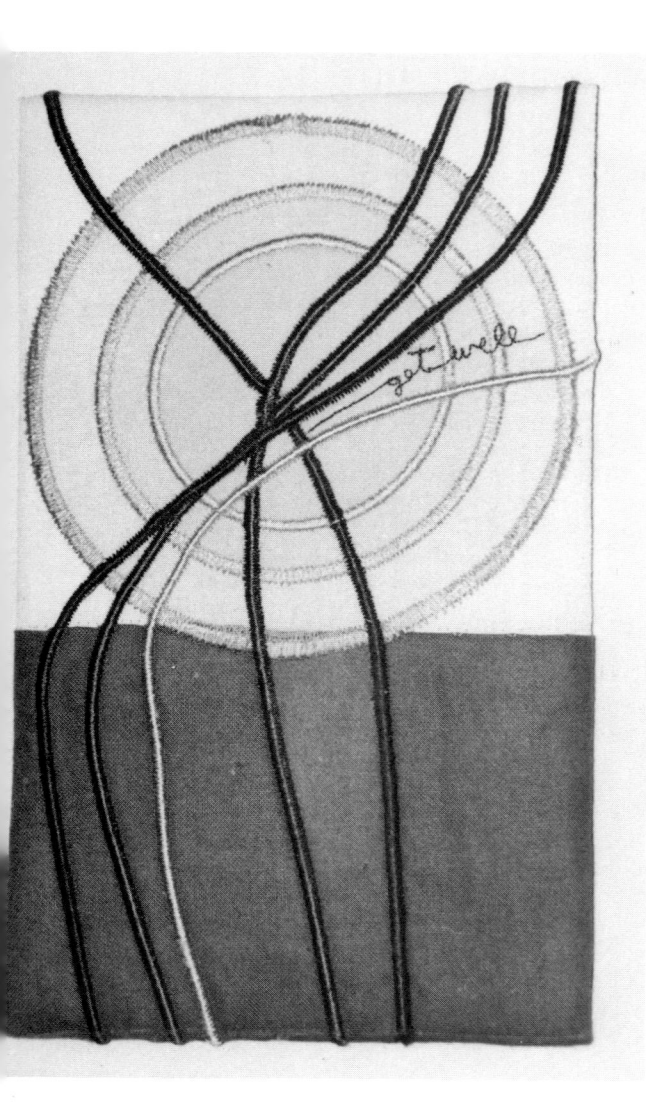

Fig. 3.9 "Even the Rainbow is Upset" greeting card.

Needle: #90/14
Feed dogs: up, down or covered
Presser foot: transparent embroidery foot N, darning foot
Tension: *top*, 3 (3); *bobbin*, normal
Fabric suggestions: 12" (30.5cm) square of white polished cotton, 6" (15.2cm) square of green polished cotton, 12" (30.5cm) square of yellow organdy
Thread: rayon in rainbow colors — yellow, red, green, purple, blue; #3 pearl cotton in the same colors; monofilament
Accessories: 7" (17.8cm) spring hoop; circle maker or thumb tack, transparent tape, cork or eraser; vanishing marker; greeting card folder (available at craft, art, and needlework shops) or picture frame; dressmaker's carbon; empty ballpoint pen
Stabilizer: tear-away

Use the pattern in Fig. 3.10 as a guide, changing measurements to fit the card folder or frame. Trace the pattern from the book, then place the drawing on top of the white background fabric, with dressmaker's carbon between. Transfer it, using the empty ballpoint pen.

Cut a piece from the green fabric large enough for the area at the bottom of the design, plus 1" (2.5cm). Fold under the top edge of the green about ½" (12.7mm) and press it. Hold it in place with pins and apply it using the transparent zigzag foot N, with monofilament thread on the top and bobbin, and the machine set on a blind hem stitch — stitch width 1, stitch length 2.

Next, stretch three layers of yellow organdy over the white and green fabric and put them all in a spring hoop. Back this with tear-away. Set up the circle maker on your machine. (If you don't have a circle maker, use the thumb tack method in Fig. 1.3.) Poke the tack through at the center of the three layers of organdy. Remove the monofilament thread and use a rayon or cotton machine embroidery thread. Place the appliqué presser foot on the line of the inner circle. Stitch on that line around the circle with a straight stitch. Take the fabric out of the hoop and cut back only the top layer of organdy to the stitching.

Place the greeting card back in the hoop, with the tack back in its original hole. Satin stitch with the machine set on a medium

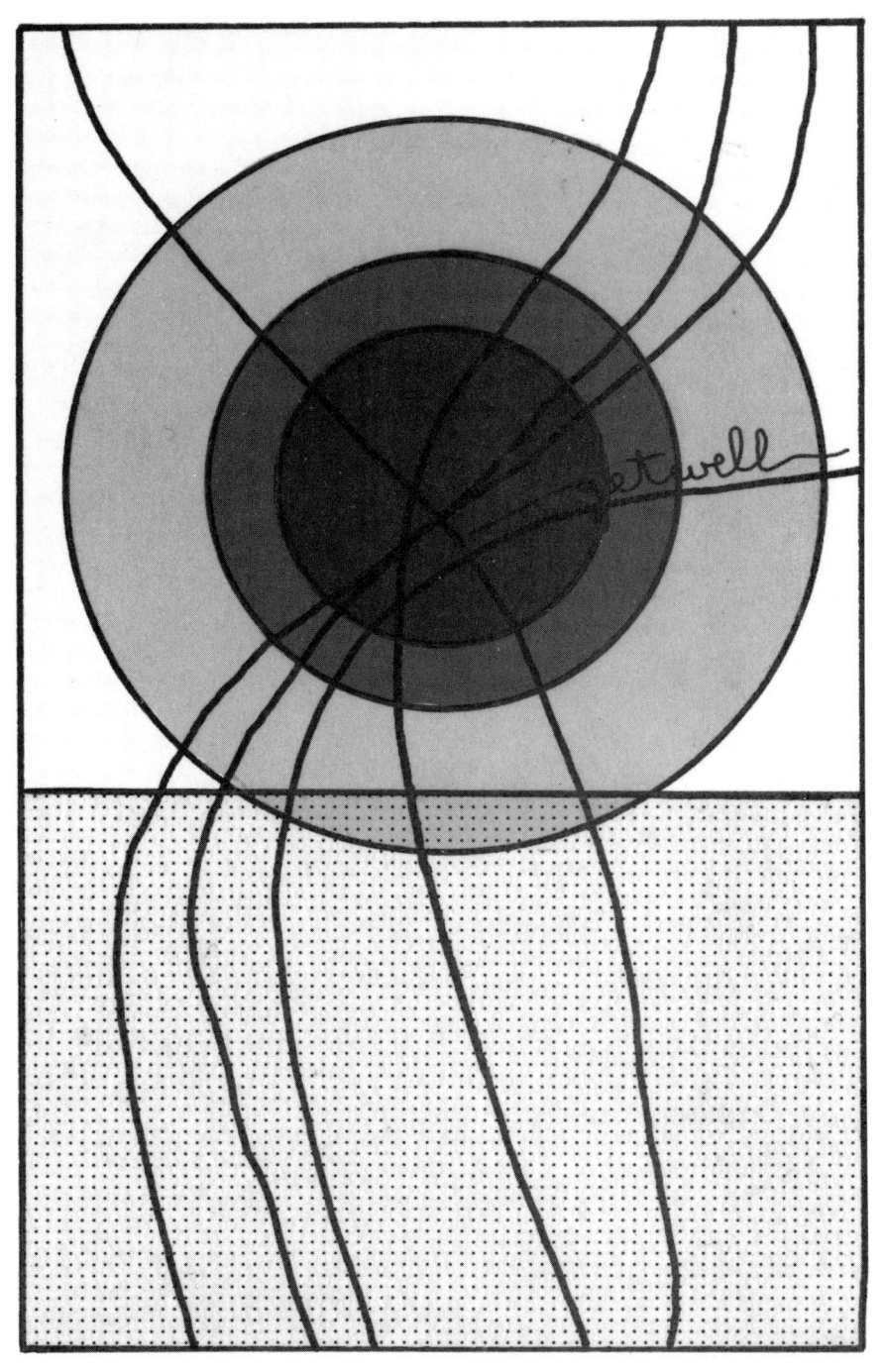

Fig. 3.10 Greeting card pattern. Enlarge or reduce to fit your card folder.

(2) width, length 1 (1/2) for smooth, close satin stitches.

Then move the tack so the line of the next circle will be centered under your presser foot. Straight stitch around the circle, cut back and satin stitch again as you did with the first. Do the same for the last layer of organdy.

Take the fabric out of the hoop while you stitch over the cords, but place tear-away stabilizer underneath. Each cord is a different color; use the cording foot to guide the pearl cotton. If you don't have a cording foot, then use N, the transparent embroidery foot. Fit the pearl cotton into the groove and guide it as you stitch. You may have to change needle positions to cover the cord perfectly. Stitch over the cords, using close satin stitches. I prefer to stitch in two passes, attaching the cord first, then stitching in close satin stitches to cover it evenly and smoothly on the second pass.

When the last cord has been covered, change to the darning foot, feed dogs down or covered, and a straight stitch. Use the color you have on your machine—unless it's yellow—to write a message along the top of one of the cords. I wrote "get well," and on the inside I'll write the message: "Even the rainbow is upset." If you have a Galaxie, raise the feed dogs, engage the presser foot lever, and program your message.

Finish the edge with a straight stitch. Trim close to stitches and slip into the card folder or finish it for a framed picture.

Stitch width: N–M (1/2–2)
Stitch length: 1–3 (1/2–1)
Needle position: auto (left)
Needle: varies
Feed dogs: up
Presser foot: transparent zigzag foot N or blind hemming foot L
Tension: *top*, normal; *bobbin*, normal
Thread: monofilament on top, polyester on bobbin
Stabilizer: tear-away

Stitch alongside the cord. At the wide bite of the needle, the cord is sewn down with a tiny, almost unnoticeable stitch. When the line of stitching is completed, go back and gently nudge the cord over toward the stitching line. Now your monofilament will be completely hidden.

Or line up several threads of pearl cotton next to each other. Use a zigzag or built-in stitch to attach them with monofilament or with a colored thread. Make colorful shoelaces this way.

Soutache is like a thick cord, and can be attached perfectly using a braiding foot. It is not easily done without this special foot, as there is no way to hold the braid in place so the needle will enter exactly in the center each time. It's sometimes possible to feed other cords, narrow braids or rickrack through the hole in this foot. To attach soutache, trace the design on the topside of your fabric, using a vanishing marker. Place stabilizer under the fabric.

Corners are not impossible if you walk the machine around them. Stop at the corner, needle down, presser foot raised. Turn the fabric 45 degrees, lower the foot, take one stitch; then, needle down again, raise the presser foot, turn the fabric to complete the corner. You'll get a good angle. If you can, though, choose a design with undulating curves, which are easier to accomplish.

Use soutache and other braids down jacket and vest fronts, around sleeves, to decorate belts and handbags.

If the braid crosses and recrosses itself, threading in and out like a Celtic interlacing cord, it is still possible to use the braiding foot. The braid will not be threaded through the foot, but will be hand basted in place on the fabric, then fit within the groove as you carefully ride over it and stitch it down.

For your next sample, use a darning foot for wool when freely couching down yarn. This darning foot may have a guide in the front to hold the yarn as you freely attach it. To get the feel of the foot, use straight

Fig. 3.11 Stitch alongside, then across the twist, to attach cord.

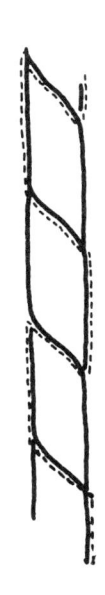

lines or gentle curves on your first samples. Try a smooth, sport-weight yarn for your first experiment. Add the result to your growing notebook.

Here's another invisible way to attach thick, twisted cord or yarn to fabric (Fig. 3.11). Leave the machine set up for free machining, but remove the presser foot or use a darning foot. Use monofilament thread on top. Iron a piece of freezer paper onto the back of the fabric. Begin by drawing the bobbin thread to the top and anchoring the threads. Stitch the end of the cord down. Then move along one side of the cord with a straight stitch. When you reach a twist in the cord, follow it to the other side by stitching in the twist. Once on the other side, follow along that side for a few stitches until you reach the top of the next twist. Cross over again, following the twist. Continue in this manner until the cord is attached.

Attaching cord with the cording foot

You can also attach thick cords with monofilament and an open zigzag or a blind stitch with the use of the cording foot. I can get five strands of #3 pearl cotton in mine—that's quite a bundle—one strand of knitting worsted, or three strands of sport yarn. Set your machine for blind-hemming with the stitch length as long as possible (Fig. 3.12). For a different look, use a thread that contrasts in value or color with the cord and sew it on with a straight stitch or use one of the decorative stitches.

Stitch a record of your experiments with straight stitch, zigzag, utility, and decorative stitches, using different colors and types of threads. Try a variegated thread in which one of the colors exactly matches the color of the cord. The stitching line will appear and disappear. You can also apply round elastic with this method.

Using thick thread in the bobbin

Cable stitching is an embroidery technique using thick thread on the bobbin. The topside of the fabric will be against the bed of the machine. It can be done with feed dogs up, using an embroidery foot for straight or built-in stitches, or it can be done freely with feed dogs down or cov-

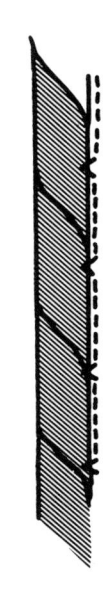

Fig. 3.12 Use the blind-hem stitch to attach cord invisibly.

ered, using a darning foot or using no presser foot at all.

Cabling can look like a tightly couched thread or like fluffy fur, depending on the thread you choose. A hard twist thread like crochet cotton will lay flatter, with less beading or looping than a soft, loosely twisted yarn like mohair. The effects you get will depend not only on top and bobbin tension, but on stitch width, stitch length, color and size of cord, color of top thread, feed dogs up or down, color, weight, and type of fabric, how fast you stitch and how fast you move the hoop.

When I say you can use thick threads, I'm not kidding. Did you know that you can use up to a four-ply yarn in the bobbin? Of course, the thicker the yarn, the less you can wind on the bobbin. Usually the bobbin can be put on the machine and wound slowly while you hold the yarn or cord to control it. If you find the yarn must be wound by hand, do so evenly without stretching it.

To use the thicker threads this embroidery requires, you must override that panicky feeling that accompanies loosening and tightening the tension on the bobbin. Perhaps you've already discovered, as you've changed bobbins, that you can recognize the feel of normal tension. If not, put a bobbin full of sewing thread into the bobbin case and click the thread into the spring. Hold on to the end of the thread and let the bobbin case hang from it like a yoyo. It should drop slowly when jerked. Memorize how this feels with normal tension before you begin to loosen the bobbin spring for cabling.

Put a bobbin filled with heavy thread in the case and bypass the bobbin tension by taking the thread straight up through the hole at the top of the case. You now have no resistance on the thread. These are the two extremes.

Replace the thread in the tension spring. Take the small screwdriver and turn the tension screw counterclockwise, one-quarter turn at a time. Each time you complete a quarter turn, pull gently on the bobbin thread to see how it feels. Loosen the spring over an empty box, as the screw has a tendency to pop out and disappear forever. I've purchased several extra screws just in case.

When adjusting tension for heavy threads, remember that the cord must feed through the bobbin case smoothly. Loosen the bobbin tension by turning the screw counterclockwise one-quarter turn at a time until the tension feels normal to you.

Practice cabling on a piece of scrap fabric. Set up your machine with feed dogs up, using an embroidery thread on top or regular sewing thread. Place your fabric in a hoop and use an open embroidery foot. Stitch and then look under the fabric to be sure the tension is set correctly—do you want tight, stiff stitches or loosely looping ones? Manipulate the bobbin tension for different effects.

Don't forget the top tension. It must be loose enough so the bobbin thread stays underneath the fabric; but if it is too loose, it may keep the stitches from staying neatly in place.

Write on your sample fabric which is the topside, which the back. Also record bobbin and top spool tensions by using + and − signs.

Most embroiderers I know buy extra bobbin cases to use for embroidery only. Buying an extra case is a good idea. It's possible to tighten and loosen the spring screw—or even remove the spring altogether—without the time-consuming adjustments needed to return to normal sewing tension.

Whatever you choose to do, don't be afraid of your sewing machine. Change tensions, lengths, speeds, and use it to its full potential. Get to know your machine.

Now prepare a cabling sample for your notebook. Choose a medium-weight cotton or blend. Use all the built-in stitches with #3, #5, and then #8 pearl cotton. Try ribbon and yarn as well. Keep the stitch long enough to prevent the cord from bunching up under the fabric. Open built-in stitches work best and simple zigzag is most effective. I like the zigzag opened up to a 2 or 3 length and a 4 stitch width. It gives a rick-rack effect.

Stretch a piece of fabric in a hoop, but don't use a stabilizer underneath. Instead, use a stabilizer on top to keep your stitches from pulling. Draw lines or designs on the stabilizer. This is actually the back of your work.

Dip the needle into the fabric, drawing the bobbin thread or cord to the top. Hold the threads to the side as you begin. If you can't bring the cord up through the fabric, then pierce the cloth with an awl or large needle and bring it up. Don't anchor the threads with a lockstitch at the beginning or end. Instead, pull the threads to the back each time you start; when you stop, leave a long enough tail to be able to thread it up in a hand-sewing needle and poke it through to the back. Later you can work these threads into the stitching by hand.

It is also possible to quilt with this technique. Using a white pearl cotton in the bobbin and a top thread to match the fabric, you can get an effect which looks much like Japanese Sashiko (Fig. 3.13).

Apply ⅛" (3.2mm) double-faced satin ribbon as shown in Fig. 3.14. Wind the ribbon onto the bobbin. The end of the ribbon will bypass the tension spring. Then place the bobbin in the case. Use the regular presser foot, needle right, stitch length about 4 or use a topstitch setting.

When you start and stop in this type of couching, the ribbon is brought to the underside and finished off by hand. This technique is used on the infant's bonnet in Chapter 5.

Next try cabling with free embroidery. Place a medium-weight fabric in a hoop with a stabilizer on top. Lower or cover the feed dogs and, using a darning foot or bare needle, freely straight stitch, then zigzag.

Plan the lines of stitching before you begin. As you work, sew and peek under your hoop so you can regulate the bobbin and top tensions to your liking. Practice turn-

Fig. 3.13 Stitching in the style of Japanese Sashiko.

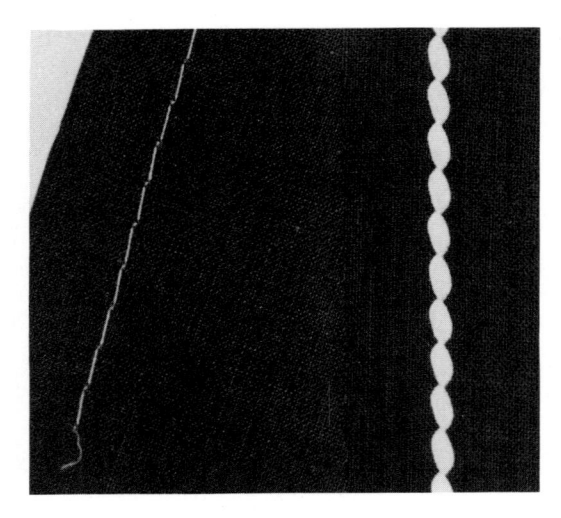

Fig. 3.14 The top and underneath of a ribbon attached by machine stitching.

ing, pushing and pulling the hoop, sewing circles and straight lines. When your stitching changes direction, the tension is also changed, so practice how fast you should move your hoop for the effects you want. Often a design can be seen from the back of printed fabric. Take advantage of that to stitch a sample piece for your notebook. Stretch the fabric in a hoop. Water-soluble stabilizer can be used underneath if the fabric is washable. Otherwise, don't use a stabilizer. Instead, be sure your fabric is very taut, and use the darning foot. Embellish these prints by outlining the designs with pearl cotton or thick rayon thread on the bobbin. If the top thread is regular sewing thread or a heavier weight and matches the fabric color exactly, the cabling line will appear broken and have more of a handstitched appearance. By using a contrasting heavy thread, you can add an additional color to the line and alter its appearance in another way.

Use bridal veiling as your fabric and create original lace. Or, decorate velveteen using velour yarn on the bobbin and monofilament thread on the top.

Project
Tote Bag Square (Cabling)

Patches of color create the background for this cabling square (see color section). All the stitching is done with feed dogs up, although you may want to try cabling with your machine set up for free-machine embroidery. Though the majority of my lines of stitching are the basic straight stitch and zigzag, I've added lines of rickrack and the triple stretch zigzag as well. Don't limit yourself to these. Choose other decorative stitches to create your original square.

Stitch width: N–W (0–5)
Stitch length: 1–5 (1–5)
Needle position: auto (center)
Needle: #80/12
Feed dogs: up
Presser foot: transparent zigzag foot N
Tension: *top*, 5 (4); *bobbin*, normal, then loosened for #5 pearl cotton
Fabric suggestions: 9"-square medium-weight white fabric for background; scraps of yellow, red, and blue medium-weight fabric (see Fig. 3.15 for sizes)
Thread: green, yellow, red, blue sewing thread; bobbins wound with #5 or #8 green, yellow, red, blue pearl cotton; one bobbin of green sewing thread
Accessories: tracing paper; pencil; ruler; vanishing marker; fusible webbing
Stabilizer: freezer paper to finish square

Transfer the outline of the fabric pieces in Fig. 3.15 to tracing paper. Use these pattern pieces to cut out the appliqués of yellow, red, and blue fabric. Press fusible webbing to the back of each piece; then press them in place on the white backing fabric. With green sewing thread on the spool and bobbin, stitch along the edges of each appliqué. These lines are your sewing guides.

Turn the square over. When cabling, you

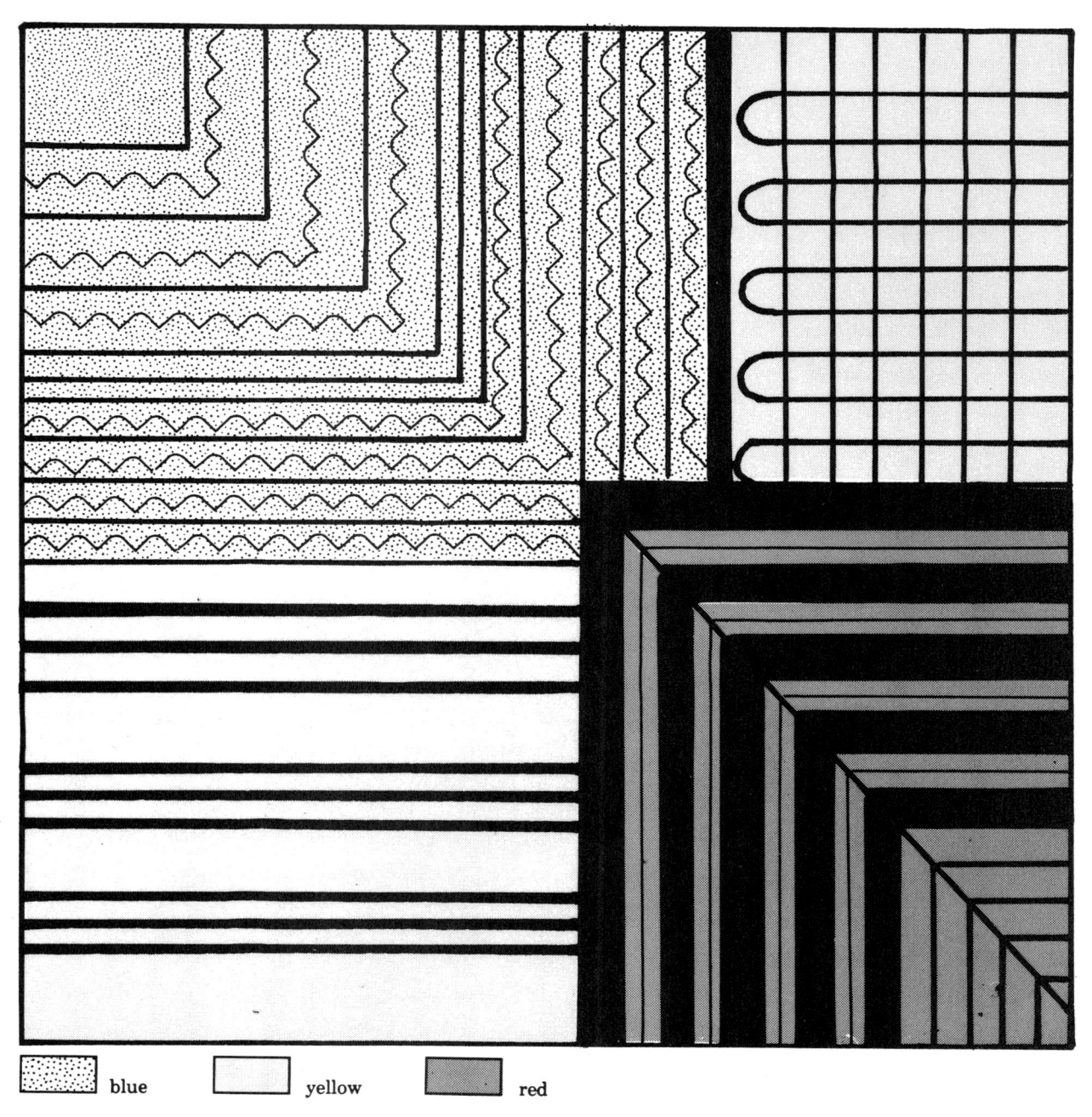

Fig. 3.15 Pattern for tote bag square.

work with the underside up and no stabilizer is used underneath. Using the ruler and marker, draw stitching lines inside the color sections. These are only guides to help keep stitching lines straight. (As I stitched this square, I used the outside edge or an inside edge of the transparent zigzag foot N as a guide, placing it on a line of stitches to keep my embroidery lines straight.) Follow the illustration as you stitch, or use your own stitches, colors, and distances between lines of stitching. One hint that shortens the time needed to finish the square: stitch with green thread first and complete everything on the square where green thread is needed. Then change to yellow and stitch everything that is done with yellow thread and so on. You'll have to switch colors back and forth on some squares, but in this way you won't have to change bobbins and thread your machine so often.

Begin with green sewing thread on the top and green pearl cotton on the bobbin. Stitch the rickrack stitch (#21, width 5) on top of the straight stitches at the edge of the red appliqué. Change to zigzag and stitch three lines as shown, leaving at least ½" (12.7mm) between the lines. Change to the longest straight stitch and sew at each edge of the zigzag stitches. The last line of green straight stitches runs diagonally from the corner of the red scrap to the edge of the square, as shown. Finish by stitching three lines of green straight stitches to fill the square.

Change to yellow thread on top, yellow pearl cotton on the bobbin. Still on the red portion, straight stitch between the lines of zigzags.

On the upper blue patch, stitch straight yellow stitches. First stitch a line of straight stitches around the edge of the area. Then stitch in other lines of yellow, some close together, some farther apart.

Change to red thread on top, red pearl cotton in the bobbin.

On the lower yellow scrap, first cover the edge with red zigzag stitches. Use a wide setting and a length that will produce satin stitches but will still feed the fabric through smoothly. Practice on another piece of fabric first to find the ideal setting.

Change to straight stitching and stitch equally spaced lines across the lower yellow rectangle. My lines are ¼" (6.4mm) apart. Change to green thread and pearl cotton and straight stitch lines to create a grid on the yellow patch.

The yellow patch at the upper left of the square is stitched with sets of wide satin stitches placed ¼" (6.4mm) apart that extend from top to bottom of the scrap. Each set is made up of a line of red satin stitches with a line of blue satin stitches on each side. Begin by covering the edge with blue. Change to red and stitch a line of satin stitches next to it, but not so close that the yellow fabric isn't visible between. Continue on until the patch is completed. Instead of changing threads constantly, measure distances this time and stitch in all three red lines first. Go back and stitch the blue lines.

The large blue area is finished using red rickrack (#21, width 3-5) in different widths and lengths. You've already stitched yellow straight stitches. Now fill in between with red rickrack stitches. Finish the square with this decorative stitch or use one of your own choice.

Finish the square as explained in Chapter 12.

Lesson 5. Fringing yarn and fabric

In this lesson you will learn to make fringe with a fringing fork, as well as with strips of fabric sewn together and clipped into fringe. Start by using a fringing fork to make yarn fringe. It can be used for wigs, costumes, rugs, and decorating edges of garments. Fringing forks are available in many different sizes. Or, you can make your own using wire, ranging from the thickness of a coat hanger to as fine as a hairpin.

Wrap the fork as shown in Fig. 3.16, sew down the center, pull the fork toward you, and wrap some more. If making yards and yards of fringe, use Robbie Fanning's method of measuring. Robbie measures the length she wants from a roll of adding-machine tape and stitches her fringe right to the tape. This also keeps the fringe from twisting. When you're finished, tear off the paper and apply the fringe.

Sometimes you may not want the fringe sewn in the middle (Fig. 3.16A). Stitch it at the edge of the fork to make fringe twice as wide as that made by sewing down the center (Fig. 3.16B). As you work with the fork, you will understand when to use each method. And don't limit yourself to yarn or string alone. Try fabric. I used it for doll hair for my denim doll.

Stitch width: auto (0)
Stitch length: auto (1)
Needle position: auto (center)
Feed dogs: up
Presser foot: transparent zigzag foot N
Tension: *top*, normal; *bobbin*, normal
Fabric suggestion: 1"-wide (2.5cm-wide) bias strips, several yards
Thread: polyester to match bias
Accessories: large fringe fork
Stabilizer: adding machine tape

I wrapped the fork with red denim and sewed down the center over adding-machine tape. When I had enough for hair, I tore the paper off the fringe and pinned the hair to her head in various ways to decide what hairdo I liked best. I sewed it on by hand; I could have left it as it was, but I decided to clip the loops (Fig. 3.17).

But you can achieve almost the same effect with fabric without using the fringing fork. Work with strips of fabrics, but don't clip them into fringe until after they are sewn to the item you are making.

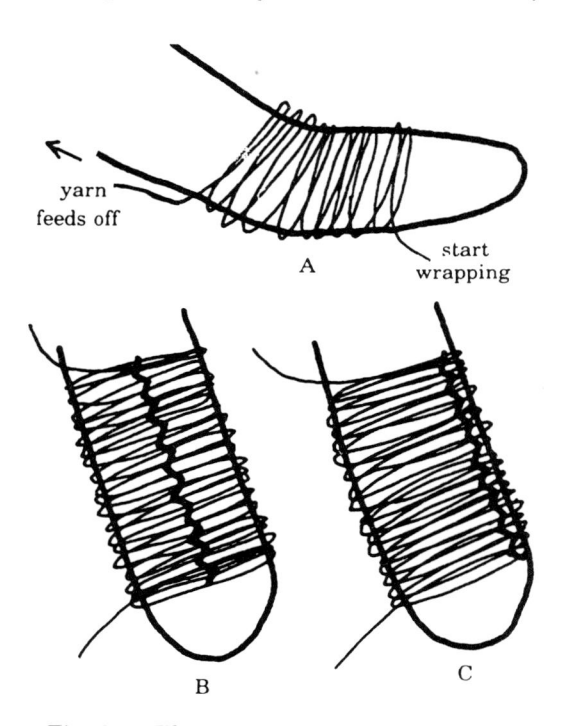

Fig. 3.16 The fringe fork. A. Wrap with yarn or fabric strips. B. Sew down in the middle. C. Or sew at the side of the fork for wider fringe.

Project
Fringed Denim Rug

This fabric-fringe project, a little rug, ate up yards of old jeans and denim remnants I picked up at sales; I kept cutting 2½" (6.4cm) strips on the bias until I had finished the rug. Set the machine for straight stitching.

Stitch width: auto (0)
Stitch length: auto (2)
Needle position: auto (right)
Needle: jeans needle
Presser foot: zipper
Tension: *top*, normal; *bobbin*, normal

Fig. 3.17 The doll's hair is fabric fringe, her eyelashes are thread fringe done with the tailor-tacking foot.

Fabric suggestion: denim, cut into 2½" (6.4cm) bias strips of blues and red; use remnants and old jeans to cut quantity needed for rug size you want; heavy upholstery fabric for rug backing
Thread: matching polyester thread
Stabilizer: 1"-wide (2.5cm-wide) fusible webbing (measure circumference of rug)

You'll need a piece of heavy fabric the size of the finished rug, plus an inch all around. Measure the perimeter and cut a piece of 1"-wide (2.5cm-wide) fusible webbing. Using a Teflon pressing sheet, press the fusible webbing to the topside of all the edges and fold them back on the topside of the fabric, pressing again (Fig. 3.18). This is the top of the rug, so the edges will be finished when the last strip is stitched down.

Fold the first bias strip lengthwise to find the center, but open it again and place it ⅛" (3.5mm) from the edge of the upholstery fabric. Stitch down the center crease of each strip from top to bottom (Fig. 3.19). Fold the left side of the strip to the right. Push the next strip as close as you can get it to the first. Sew down the center again; Fig. 3.19 shows the first three fabric strips stitched down. If you run out of fab-

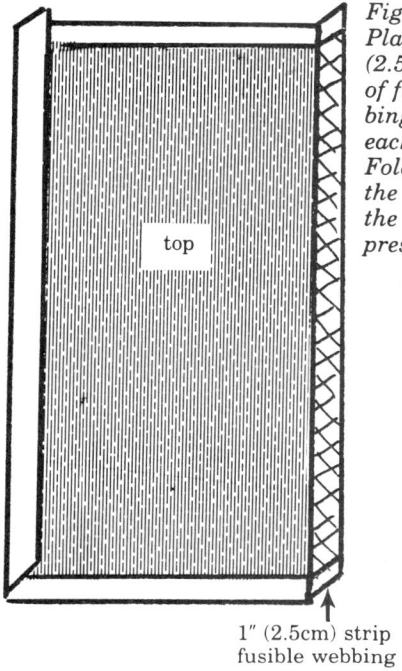

Fig. 3.18 Place a 1" (2.5cm) strip of fusible webbing along each edge. Fold toward the topside of the fabric and press in place.

1" (2.5cm) strip fusible webbing

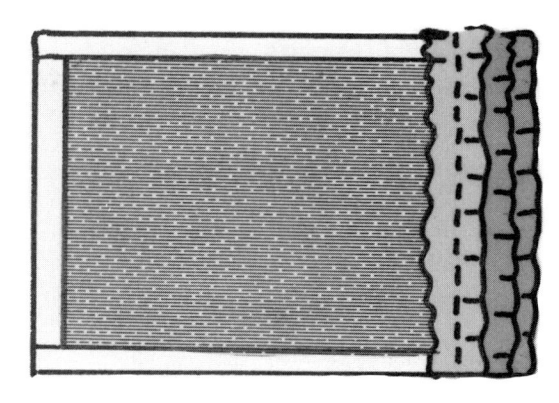

Fig. 3.19 Stitching bias strips onto the rug.

ric for a strip, add another by overlapping the last strip at least 1" (2.5cm).

When you're all done stitching, clip each strip every ½" (12.7mm), staggering the clips for each row. My rug (Fig. 3.20) went into the washer and dryer to soften.

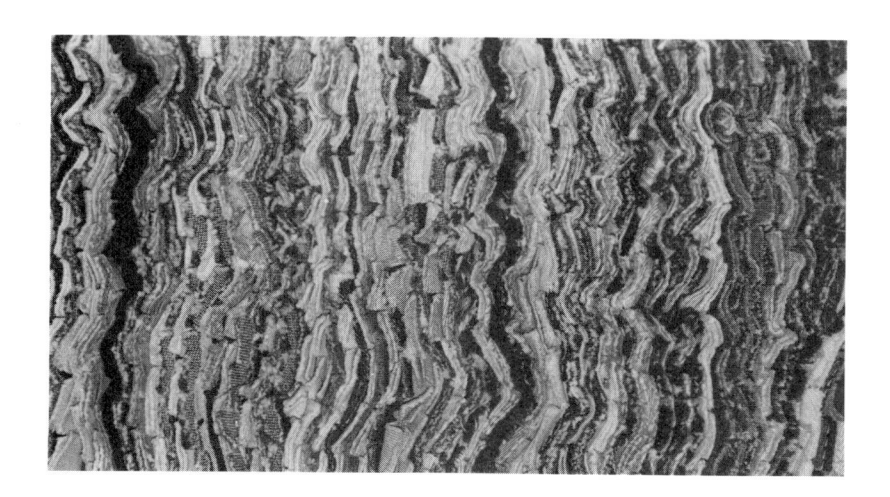

Fig. 3.20 The bias strips are clipped into fringe.

43

Lesson 6. Adding buttons, beads, shisha

Attaching buttons

Once you've attached a button by machine, you won't want to do it any other way, it is so speedy. If you are applying buttons to a garment you've made, be sure the button area is interfaced. Dab glue stick on the underside of the button and position it.

> Stitch width: auto 3.9mm or 2.5mm (space between holes in the button)
> Stitch length: 0
> Needle position: auto (left)
> Needle: #80
> Feed dogs: lowered (covered)
> Presser foot: button foot M (button foot)
> Tension: *top*, normal; *bobbin*, normal
> Thread: polyester
> Accessories: Viking button reed, pin or toothpick are optional, transparent tape, glue stick, scrap fabrics, buttons, beads and shisha mirrors (see Sources of Supply)

Set the Galaxie for button sewing, either 2.5mm or 3.9mm, and the machine will do all the steps for you. On the 950 place the button foot on top of the button and stitch in the hole to the left three or four times to anchor the threads (stitch width 0). Raise the needle and move the stitch width so the needle clears the button and falls into the hole at the right. On that setting, stitch back and forth several times. When you have finished, move the stitch width to 0 and anchor again. That's all there is to it.

If the garment fabric is thick, such as coating, you will need to make a button shank; otherwise, the buttonhole will pucker whenever the coat is buttoned. On the Galaxie simply move the front leg lever on the button foot M to the front. On the 940/950, raise the stitches to create a shank by taping a darning needle or round toothpick between the holes on top of the button before you stitch (Fig. 3.21A).

When finished, pull off the tape and remove the darning needle. Leave a long thread to wrap around the shank and anchor with a hand needle, strengthening the shank.

Or use the Viking button reed (Fig. 3.21B). It is a small gadget made to slip under the button to raise it off the fabric and create either of two shank heights. A button elevator, which accomplishes the same thing, is available at notion counters.

Attaching beads and baubles

Beads can be attached by machine if the hole in the bead is large enough and your needle fine enough. The thickness of the bead also matters if you zigzag it in place. Lower or cover the feed dogs, remove the presser foot, adjust the stitch width as directed. Hand-walk the machine first to see if the needle will clear the bead, and if the sizes of the bead and needle are compati-

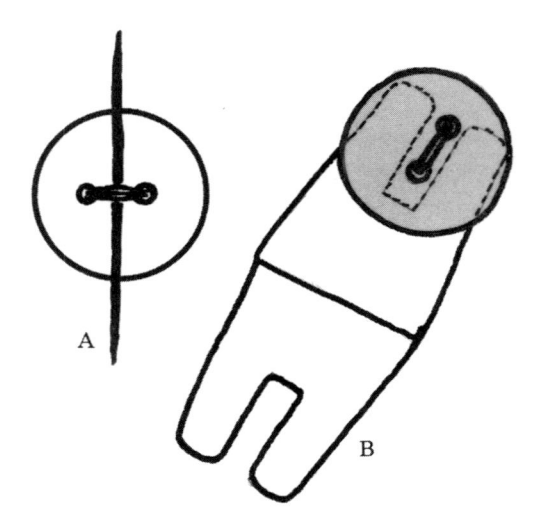

Fig. 3.21 Sew on a button with a shank.
A. Use a toothpick on top of the button.
B. Use the Viking button reed.

44

ble. If attaching the bead by hand-walking only, attach the rim of the bead to the fabric by first holding it in place with a dot of glue from a glue stick. Anchor the thread in the center of the bead by stitching in place three or four times. Raise the needle. Move the fabric over to anchor the thread on the side of the bead. Go back to the center and anchor again. Repeat until the bead is securely sewn in place and will stand up (Fig. 3.22). Nudge the bead to stand on its outside rim when you finish stitching. Wipe off the glue.

If you go back and stitch down the other side as well, your bead will lay flat, hole up (Fig. 3.23).

Attaching seed beads, or other fine or oddly shaped beads can be done in the following way. First string the beads onto a thread. Using monofilament, stitch one end of the beaded thread down on the fabric. Stitch along the thread the width of one bead. Push the first bead near that end and then stitch over the thread to keep the bead in place. Stitch again the distance of the next bead. Push the bead up to the first, stitch over the thread and repeat, as shown in Fig. 3.24.

Or sew beads down by stringing them singly on thick threads and stitching both ends of the threads down (Fig. 3.25).

You can attach beads invisibly, using monofilament thread to couch them down or to string the beads on. Or choose your thread wisely and use the stitching as a part of the decoration.

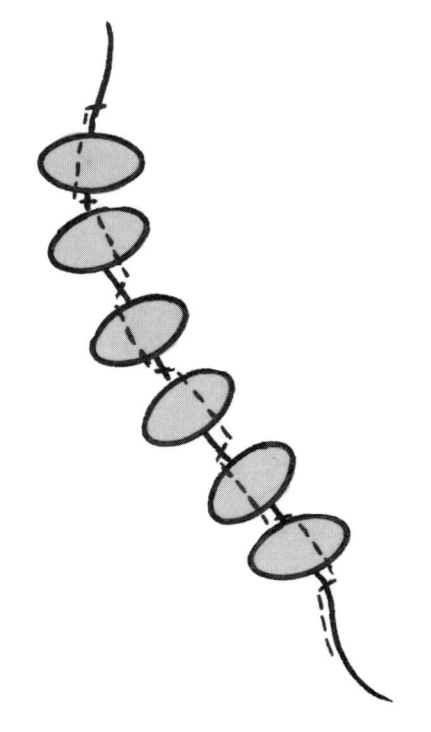

Fig. 3.24 A string of seed beads, attached by machine along dotted line (solid line is thread).

Another way to hold down beads is to first stitch strips of needlelace on water-soluble stabilizer. When the lace has been stitched, merely pull off the excess stabilizer and hold your work under a faucet to wash out most of what remains, but leave

Fig. 3.22 If beads are stitched down on only one side, they can be nudged to stand up.

Fig. 3.23 Stitching down both sides to make beads lie flat.

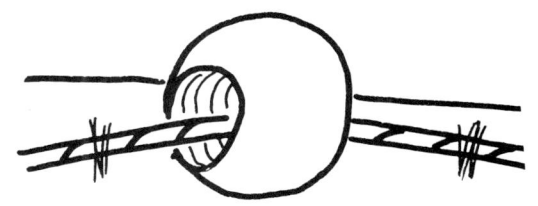

Fig. 3.25 Attach a large bead by threading a cord through it and stitching on either side of the cord.

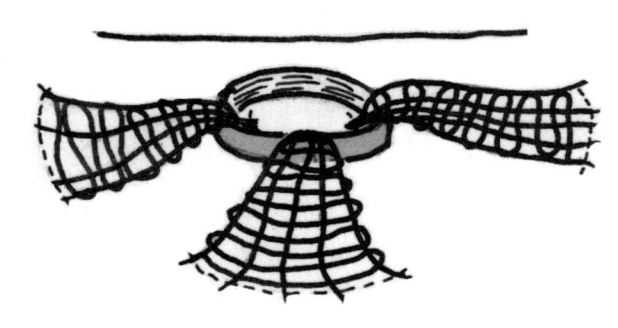

Fig. 3.26 Using needlelace to attach beads.

a bit of the sticky residue. When it is almost dry, shape the needlelace strips and they will dry in that shape. Use two or three of these strips to hold down beads or washers (Fig. 3.26). Thread a strip through the object and stitch down one end. Move the bauble down over your stitching. Arrange the strip, twisting it if you wish. Then stitch down the other end freely and invisibly. Use this method, as I have, on decorative box tops and collages (Fig. 3.27).

Fig. 3.27 "The Flop Box," made by Pat Pasquini, has a machine-embellished top by the author. It includes beads held down with needlelace, other beads strung with cord and porcupine quills and couched in place, textures created by stitching cords down, using a double needle to pintuck suede, and stitching blobs and satin stitches in the background. Photo by Robbie Fanning.

Tote Bag Squares: (upper left, clockwise) Chapter 4, Lesson 10—Straight Stitch Applique; Edge-Stitch Applique; Modified Reverse Applique; Chapter 3, Lesson 4—Cabling.

(upper) Earrings worked with metallic thread on water-soluble stabilizer can be shaped when the stabilizer is washed out.

(lower) Chapter 2, Lesson 2—Pendants are a fast way to practice free machining and satin stitches.

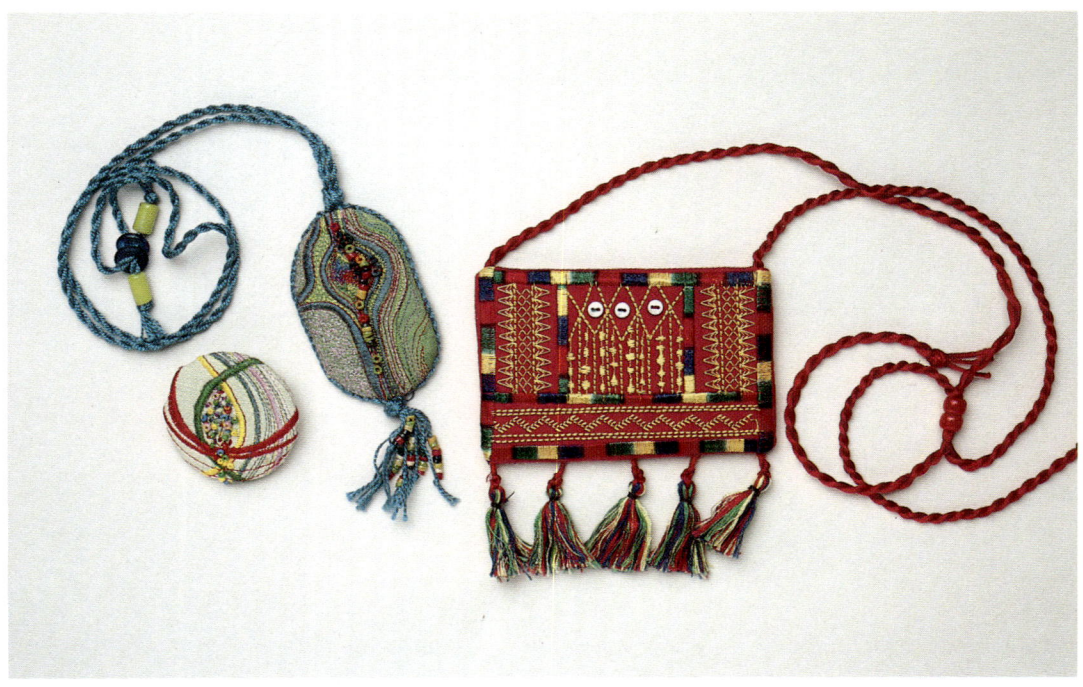

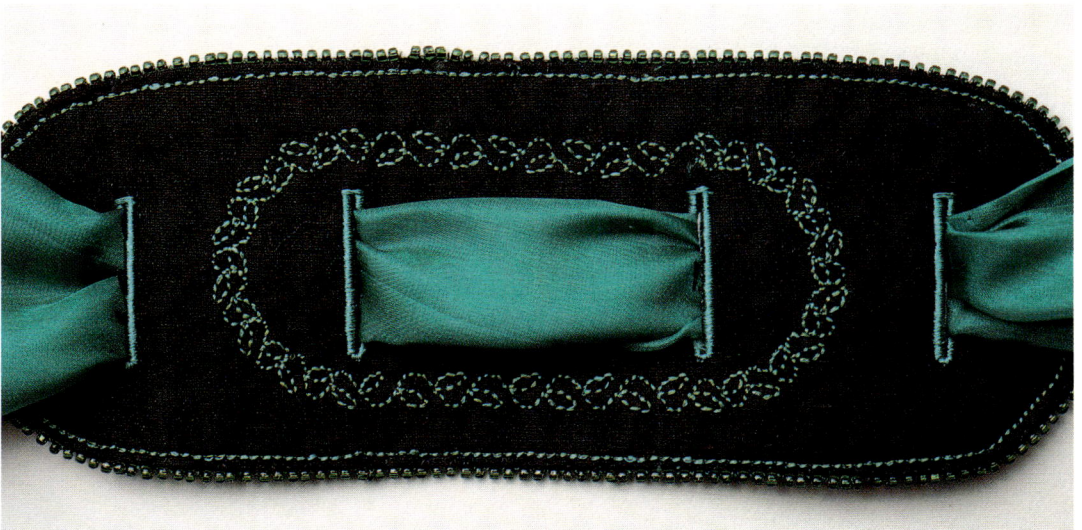

(upper) Learn to use your decorative stitches to direct the eye on a specially shaped scarf and shoe ornaments.

(lower) Practice making perfect (half)circles and applying cross-locked beads by machine in this belt ornament.

The best way to learn is to make lots of small samples. And the best way to store those samples is in a notebook, with a cover recording all your stitches.

Pre-strung, imported glass beads that are cross-locked onto 100% cotton thread are easy to stitch in place. They are sold on cards in two-yard lengths at local craft stores or through the mail and make a lovely trim at the edge of a collar, cuffs, pendant, etc. You can cut the thread anywhere along the length without losing any beads. (The belt in Chapter 11 uses them.)

Another method of using stones and jewels for wall hangings or pictures is to cover them with net or transparent fabrics, and then stitch down the fabric. Then cut holes in the fabric large enough to let the objects show through and small enough so they don't fall out.

Or make needlelace in the center of wire bent into a circle, rectangle, or other shape. Stretch the lace over an object placed on a background fabric. Attach the lace to the fabric by stitching freely, close to the wire, around the inside of this frame, and cutting off the wire. Embroider the edges if you wish.

Attaching shisha mirrors

Shishas are small pieces of mirrored glass. They are about 1" (2.5cm) in diameter, but are never exactly circular. It is possible to attach them to fabric if you follow the methods Caryl Rae Hancock of Indianapolis, Gail Kibiger of Warsaw, Indiana, or Jane Warnick of Houston, Texas, invented.

This is Caryl Rae Hancock's method, illustrated in Fig. 3.28. First, stretch organdy in a hoop. The shisha is placed on top of the organdy and its outline traced. The back of the shisha is dabbed with glue stick and placed on a background fabric, not the organdy.

Sew around — and about 1/8" (3.2mm) inside — the drawn circle. Stitch around two more times. Without taking the fabric out of the hoop, cut out the circle of fabric within the stitching. After anchoring threads, the machine should be set on a medium width zigzag and the circle stitched freely around the cut edge. Turn the hoop as you sew around it, letting the stitches radiate from the edge of the hole to about 1/2" (12.7mm) beyond. The organdy must be covered with stitches at this time. Anchor threads and take the organdy out of the hoop. Cut very closely around the outside stitching.

With the machine changed back to straight stitch, place the piece of embroidery over the shisha and background fabric and pin organdy in place. Stitch around outside edge of the shisha. Be careful: if you stitch into the glass, the needle and probably the shisha will break.

Leave the machine as set or change to zigzag again and stitch over those straight stitches, following the radiating direction of the original zigzagging. Blend the outside edge of the organdy with the background fabric by radiating stitches onto the background fabric.

Gail Kibiger has a slightly different method. She applies shisha by first placing the mirror on the background fabric, not on organdy, and tracing around it. Removing the shisha, she stitches 1/8" (3.2mm) within this circle three times and cuts out the circle. Gail embroiders on the background fabric as Caryl Rae did the organdy.

The shisha is then glued to a piece of organdy and placed under the finished hole. After pinning it in place, she straight stitches around the mirror to hold it in place.

One of Gail's variations is to work a spiderweb across the hole before the edges are zigzagged.

Jane's method differs from the other two because it's a one-step method. The shisha are attached directly to the fabric, not to a separate piece. Set your machine for darning. The thread you will see on the front will be the bobbin thread pulled to the top, so fill your bobbin with a fine thread in the desired color. Place the bobbin in the case and bypass the bobbin tension. Set your upper tension to 5 or above,

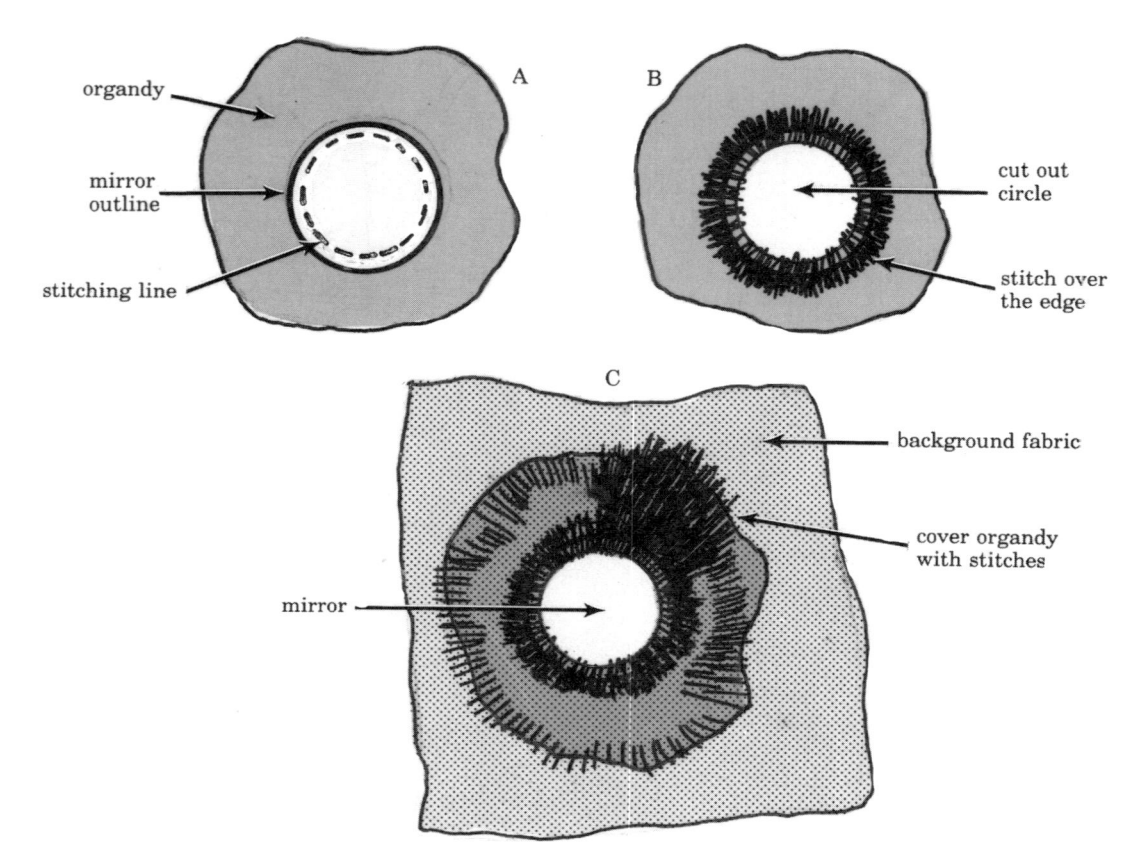

Fig. 3.28 Glue the shisha to the background fabric. A. On organdy, stitch around a circle slightly smaller than the shisha. B. Cut out the center and embroider over the edge. C. Place the organdy over the shisha and stitch it in place on background fabric by straight stitching. Embroider the background to conceal the edge.

and set your speed to medium or slow. Stretch your fabric in a hoop and glue the shisha down with a dab of basting glue. Now stitch around and around the outside of the mirror. Be careful not to hit the shisha. Stitch around as many times as you want. Do some free decorative stitching around the mirror if you like (see Fig. 3.29). Set the upper tension to 2 and stitch in place to tie off the threads. Practice this technique first using bits of index card, acetate or mica in the place of the mirror until you're confident of the process. Do try some of the laser-printed optical papers with patterns that dance and shift before your eyes. This technique also makes great craters, barnacles, and spiky flowers (Chapter 2, Lesson 2). Now turn your fabric over and you will find "mountains." You can use this technique to attach all sorts of flat bits to fabric, whether it is a rock, a slice of a mineral, etc.

Silver bangles, the large sequins found in craft and knitting shops, are an excellent substitute for shisha. Not only are they exactly round, unlike the uneven

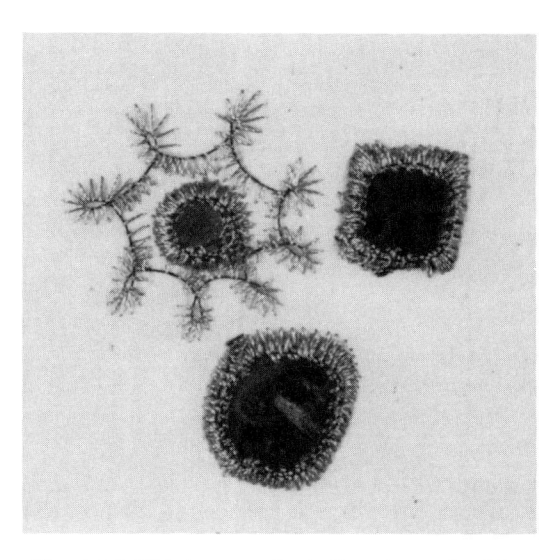

Fig. 3.29 Shisha attached directly to the fabric with and without additional free stitching. Zigzag feather stitching at the top.

shape of shishas, but they are durable. If you sew into them, your needle doesn't break. Make a record for your notebook of how you have applied buttons, beads and shishas.

Project
Bird Collage

I work with transparent fabrics almost exclusively, so I collect them. Besides fabric stores, garage sales and thrift shops are wonderful sources. I check out the chiffon scarves, colored nylons, lingerie, curtains, as well as glitzy dresses—though it takes courage to buy some of these because of the double-takes at the checkout counter.

This is a beadwork project, which includes appliqué as well. Bird shapes are my favorites. I like them plump like baby chicks, sleek like soaring eagles, even whimsical like African Dahomey appliqués. I've used them on quilts, wall hangings, and in fabric collages.

In this small picture, shown in Fig. 3.30, I added small clay beads by machine to the appliquéd picture. Set the machine for darning.

Stitch width: auto (0)
Stitch length: auto (0)
Needle position: auto (center)
Needle: #90/14
Feed dogs: lowered (covered)
Presser foot: darning foot or spring
Tension: *top*, slightly loosened; *bobbin*, normal
Fabric suggestions: green and gold suede or felt for bird's body and wings; transparent fabrics, such as organdy, chiffon, yellow mesh grapefruit bag, for the wings; moss green bridal veiling to cover the picture; 12" (30.5cm) square of coarse beige upholstery linen for background; loosely woven taupe-colored fabric for the nest; gold lamé for the eggs; nude-colored nylon stocking; also needed are small clay beads
Thread: several strands of brown and beige coarse thread or string, cut into 1" (2.5cm) pieces; brown, green and beige shiny rayon; monofilament
Stabilizer: freezer paper

If this sounds overwhelming, you can substitute any colors you wish, and use only one, instead of a variety, of transparent fabrics. Although I used transparent thread for most of this collage, I added browns, greens and beiges in rayon stitches when my piece was almost complete.

Begin by pulling off a half-dozen threads from the square of background fabric. Cut these threads into small lengths of 1 and 2 inches (2.5–5.0cm) and add them to the other threads you've cut—you will need several dozen. Put them aside.

Iron freezer paper to the back of the linen fabric for stability, as you will not use a hoop for this project. Although not necessary, I always cut the background fabric at

Fig. 3.30 Bird collage.

least 6"–8" (15.2–20.3cm) bigger than the finished size so I can practice stitching or layering on the edges. Also, I plan my pieces so they look as if they go on beyond the frame. I don't want them to look as if they end inside it.

Fig. 3.31 shows the arrangement, and Fig. 3.32 is the pattern. Cut out the fabric pieces as follows: Cut out the oval nest from the taupe fabric and place that slightly below the center on the background. When I cut fabric for collages, I use a cut/tear method. By pulling slightly on the fabric as I cut, I fray the material a bit to keep the edges soft. The bird should be cut from green suede or felt so it will not roll when you cut it out. Be sure to use fabric that has some body, so it will be easy to control. Place the bird on the nest (Fig. 3.31). Cut a gold wing from suede and position that on the bird. Cut out the transparent wings. Place one on top of the gold wing, but shift it a bit so it is not exactly in the same place as the first. Do the same with the other sheers. Your wings will cross, meet, blend, as if in a watercolor. Over the last wing you will use one cut from a yellow mesh grapefruit bag or a coarse yellow net. Rearrange until the wings look pleasing to you.

Cut the foot and top off a nude-colored nylon stocking and slit the stocking from

50

Fig. 3.31 Follow this design for assembling the bird picture.

top to bottom. Stretch it over the picture and pin it down just beyond the image area. As you stretch the stocking, it will lighten in color. It should be almost invisible, but not stretched so tightly it buckles the picture. This holds all the pieces in place, and softens, but does not change, the colors of your picture.

Lower or cover the feed dogs on your machine. Use a darning foot, as you will have many layers to stitch together. Begin by freely sewing around the bird with transparent thread. Stitch just off the edge of the body and wing pieces. It is not important to be completely accurate; it's fine if you stitch into the body or wings. You might want to stitch in a few feathers on the gold wing as well, giving the bird an attractive, padded look. Stitch to the outside of the nest and sew that down freely. Then sew all around the outside edge of your picture. Cut off the stocking from the outside edges.

Add three gold lamé eggs under the bird. Over the edge of the nest, scatter half the thread pieces you've cut. Hold all this down by laying a piece of moss green bridal veiling over the picture and pinning it in place.

Again, with transparent thread and a free machine, sew around the eggs, around the outside of the bird and around the nest, managing to catch threads to anchor them. Yes, you will be sewing in a haphazard manner around the nest—and you do not have to sew every thread in place. With very fine embroidery scissors, cut out the veiling from in front of the bird and the eggs.

String the small clay beads onto some of the remaining "nest" threads. Arrange the threads around the nest on top of those you have already sewn in place. Be very careful as you sew these threads in place; you don't want to hit beads with the darning foot. With transparent thread, sew above and below the beads to hold them in place (see Fig. 3.25).

An alternative method is to remove the darning foot. Press the fabric firmly

51

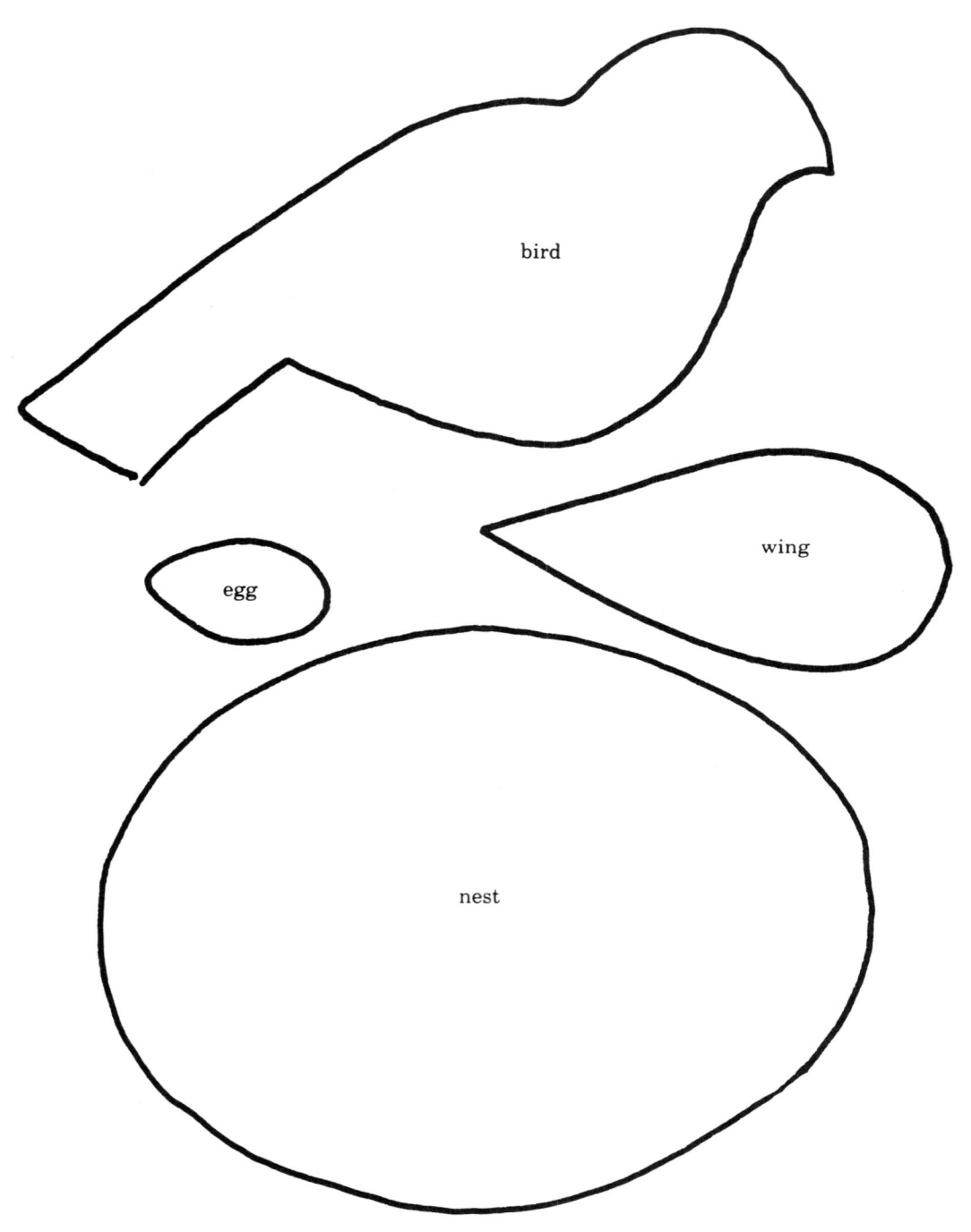

Fig. 3.32 Patterns for the Bird Collage.

against the needle plate as you sew down the threads. Be careful of your fingers. Thread up with a shiny brown rayon thread. With your machine set up for zig-zag stitching, add texture and color to the nest by stitching a blob, lifting the presser foot lever and pulling the picture to stitch again in another spot. Cross and recross threads. I change colors several times (browns, beiges and greens). This also helps anchor the coarse threads.

The bird's eye can be added by sewing on a gold bead by hand, or with your machine, by building up a blob of thread. Your picture is complete. Pull off the freezer paper, or leave it in place. Cut off that extra margin from around your piece. Stretch the picture over a piece of batting and plywood and frame it. These pictures are so much fun to put together, and no two are alike.

Lesson 7. Smocking and gathering

Smocking

In hand smocking, fabric is gathered tightly into channels and embroidery is worked on top of the channels. Stitches chosen are open and stretchy.

Smocking by machine, on the other hand, will not be stretchy like hand smocking. After gathering with thread or cord, machine embroidery stitches usually hold the gathers in place. But if you use elastic, the gathering will stretch—but then, of course, you won't embroider over it.

There are at least a dozen ways to smock on your sewing machine, varying the method of gathering or embroidering, or varying the threads used. Here are several methods you can try. In each one, start with at least 2½ times the width needed for the finished pattern. For any garment, do the smocking first and then cut out the pattern.

Stitch width: N–W (0–5)
Stitch length: varies
Needle position: auto (center)
Needle: #90/14
Feed dogs: up
Presser foot: transparent zigzag foot N
Built-in stitch: zigzag or open embroidery type
Tension: *top*, normal; *bottom*, varies

Fabric: 2 or more 18" × 45" (45.7 × 114.3cm) pieces of medium-weight cotton; 1 yard (.9m) strip for gathering ruffles; several 12" (30.5cm) or larger pieces of scrap fabrics
Threads: machine embroidery; monofilament
Accessories: water-erasable marker
Stabilizer: water-soluble, tear-away type

Simple gathered smocking

First draw at least four lines across the 45"-wide (114.3cm-wide) fabric with a vanishing marker. The lines should be about ½" (12.7mm) apart. Leave the seam allowances free of stitching. Anchor the threads, and then straight stitch along your drawn lines, leaving long ends of thread at the ends of the rows (Fig. 3.33A). Pull on the bobbin threads to gather the fabric to 18" (45.7cm) and knot every two threads together. Pin this to tear-away stabilizer.

Choose a decorative stitch and embroider across the fabric between the gathering lines of stitching (Fig. 3.33A). Then take out the gathering stitches and tear off the stabilizer.

Smocking with cordonnet

Use another piece of 18" x 45" (45.7cm x 114.3cm) fabric and mark lines ½" (12.7mm) apart with a vanishing marker.

53

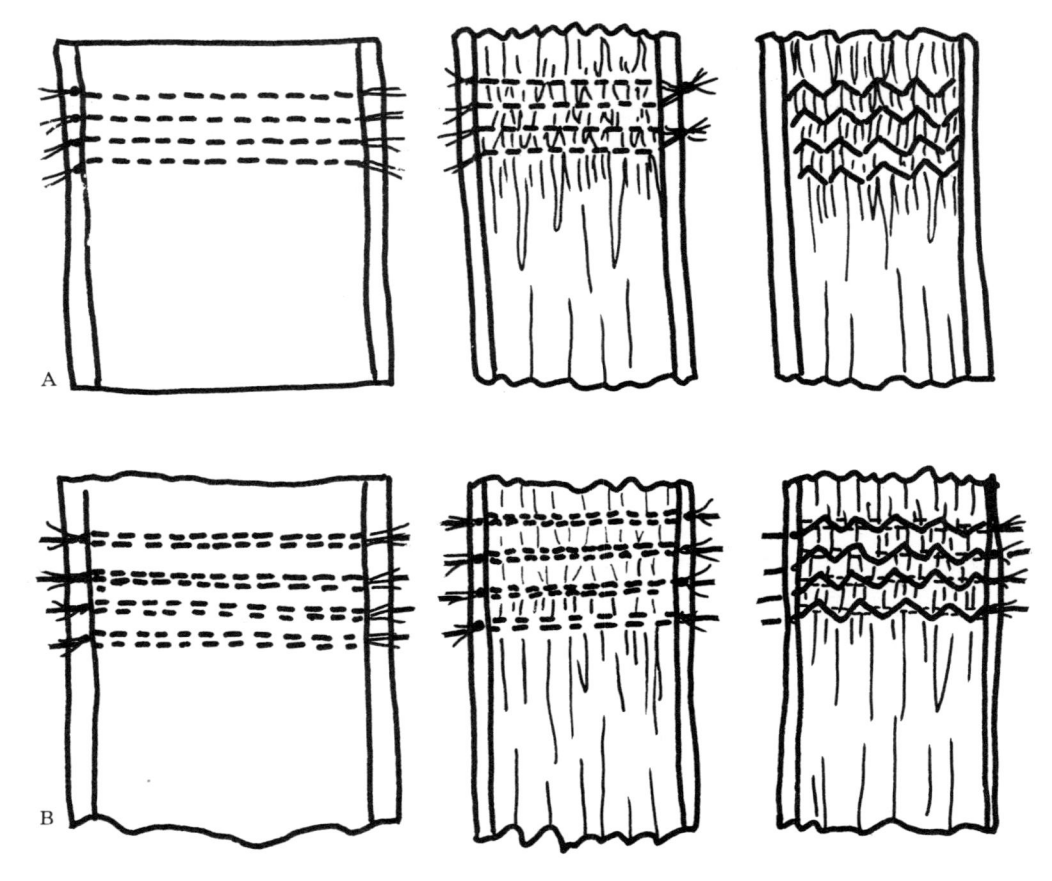

Fig. 3.33 Two ways to machine smock. A. Gather up rows of stitching and embroider between them. B. Gather the fabric, then using a cord and double needle, embroider over the gathers.

Place the cording foot on your machine; thread the cordonnet through the foot. Zigzag along the lines, using a narrow width, just enough to clear the cordonnet (Fig. 3.33B). Again, leave the seam allowances free of stitching. Stitch an even number of rows, at least four. Leave tails of cord at the beginning and end of each line.

Tie off pairs of the cords at the start. Pull the cords to gather the material to 18" (45.7cm). Then tie a knot at the end of each. Remove the cording foot and replace with the transparent zigzag foot N.

Place a stabilizer under your work. Embroider over the cords and then remove the stabilizer.

Embroidering with thick thread in the bobbin

This may be used with either of the preceding methods for gathering. First complete the gathering. Turn the fabric over, topside down on the bed of the machine.

Place water-soluble stabilizer under the gathers.

> Stitch width: widest
> Stitch length: varies
> Built-in stitch: zigzag or open embroidery type
> Needle position: auto (center)
> Needle: #90/14
> Feed dogs: up
> Presser foot: transparent zigzag foot N
> Tension: *top*, normal; *bobbin*, varies with cord
> Fabric: medium-weight cotton
> Thread: monofilament or sewing thread for top; #5 or #8 pearl cotton for bobbin
> Stabilizer: water-soluble

When you stitch up the samples, sew a short way; then look underneath to see if the pearl cotton is attached evenly and smoothly. Adjust tensions and stitch width as necessary.

Open built-in stitches (#84 and #79 on the Galaxie; #12 and #26 on the 940/950) look best—the simple zigzag is effective. Remove the stabilizer when your stitching is completed.

Smocking with elastic

Wind the bobbin with fine, round elastic. Do this by hand so it doesn't stretch. Again, stitch down rows ½" (12.7mm) apart, gathering as you sew. The thread on top will show, so choose the color carefully. You can use this for bodices of sun dresses, nightgowns or swimsuits. This works best on delicate to lightweight fabrics.

Another way to make fabric stretch, giving a shirred effect, is to use a round elastic through the hole of the cording foot. Use regular thread on top and bobbin, and a zigzag setting that clears the elastic.

Alternately, stitch with a double needle and a straight stitch. Stitch several rows across the fabric using the presser foot as a guide, or draw the rows on the fabric with a vanishing marker before stitching. Don't pull the elastic for gathering until all the stitching is completed. I use this method at the top of children's knit skirts, as well as on waistlines of T-shirt dresses.

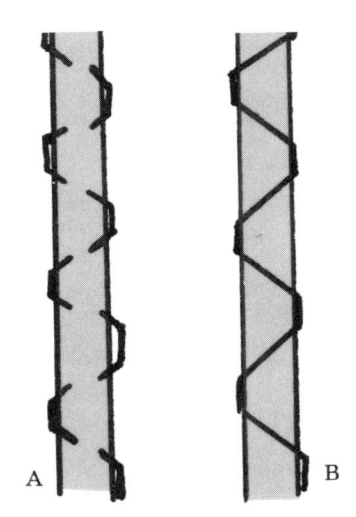

Fig. 3.34 Two ways to attach flat elastic. A. 940/950 #4. B. Galaxie #93.

With ⅛" (3.2mm) flat elastic, use either the multi-zigzag, the overlock or decorative stitch #93 (#3, #4), width 5 (3), length 4 (3). Use the groove in the transparent zigzag foot N to guide it (Fig. 3.34).

With the multiple (#3) zigzag settings, the gathers can't be changed after they are sewn in, because the needle stitches into the elastic. Stretch the elastic while sewing. The more you stretch it, the more gathers it will create.

The universal stitch will sew on either side of the flat elastic and will not pierce it as the multiple zigzag stitch does. After stitching, adjust the gathers.

Gathering
Using cord

To gather light to heavyweight materials, use this, my all-time favorite method. Set the machine for zigzag.

Stitch width: M (2)
Stitch length: 4 (2)
Needle position: auto (center)
Feed dogs: up

Zigzag over a cord, such as gimp or cordonnet. To keep the cord in position while stitching over it, use a cording foot. Place the cord in the hole and it will be fed through and covered perfectly (Fig. 3.35). Pull up the cord to gather the fabric. Leave the cord in the fabric.

I use this for everything from skirts to dust ruffles to slipcovers. You won't break the gathering stitch as you often do when pulling on a basting thread. It saves hours.

Using elastic

Using the same settings as you did for cord, thread the elastic through the hole in the cording foot. Knot the elastic in back. Pull on it from the front while sewing a zigzag over it. I use this for quick sleeve finishes for little girls' dresses. If sewn about 1" (2.5cm) from the finished edge, it creates a ruffle.

Using a gathering foot

Gathering yards of ruffles is easy with a gathering foot. It simultaneously gathers and applies the gathers to another flat piece of fabric. The only drawback is that without seeing your fabric, I can't give you an iron-clad formula for how much fabric is needed to gather into, say, a 15" (39.1cm) ruffle.

The key to your estimates is to stitch a sample. Work with the same material you're going to use for the ruffle. Finer materials need to be gathered more fully than heavy fabrics do. Gathering depends upon fabric weight, tension and stitch length. The tighter the tension, the more gathering. The longer the stitch, the more fullness that can be locked into each stitch and the tighter the gathers—and the more

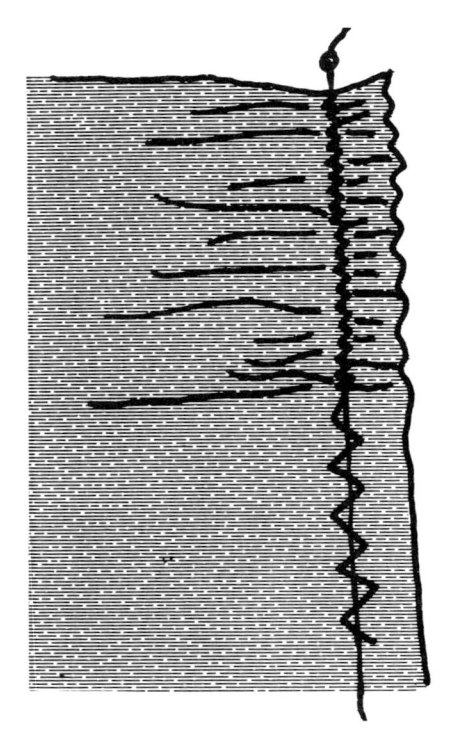

Fig. 3.35 Use an embroidery foot when zigzagging over cord to gather fabric.

fabric you'll need. I admit I'm a coward and always add inches to be sure.

Even though this foot will gather a ruffle and apply it to fabric at the same time, I prefer gathering and attaching the gathers in two steps because of the difficulty in estimating the yardage I'll need for the ruffles. But, to do both steps at once, place the fabric to be attached to the ruffle in the slot of the gathering foot and the ruffle fabric under the foot. Keep the edges of both pieces of fabric even with the right side of the foot.

This does not exhaust the methods of gathering and smocking on the machine. Check sewing books for others.

Lesson 8. Pulling threads together

Satin stitching on top of loosely woven fabric builds up texture quickly by drawing the threads of the fabric together into ridges. Then you can connect the ridges for even more texture. As you can see in the sample (Fig. 3.36), this technique looks like lace.

If you're hesitant about stitching in open areas, place water-soluble stabilizer behind the fabric before stitching. Set the machine for darning.

Stitch width: N–W (0–5)
Stitch length: 0
Needle position: auto (center)
Needle: #90/14

Feed dogs: lowered (covered)
Presser foot: darning foot or spring
Tension: *top*, 3 (3); *bobbin*, normal
Fabric: loosely woven cheesecloth type
Thread: machine embroidery, desired color top and bobbin
Accessories: spring hoop, water-soluble stabilizer (optional)

To learn this technique, stitch an imaginary tree of satin stitches and lacy straight stitches. It's not necessary to trace my design as this is done freely.

Put the fabric in a hoop. It must be stretched tightly. Bring the bobbin thread to the top and anchor the threads. Using the widest stitch setting, sew up and down in straight lines. At the down points, move the fabric over a bit and go up and down again. Continue until you have three or four rows of satin stitches. Then go back over them, zigzagging in between. This draws the previous lines together. Cut fabric threads if there is too much pulling and puckering.

Create branches on top and, when you come down to the bottom again, flare the line of stitching to resemble roots. Use the widest zigzags to stitch up and down again. Go back and zigzag over the whole tree again and again until the stitches are built up to your liking.

Change to a straight stitch and begin to stitch small circles at the top to crown the branches. Go from one to another. Cut or poke out the centers of some or all of the circles in the tree top, thus creating a lacy effect.

If you've used water-soluble stabilizer, then wash it out on completion of your work.

In the sample, I trimmed the tree from the background to show you the type of ap-

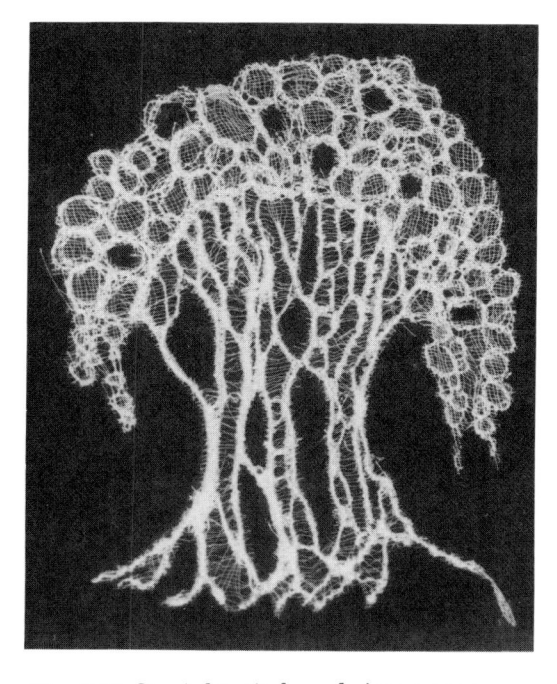

Fig. 3.36 Straight stitch and zigzag over loosely woven fabric produced both lacy and textured embroidery.

pliqué I add to my collages. It has a lacy look you can see through, which adds depth to the embroidery it's placed over. But sometimes I place the untrimmed appliqué over a background fabric and stitch it in place. After trimming it back to the stitches, I freely embroider over it with more satin stitches, with more ridges, building up more and more texture.

If you do a large enough square of threads pulled together with satin stitches, it can be used as a design for your tote bag. Or leave it untrimmed and still in the hoop for a window hanging.

CHAPTER **4**

Adding Fabric to Fabric: Appliqué

- Lesson 9. Methods of applying appliqués
- Lesson 10. Appliquéing with feed dogs up
- Lesson 11. Appliquéing with feed dogs lowered

Once you know your Brother as I know mine, you won't be satisfied stitching down all your appliqués with satin stitches. This chapter will show you several ways to place an appliqué onto a background successfully and teach a variety of methods for stitching it in place, including satin stitch, straight stitch, blind hem, and three-dimensional applications.

You'll make tote bag squares, Carrickmacross lace, and shadow work in these lessons. You will also work samples for your notebook to practice other appliqué methods.

Lesson 9. Methods of applying appliqués

Applying fabric to fabric takes two steps. Both are equally important. The first is to place the appliqué on the background in a way that keeps it in place, without puckering the fabric and with edges held down firmly, to enable you to do a perfect final stitching. The second step is the stitching. In Lessons 10 and 11, we'll try blind hems, straight stitching, blurring, scribbling and corded edges.

In appliqué, the best results are achieved when the applied and background fabrics have similar properties. For example, if using a cotton background fabric, it is best to use a similar weight appliqué fabric, and one that can be washed like the cotton. If washable, prepare the fabrics by washing and ironing them. They may be easier to work with if they are starched.

Match the grain lines of the appliqué to those of the background fabric unless you wish to create a certain effect, such as stripes or plaid on the diagonal. For consistent results, always use a stabilizer under the fabric to prevent puckers when stitching. There are several methods for the first step. The first one wastes fabric, but the results are worth it.

Method A

Stretch both fabrics tightly in a hoop. I use a wooden hoop for this step because the fabric can be stretched and held more tightly than in a spring hoop. The fabric for the appliqué should be underneath–on the bed of the machine–with the topsides of both fabrics down. Draw the design on the wrong side of the base fabric, or place a paper pattern in the hoop, either pinning it there or catching it in the hoop with the fabric.

With the machine set up for free machining, single stitch around the design. Take the fabric out of the hoop, turn it

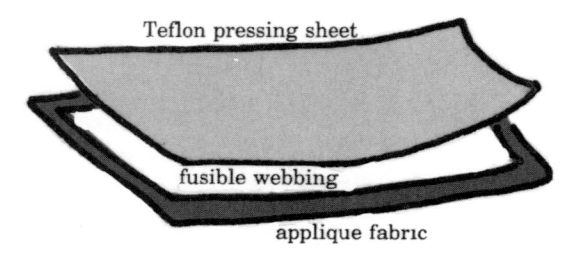

Fig. 4.1 To prepare an appliqué with fusible webbing, first place a piece of the fusible on the back of the appliqué fabric, cover it with the special Teflon sheet, and press in place.

over and cut the applied fabric back to the stitching line. Place the fabric back in the hoop with the appliqué on top this time. Use one of the methods for final stitching discussed in Lessons 10 and 11.

Method B

For the next method, fusible webbing and a Teflon pressing sheet are needed. This will produce a slightly stiffer appliqué than the first method, but if done correctly, it will never produce a pucker.

Cut a piece of fabric and a piece of fusible webbing slightly larger than the appliqué (Fig. 4.1). With the fusible webbing on top of the appliqué fabric, place the Teflon sheet over it and iron until the fusible webbing melts. When it cools, the Teflon can be peeled away. Then cut out the appliqué from this piece of fabric and iron it to the background fabric (Fig. 4.2), using a Teflon sheet on top to protect your iron. Or use the paper-backed fusible webbing described in Chapter 1.

Method C

An alternative to fusible webbing is the appliqué paper backed with "glue." To use this paper, cut a piece of it and fabric approximately the size of the appliqué. Draw the design on the non-adhesive side of the paper, then iron the paper to the back of the fabric. After it adheres and cools, cut around the design and fabric, then peel the paper off the appliqué. The glue will have been transferred from the paper to the fabric. Iron the appliqué to the background.

If doing lettering or an appliqué where

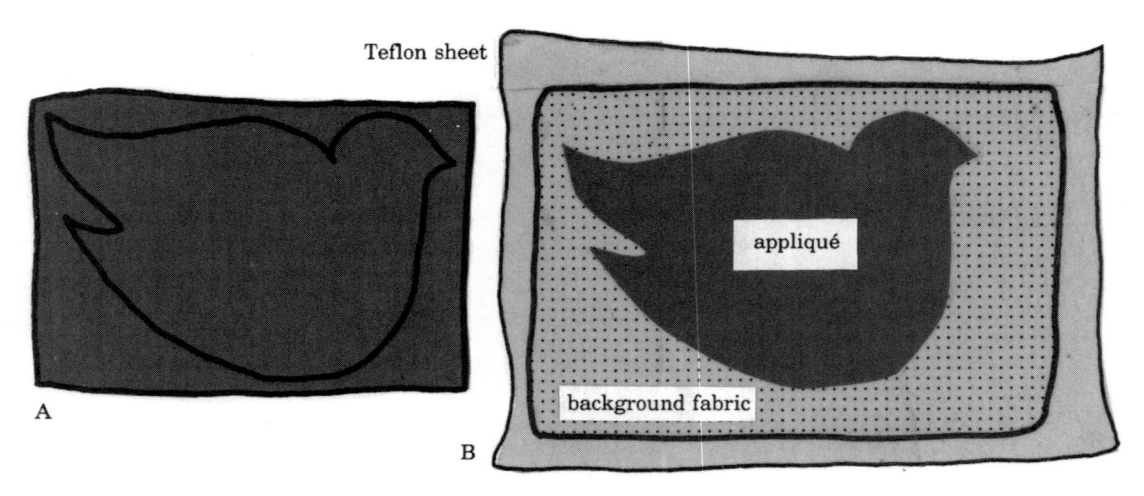

Fig. 4.2 A. Cut out the design from the appliqué fabric. B. Cover the design with the Teflon sheet again to press in place on the background fabric.

direction is important, then remember that this method gives you a flipped or mirror image of the original.

Method D

Plastic sandwich bags can also be used as a fusible–or try cleaners' garment bags. Cut out a piece of plastic the size of the appliqué and place it between the backing fabric and appliqué.

Put brown wrapping paper over and under this "sandwich" so any plastic that is peeking out will be ironed onto the brown paper and not your iron or ironing board. Press it with an iron hot enough to melt the plastic and fuse the fabrics together.

Method E

If you wish to blind hem around the edge of an appliqué for step two, the appliqué must be prepared in another way (Fig. 4.3).

First, straight stitch around the appliqué on what will be the fold line. Cut the appliqué from the fabric, leaving a ¼" (6.3mm) seam allowance. Clip the edges and turn under on the stitched line. Trim off more seam allowance wherever fabric overlaps or creates bulk. Baste with stitches or a glue-stick. Press the edges flat. Baste in place on the background fabric–I find it more accurate when done by hand. There is a wash-away basting thread on the market. If you use this it eliminates the need to pull out the basting later, and if it gets caught in your final stitching, there's no problem because it simply washes away. Now you can blind-hem the appliqué to the foundation.

If the appliqué is to be embroidered, it is sometimes best to do it first to prevent puckers in the background fabric. Embroidered patches can be appliquéd in many ways, the most common being satin stitching around the edge. But another way is to leave the edge almost devoid of stitching, cut out the appliqué and apply it with the same free stitches as the embroidery, to blend it into the background.

Even if fabric is to be heavily embroidered, embroider first on another piece of fabric, cut it out, and make it an appliqué. Use a glue stick or pin it in place. These appliqués are usually too thick to attach with fusible webbing.

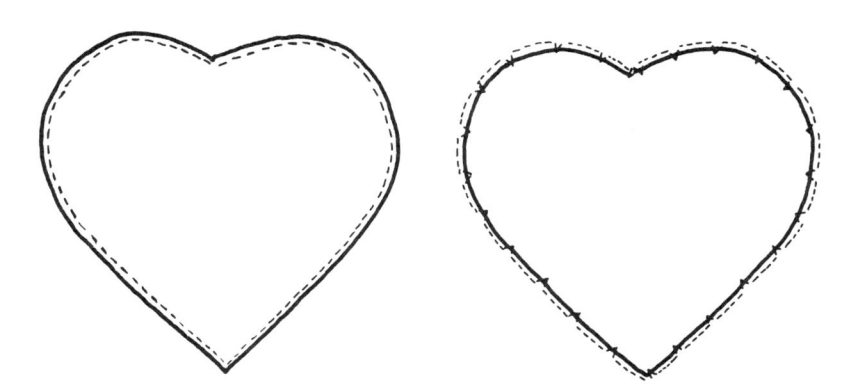

Fig. 4.3 To prepare and apply an appliqué for blind hemming, stitch all around it ¼" (6.3mm) from the edge (left). Fold under on the stitching, apply to the background and blind-hem-stitch in place (right).

Lesson 10. Appliquéing with feed dogs up

Satin stitches three ways

In addition to keeping your machine in excellent condition, the perfect satin stitch is achieved by matching of fabric, needle, and thread. Always sew a sample, using the same fabric, needle and thread that will be used on the finished piece. Don't watch the needle, but keep your eyes on the line you'll be stitching. Check to see if the fabric is being fed through evenly. Open or close the length of the zigzags. Each machine has its own personality, so you must work this out for yours.

Standard method

Keep a few things in mind when attaching an appliqué with satin stitches: First, the stitch width should not overpower the appliqué. I almost always use a setting no wider than medium (2), along with the transparent zigzag foot N, because the satin stitches fit perfectly inside the groove on the underside of the foot. The groove guides my stitching so that satin stitches are perfect. Set the machine for zigzag.

Stitch width: M–W (2–5)
Stitch length: 2 (1/2)
Needle position: auto (center)
Presser foot: transparent zigzag foot N
Feed dogs: up
Tension: *top*, 3 (3); *bobbin*, normal

I prefer to cover the edge of an appliqué in two passes rather than one. Instead of a 1/2 length, start with 3/4. At the same time, dial the first pass slightly narrower than the final one. Instead of 4 width, dial down to 3 3/4 for the first pass.

Use a needle appropriate for the thread. The needle must be large enough to let the thread pass through freely and it must punch a large enough hole in the fabric to prevent the thread from fraying. For example, with rayon embroidery thread I use a #90 needle; on cotton embroidery thread, I use a #80 needle. On woven materials, I use a pierce-point needle instead of a universal point because I feel it gives me a more perfect edge. (The universal point is slightly rounded, so it deflects off the fibers and slips between them. When satin stitching on closely woven materials, this needle may create an uneven edge.)

Stained-glass method

Stained-glass is a type of satin-stitch appliqué in which your satin stitches are gray to black and extend out from the appliqué to the borders of the design. It is important to remember this, since not every design is appropriate for stained-glass.

Reverse appliqué

Reverse appliqué is the technique of layering from one to many fabrics on top of a background material. A design is straight-stitched through layers, then the fabric is cut away from portions of the design to reveal the fabric beneath. It is finished by satin stitching over the straight stitches. Reverse appliqué can be combined with appliqué from the top as well. To do a perfect reverse appliqué, put both fabrics in a hoop, topsides up, your appliqué fabric underneath. Draw the design on the top fabric or place the pattern on top of the fabrics in the hoop and straight stitch around the design. Remove the paper.

Take the fabrics out of the hoop and cut out the top fabric inside the design area. Put the fabric back in the hoop, slip stabilizer between hoop and machine, and then satin stitch the edges. When finished, you may want to cut away the extra appliqué fabric on the back to eliminate bulk.

This method often affords better control of the appliqué when applying small pieces to a design.

Project Tote Bag Square (Modified Reverse Appliqué)

This square, shown in the color section, is modified reverse appliqué. I used red, yellow, and blue fabric, but added even more color with lines of green satin stitches.

In the method I use for this square, I'm able to cut the fabrics easily and accurately. Beginning at the top of the appliqué, I cut out the blue areas shown, then fuse this to the second layer of yellow. The two pieces are treated as one (notice that I've done no stitching) and then the second layer (yellow) is cut where needed. When that is completed, I fuse the top two layers to the red base fabric.

When the fabrics are fused together layer-by-layer and treated in this manner, instead of layering and stitching all three fabrics together at once (without the use of fusible webbing), there's no fear of my poking or clipping through too many layers when trimming out the areas.

Stitch width: 0–7 (0–5)
Stitch length: 2–5 (1–4)
Needle position: auto (center)
Needle: #80/12
Presser foot: transparent embroidery foot N
Tension: *top*, 3 (3); *bobbin*, normal
Fabric suggestion: lightweight cotton, 9" squares of yellow, red and blue
Thread: blue, yellow, green cotton machine embroidery
Accessories: fusible webbing; Teflon pressing sheet; dressmaker's carbon; empty ballpoint pen; tracing paper; ruler; vanishing marker
Stabilizer: freezer paper

Begin by backing the blue and yellow fabrics with fusible webbing, using the Teflon pressing sheet. Transfer the design in Fig. 4.4 onto tracing paper. Use dressmaker's carbon between the design and the blue fabric. Then, with the ballpoint pen, transfer the design to the blue fabric. Cut out the open areas as shown.

Place the blue fabric on top of the yellow square and fuse in place. With ruler and vanishing marker, draw cutting lines on the yellow fabric; then cut out the areas as indicated. Place this on top of the red fabric and fuse in place. Iron freezer paper to the back of the square.

Using the color of the fabrics, straight stitch at the raw edges where satin stitches are indicated. This holds down any edges that may tend to open and fray as you work; and, in the case of the blue fabric, it's a guide for satin stitch replacement.

Using yellow thread, satin stitch along the right edges of the yellow fabric. Use two passes for all the satin stitches on this appliqué. The first pass is narrower and longer than the final, smooth satin stitch. Change to green thread. Stitch a narrow satin stitch at each side of the yellow stitching.

With blue thread, stitch all the horizontal lines first. Then go back and stitch the vertical lines where needed. If you wish, change to straight stitching and stitch at the sides of these blue satin stitches to clean up the edges and emphasize them even more.

Finish the square as described in Chapter 12.

Blind hemming

A second way to attach appliqués to a background is with the blind stitch. Use the blind hemming foot L. Prepare the appliqué according to Method E (see Fig. 4.3) and use monofilament thread on the top. Use the blind stitch (#5), starting with the automatic settings (length 1–2, width 3) and altering them if desired.

Stitch around the appliqué, letting the straight stitches fall just outside the appli-

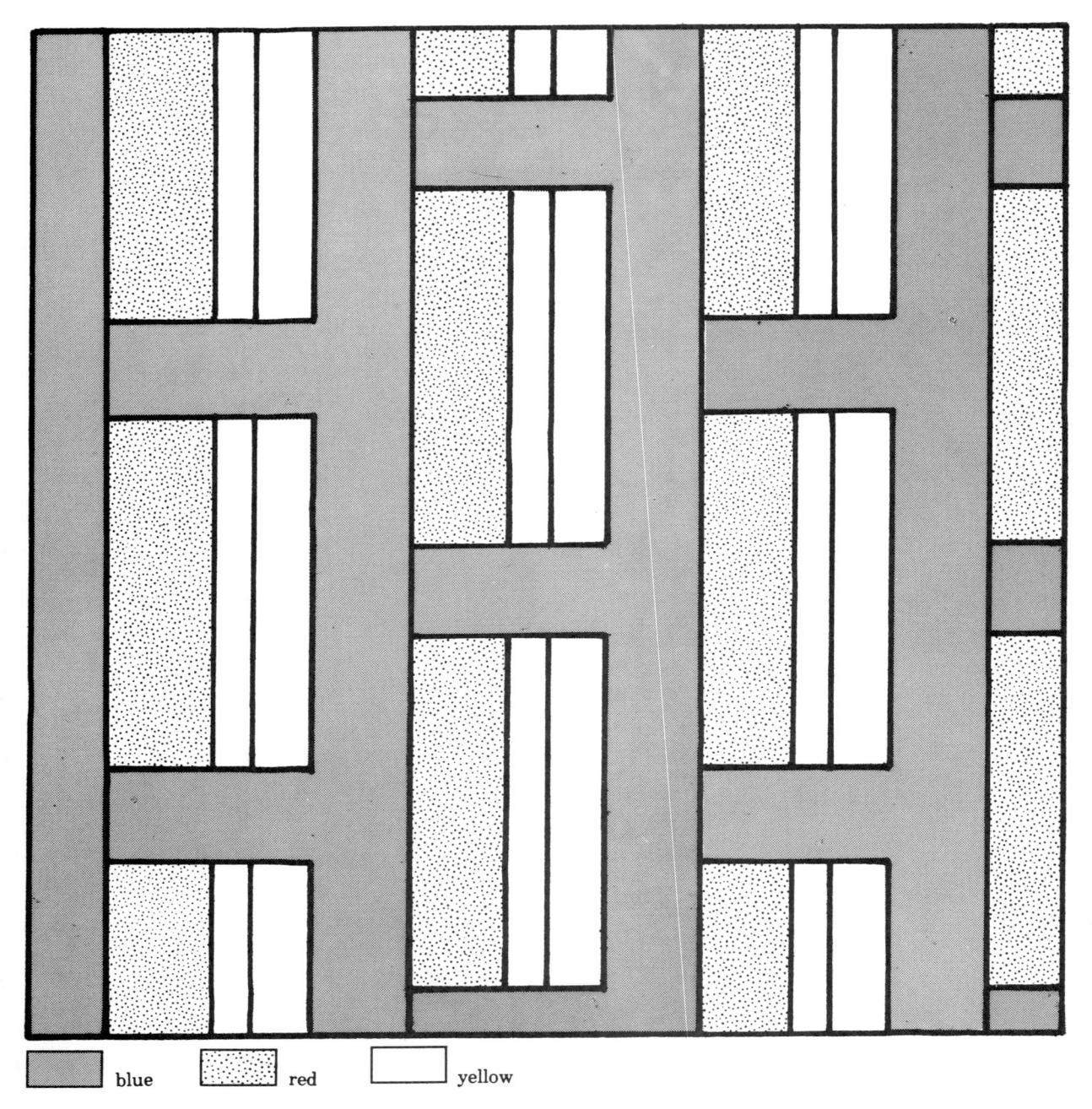

Fig. 4.4 Appliqué tote square design, modified reverse technique.

qué, with the bite of the widest stitch catching the edge. You can set up the machine to give the look you want. Do you want a wide bite? Then set the width to a higher number. The length of the stitch determines the closeness of those two stitches that go up and back, holding the appliqué in place. Find the right length by doing a sample. Use this method to attach patch pockets and to couch down heavy threads and cords. Usually monofilament is used on the top because it is almost invisible.

If you change the monofilament to a thread that will contrast with the fabric, this stitch gives the look of buttonholing by hand.

A line of blind stitching is used in the greeting card project in Lesson 4 (Fig. 3.9).

Straight stitching

To apply fabric with a straight edge-stitch, you will place the appliqué on the background as you did for blind hemming (if you are working with non-wovens like suedes or felt, don't press the edges under). Use the blind hemming foot. Set the Galaxie for straight stitch (length 2, width 0).

With the presser foot in place on the fabric, set the needle position to slightly within the appliqué. Stitch around the motif.

Project
Tote Bag Square (Edge-Stitch Appliqué)

The next tote bag square, shown in the color section, uses straight stitching on felt.

Stitch width: auto (0)
Stitch length: auto (2)
Needle position: auto (center)
Needle: #80/12

Feed dogs: up
Presser foot: zipper
Tension: *top*, normal; *bobbin*, normal
Fabric suggestion: 9" (22.9cm) square green felt; 6" (15.2cm) squares red and yellow felt; 3" (7.6cm) squares blue and purple felt
Thread: clear monofilament
Accessories: fusible webbing; Teflon pressing sheet; tracing paper; glue stick; dressmaker's pins; glue stick
Stabilizer: freezer paper

Press fusible webbing behind the yellow, purple and blue felt. The yellow will be the background onto which you will appliqué the other fabrics. Those in turn are appliquéd to the green base fabric.

Transfer the design in Fig. 4.5 to tracing paper. Using the tracing paper pattern, cut out the red and yellow fabrics. They are the same size and shape. Fuse the yellow fabric to the green felt background as shown.

Again, using the tracing paper pattern, cut out the red triangles as shown. Flip back the cutouts. Cut triangles out of the flipped piece as shown, and flip those pieces back onto the yellow felt. Pin these pieces in place. Cut out the two blue shapes and purple shape from the 3" squares and slip them under the red fabric as indicated by the illustration. Refer to the color photo as you proceed. Remove pins as you glue all the pieces in place.

With the zipper foot placed at the edge of the appliqué, straight stitch along each edge to attach the felt pieces.

Finish the square as described in Chapter 12.

Project
Tote Bag Square (Straight Stitch)

The next sample also uses straight stitches to hold appliqués in place, but is

Fig. 4.5 Design for tote bag square, edge-stitch appliqué technique.

otherwise quite different. I used blue, yellow, green and red fabric with green thread.

The background is yellow. The blue overlay is cut in one piece, instead of cutting out each umbrella outline separately. One umbrella is green, which I slipped under the blue fabric (see color section). At the top of each umbrella is a tiny red rectangle.

- Stitch width: auto (0)
- Stitch length: auto (2)
- Needle position: auto (center)
- Needle: #80/12
- Feed dogs: up
- Presser foot: transparent zigzag foot N
- Tension: *top*, 5 (4); *bobbin*, normal
- Fabric suggestion: light or medium-weight cottons for 9" (22.9cm) blue and yellow squares, scraps of green and red (see Fig. 4.6 for sizes)
- Thread: green machine embroidery on top, green sewing thread on bobbin
- Accessories: fusible webbing; Teflon pressing sheet; vanishing marker; tracing paper, pencil
- Stabilizer: freezer paper

Apply fusible webbing to all fabrics except the yellow background square, using the Teflon pressing sheet. Trace the appliqués from Fig. 4.6 using tracing paper and pencil. Cut out the blue pattern, using the tracing paper pattern as a guide. Place on top of the yellow fabric. Slip the scrap of green under one of the umbrellas. Trim as necessary. Cut up small red rectangles and put in place at the top of the umbrellas. Press, fusing all the appliqués in place.

With the vanishing marker, draw lines diagonally from top right corner to bottom left corner and every ½" (12.7mm) on both sides of the line across the square. Stitch from top to bottom on the first line. Turn and stitch back, bottom to top, on the next line. Continue across the square.

Go back and stitch between those lines. Make one last pass and stitch between the lines again. There are now straight-stitch lines from top to bottom every ⅛" (3.2mm).

Finish the square as described in Chapter 12.

Cording edges

Corded edges give appliqués and decorative patches a neat, exact finish. Use a cording foot if cord is fine enough to be threaded through it. You may also use the narrow hemmer (with zigzag opening) to guide cord.

When finishing patches, sew the corded edges in two passes. Place the patch over typing paper or tear-away stabilizer. You'll need two pieces–one for each pass–and they must be large enough to extend past the edge of the patch.

On the first pass, apply the cord, sewing at a narrower stitch width, and with stitch length slightly longer than the final pass.

The final stitching is done with a close satin stitch, the needle stitching down in the fabric on one side of the cord, but stitching off the cord and fabric on the other side. Leave enough cord at the beginning and end to poke to the back and work into the stitches. Use a needle with a large eye to do this by hand. Or, when you reach the end of the first pass, cut the cord to slightly overlap the start. If you can cut it on an angle, the join will not be noticeable when the second pass is completed.

It is not necessary to cover the entire cord if the cord itself is decorative or is a color that adds to the effect you wish to achieve. When I had to appliqué dozens of velveteen crosses to a woolen ecclesiastical garment, I used a velour cord and an open zigzag, and sewed with a thread the color of the velour. When finished, the velour edges looked like an extension of the velveteen.

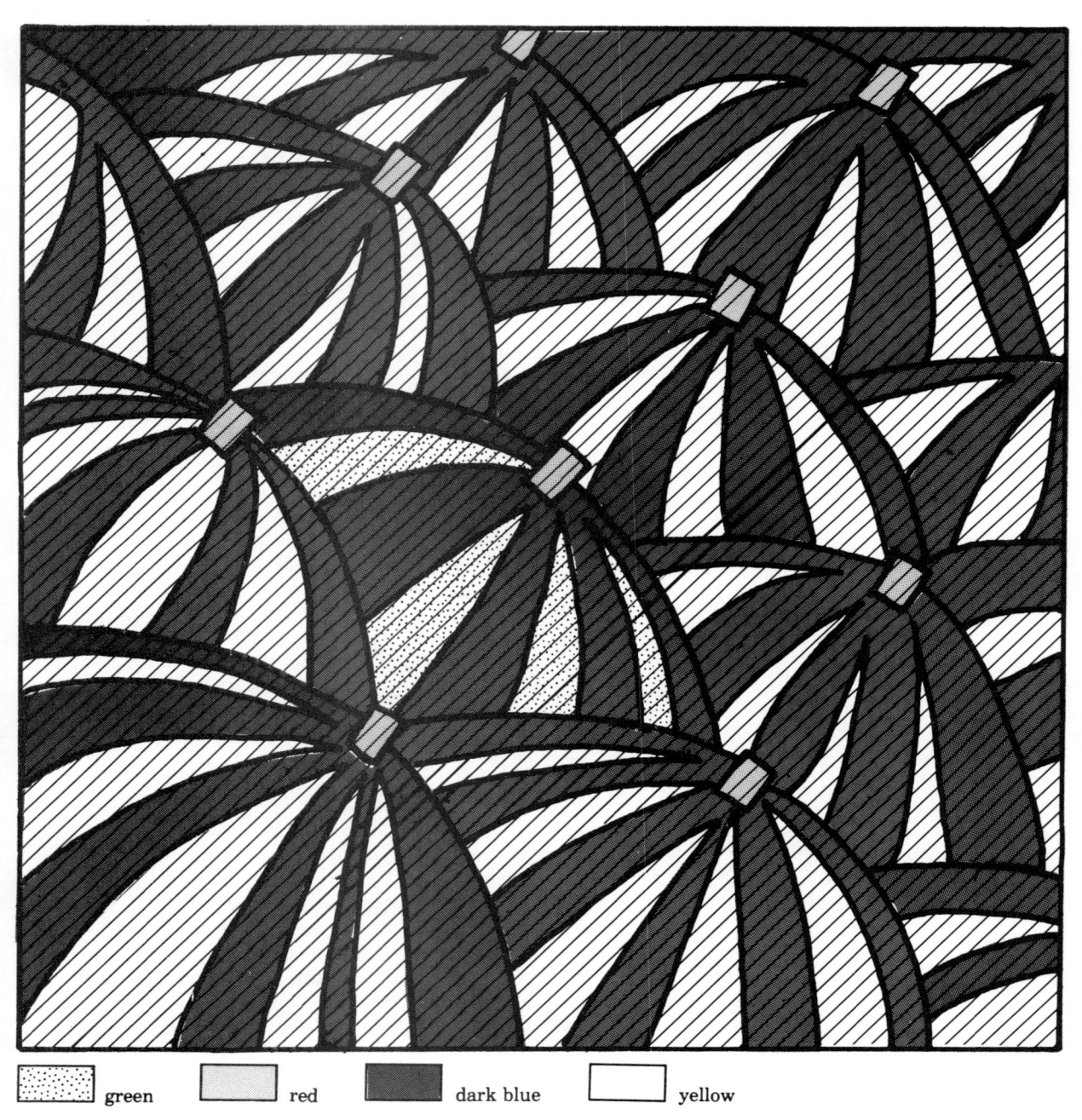

Fig. 4.6 Pattern for tote square. Use the fusible webbing method to attach the blue overlay, one green umbrella and the tiny red rectangles to the background fabric. Then stitch evenly spaced lines of straight stitching to hold them.

Lesson 11. Appliquéing with feed dogs lowered

In this lesson, the appliqués are sewn in place freely; sometimes edges are not completely covered.

Set up your machine for darning (using a darning foot, spring, or bare needle as you choose), loosening the top tension slightly, and using either a hoop or iron-on freezer paper.

Blurring

What is blurring? Apply a fabric to another by starting to stitch within the appliqué. Then, following the shape of the appliqué, stitch around and around it, extending the stitching out into the background fabric. It's difficult to tell where one begins and the other leaves off. That is called blurring.

Although the sample here uses transparent fabrics, blurring can be done with any type of fabric. I chose to combine blurring with sheers and overlays to show you how to create pictures that look like watercolors. Thread color is usually the same as the appliqué, but never limit yourself. Use other colors as well.

When working with transparent fabrics, use pins to hold the appliqués in place. If possible, hold both in a hoop while sewing. Attach one layer at a time, sewing a straight stitch around the appliqué and then cutting back to the stitching. Blur the edges. Then stretch the next transparent fabric in the hoop, stitch and cut away excess, then blur the edges.

To blur edges, find any point inside the appliqué. Stitch round and round, in ever-widening circles, until the edge of the appliqué is reached. But don't stop. Keep stitching past the edge and into the background. Three transparent circles applied in this way, one overlapping the next, the third overlapping the others, makes a good sample (Fig. 4.7). Possibilities will grow from this one idea: try many colors, overlapping them to make other colors; give depth to a picture by overlapping so that the color becomes more intense as the layers are built up, and recedes where only one layer is used.

Project Flower of Sheers and Overlays

Use this floral piece as a pillow top or slip it into your notebook. To do the flower sample (Fig. 4.8), set up the machine.

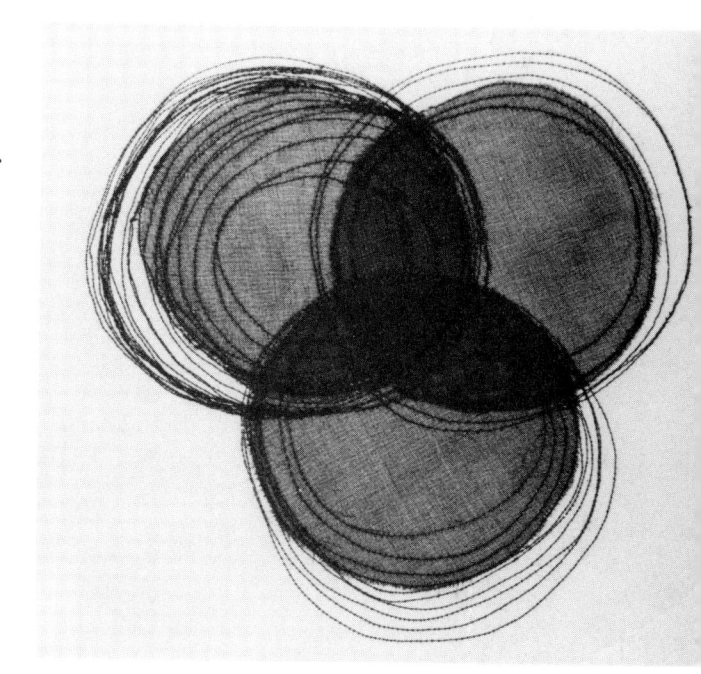

Fig. 4.7 Blurring the edges of appliqués.

Fig. 4.8 Use bridal veiling to hold small pieces of appliqué fabric in place.

Stitch width: N–W (0–5)
Stitch length: 0
Needle position: auto (center)
Needle: #80/12
Feed dogs: lowered (covered)
Presser foot: darning foot or spring
Tension: *top*, 3 (3); *bobbin*, normal
Fabric suggestion: 10" (25.4cm) square medium-weight white fabric for the background; ¼ yard (22.9cm) green transparent fabric; ⅛ yard (11.4cm) pink transparent fabric; 12" (30.5cm) square off-white bridal veiling
Threads: machine embroidery in yellow, green, and pink
Accessories: 7" (17.8cm) spring hoop with tear-away stabilizer or iron-on freezer paper without a hoop

Use the circle and leaf shape to make the patterns. Cut out several dozen 1" (2.5cm) circles in pink transparent fabric. Also cut the same number of 2" (5.1cm) long leaf shapes from green transparent fabric. Patterns are provided in Fig. 4.9. You may not use all of these petals and leaves: It will depend upon how much they are overlapped and how large an area you're covering with the design. If using freezer paper, iron it to the background fabric.

Arrange and overlap the leaves in a circle on the background fabric, points toward the center. Plan so they will fit within the hoop (if you have chosen to work with one), keeping the leaves at least an inch (2.5cm) inside. If the presser foot gets too close to the edge, it will be difficult to sew around the appliqués without hitting the darning foot on the hoop.

Lay down the circles of color for the flower head, starting in the middle of the leaves. New colors pop out for the leaves and petals as you overlap, arrange and rearrange. Leave the center of the flower open. Don't pin down any of these small pieces.

After completing the arrangement of the sheers and overlays, cover with the piece of bridal veil to help hold them all in place. Pin the veiling down in several places near the center of the flower and at the edges of

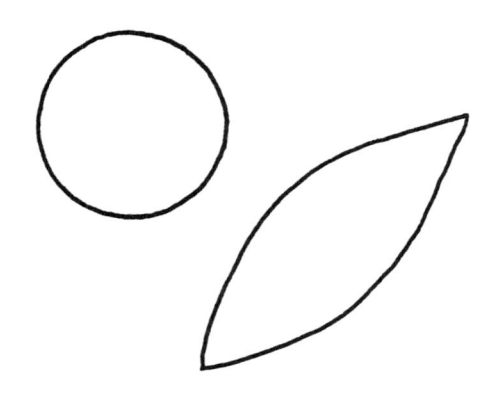

Fig. 4.9 Patterns for the flower design.

the fabric. If working with a hoop, lift your piece carefully from the table and place it in the hoop. Slip stabilizer under it.

Start by sewing around the petals of the flower. Use pink thread on the top, green thread on the bobbin. Stitch the petals very freely. Bring the stitching out past them, or inside, or make stitched circles between them. Stitch circles within circles.

Then change the top thread to green. Stitch around the leaves in the same free-flowing way. Go up the centers and down, stitching in veins on some and leaving others without.

Now only the center is left to stitch. Change the top thread to yellow and set stitch width to the widest zigzag, stitch length 0, needle position to the left. Anchor your threads in the center of the flower. Stitch in the same spot at least a dozen times to build up a nubby "seed" (see Fig. 3.2). Anchor the threads again. Lift the presser foot and move to another place. Do another seed. There's no need to clip threads until all the seeds are completed. Keep building up the nubs and moving your needle from one place to the next until the flower center is to your liking. Then clip the threads between the zigzag areas.

Change the top thread back to green. Set stitch width back to 0, needle position center. Sew around the seeds. Go from one to another until all are outlined. When the picture is complete, take it out of the hoop if you've used one. Most of the stabilizer will drop away; the rest can be pulled off (or left on, since it won't show).

The bridal veil can be left as is. However, I often clip out areas to create color changes.

Scribbling

Scribbling is like darning over appliqués, but you will use both straight and zigzag stitches. It's a good way to lay in big areas of color without having to cover the areas with heavy embroidery.

The appliqué picture in Fig. 4.10 was

Fig. 4.10 This is part of a design that has been appliquéd to a tote bag, using free-machining to hold the appliqués in place.

placed on the outside of a tote bag. Use the patterns in Fig. 4.11 as a guide, enlarging or reducing to fit your purpose.

Stitch width: varies
Stitch length: 0
Needle position: center
Needle: #90/14
Feed dogs: lowered
Presser foot: darning foot

Fig. 4.11 Use these patterns to create one element of the design shown in Fig. 4.10.

Tension: *top*, 3 (3); *bobbin*, normal
Fabric suggestion: medium-weight cotton
Thread: machine embroidery on top; sewing or darning thread on bobbin
Accessories: glue stick
Stabilizer: ironed-on freezer paper

Apply the appliqués with a dab of glue stick and begin to stitch the edges down freely with either a straight or a zigzag stitch. Sew freely over the entire appliqué first to anchor it before embroidering the designs. Stitch inside and over the edges of the appliqués. If you can live with raw edges, then don't be too particular about covering them exactly. Here is a good place to blur edges. Add to the design by laying in different colors with the same free ma-

72

chining. Add as much stitching as you wish, but don't cover the entire appliqué, as that would defeat the purpose. Let most of the color show through. It's like sketching with colored pencils.

Stitching Carrickmacross

Carrickmacross is an Irish lace made with appliqués of batiste. Tiny pops, or eyelets, are embroidered in the fine hexagonal net which is used as the ground, and it has a picot edge. If hand done, this type of lace is very fragile, but our machine version is both beautiful and sturdy (Fig. 4.12).

Project Carrickmacross Doily

Instead of batiste, we'll use organdy. I've used a polyester for the veiling; so my fabric will be the same. It will be white on white, typical of Carrickmacross lace. Set your machine for darning.

Stitch width: 0
Stitch length: 0
Needle position: auto (center)
Needle: #80/12
Feed dogs: lowered (covered)
Presser foot: darning foot
Tension: *top*, 3 (3); *bobbin*, normal
Fabric suggestion: white polyester organdy; fine white polyester hexagonal veiling
Thread: white cotton machine embroidery thread and white cordonnet (optional)
Accessories: 7" (17.8cm) spring hoop; vanishing marker
Stabilizer: water-soluble

Copy the design in Fig. 4.13 onto the organdy, using a vanishing marker. Slip the net underneath the organdy and put them both into a spring hoop. If possible, always use a hoop large enough so you can do the entire design without having to move the fabric and net.

Set up your machine for free embroidery. Anchor threads and stitch on the lines around each motif at least three times. It may be necessary to stitch a fourth pass on some, but make it look consistent: Don't leave some lines with one pass, others with four. Plot the course of the needle ahead of time so there won't be too many stops and starts.

When the design is finished, take it out of the hoop and cut out all the areas that are to be free of organdy. Use sharp, fine-pointed scissors. It helps to lift areas away from the net with the point of a seam ripper and then clip.

Should you cut the net, don't panic. Put it back under the needle and stitch a few

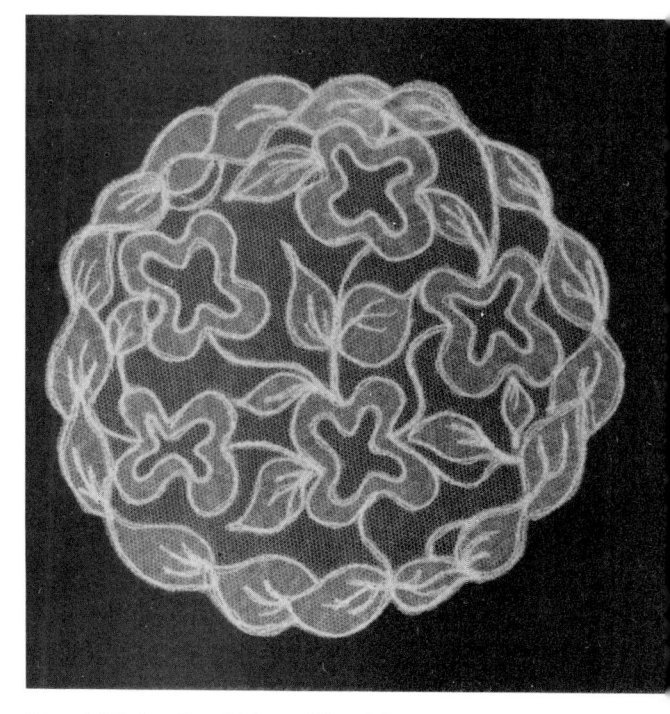

Fig. 4.12 Appliquéd lace (Carrickmacross), is made quickly using organdy and fine hexagonal net.

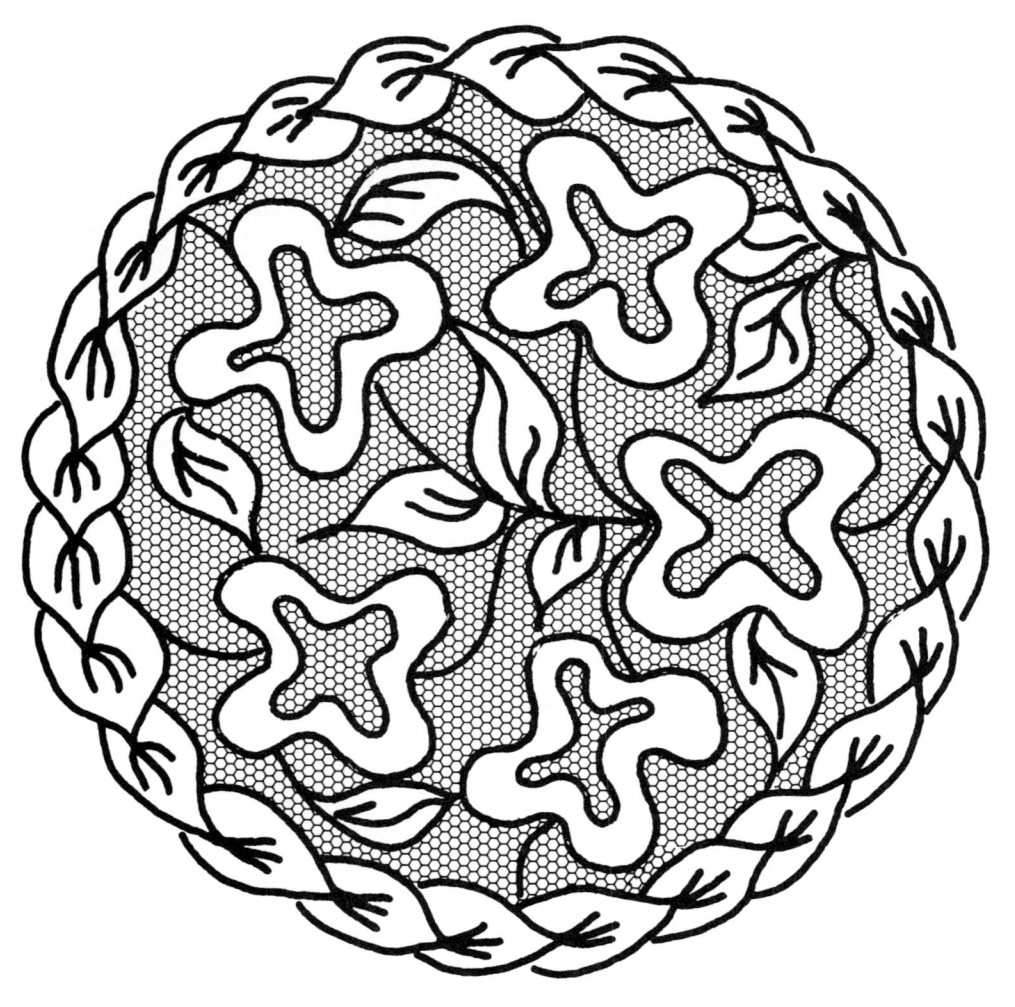

Fig. 4.13 The pattern for appliquéd lace.

lines of straight stitching over the cut, blending it into the other stitches already there. It will look like it was meant to be there all the time.

When that is completed and looks great, decide whether to go on or to stop while you're ahead. You may go one step further, as real Carrickmacross lace always has a picot edge and small eyelets in the net, as shown in Fig. 4.14.

To stitch the eyelets, mark some places, such as the middles of the flowers, that you think need pops. Stitch freely around those tiny spots. Then go back and poke holes in the centers with a darning needle. Set the stitch width to N–M (2), and slowly (use the moderate speed setting on your machine), almost hand-walk the stitching from center to outside with the zigzag. Stitch twice, turn the hoop a hair, stitch 2

Fig. 4.14 Eyelets and picots in Carrickmacross.

more times, turn the hoop, stitch again, all around the pop.

Hand-worked Carrickmacross lace has a cord couched down around the appliqués to hold them in place. To do this by machine, stitch around the appliqués only once before cutting back. Do not trim around the outside edge. Put the piece back in the hoop upside down. Use cordonnet or pearl cotton in the bobbin.

Before beginning to outline the appliqués, dip the needle down and bring the cord up to the top. Hold both threads to one side as you take several stitches along the design. In other words, don't anchor the cord, as is usually done with thread. Later go back and work the threads into the stitches on the backside of the design.

Picots around the edge should be left until the rest of the stitching is completed.

Cut back to the edge. Use two layers of water-soluble stabilizer. The topside of the appliqué should be pinned against the stabilizer. Put all this into the hoop. First stitch the cord around the leaves at the inside edge. Then, with a vanishing marker, mark small dots every 1/8" (3.2mm) along the edge to use as a guide for the picots.

Stitch in by following the edge and making small loops at each mark. Take it out of the hoop and wash the stabilizer and blue pen marks out of the fabric.

What we've made is a small doily but, if you're like me, you are not big on small doilies. This is a fast technique, so think big. Try it for the edge of a bridal veil or for the bodice and puffed sleeves of the wedding dress itself. Now that's what I call a long-cut, but definitely worth it.

Layering transparent fabrics

Shadow work is my favorite. I love the painterly effects of combining colors and toning down with whites. It's done using sheers and overlays. In the picture made in the following project, the color does not come from a colored cotton fabric layered between organdies; instead, these flowers are created only from transparent fabrics.

Project Shadow Work Picture

In this project, I switch from feed dogs up to feed dogs lowered or covered, but most of the stitching is done freely, so I've put it in this lesson. This design (Fig. 4.15) will give you an idea of what can be done with only white, mauve and green organza.

Stitch width: 0–4
Stitch length: 0–1/2
Needle position: center
Needle: #70
Feed dogs: up, lowered
Presser foot: appliqué, open embroidery, or darning foot
Tension: *top*, slightly loosened; *bobbin*, normal
Fabric: white, mauve, and green organza
Thread: green machine embroidery

Fig. 4.15 Layers of transparent fabrics give a painterly effect to shadow work.

Accessories: spring hoop; water-erasable marker
Stabilizer: water-soluble

Place the white organza over the design (Fig. 4.16) and trace it off with a vanishing marker. Layer two mauves behind each flower on the white organza and pin them in place. Put this in a hoop.

With the machine set for free machining, without anchoring the threads, straight stitch around the flowers twice. Lift the needle and go to the flower centers. Stitch twice around each center, also: The lines should be next to each other, not on top of each other. Cut back to the stitching around the outside edge, but not too close.

Place the green organza behind the leaf areas and stitch in place with two lines of stitching. Cut back to the stitching at the edges.

Set up your machine for normal sewing. Put feed dogs up and use the transparent embroidery foot N. Use stitch width 4 (2), stitch length 2 (1/2) or a setting that will produce a smooth satin stitch. Sew around the flowers and leaves. Be careful: sew too closely and the stitches will cut the fabric.

From the front of your picture, cut the white organza from one flower, the white and one mauve layer from another. Turn the hoop over. Cut out one layer of mauve from the back on another. Or from the back, cut out both layers of color, leaving only the white organdy and the flower center intact. Can you imagine the combinations and shades of mauve you can create?

The large leaf is divided into four sections. In the first section, cut out the top white layer and place a layer of green behind the remaining green layer to darken it. In the second area, cut out the white and leave just green. In the third, place white behind the section to make it three layers. The fourth is left as is, the white in front of the green.

Once you have finished the flowers and leaves, go back to the flower centers and blur them out by stitching spirals from the centers out to the edges. Or start at the edges and travel to the outside of the flowers. Leave some flowers with only the first stitching around the center.

Satin stitches should be sewn through at least two layers of fabric. Ordinarily, we'd add stabilizer, but tear-away could leave specks in the fabric that might show through. To prevent this, use green organza as a backing for the stems. The lines are satin stitched, then the stabilizing organza is cut back to the stitching.

Finish up with straight stitching. Set up again for free machining. Using water-soluble stabilizer behind the fabric, set the machine on stitch width 0, stitch length 0, to sew in the accent lines.

Fig. 4.16 Shadow work design.

If one of the fabrics has pulled away from the satin stitches, don't give up. Layer a piece of transparent fabric underneath and stitch it on. Then cut away the original one. Or put a piece of organza underneath, use straight stitching or zigzags to sew in some lines, and pretend you wanted it that way. On the flowers, too: If by mistake you cut through two layers instead of one, leave it or layer something behind it. Sometimes blurring out more lines of stitching will attach and hide any mistakes.

Keep the stitching light and airy, with no wide satin stitches. There should be more fabric showing than stitching. When finished, wash out the stabilizer and pen marks.

This type of shadow work is quite fragile and I suggest using it for pictures or window hangings, rather than for clothing.

Project
Stitching Three-Dimensional Appliqués

One of the prettiest dresses I've ever seen was at a fraternity dance back when we thought we had to wear yards of tulle and gobs of ruffles. This dress was a beautiful white organdy exception. Over the entire skirt were scattered lavender and peach pansy appliqués of organdy. They were attached only at the centers. It was a plain dress except for this scattering of flowers.

Detached appliqués do not have to have a heavy satin stitch edge, and I think you'll agree that straight stitching on fine fabric is easier and more beautiful. After all, that was a long time ago and I've never forgotten that dress. Set the machine for darning.

Stitch width: 0
Stitch length: 0
Needle position: auto (center)
Needle: #60/9 or #70/10
Feed dogs: lowered (covered)
Presser foot: darning foot or no presser foot, tailor-tacking foot (optional)
Tension: *top*, 3 (3); *bobbin*, normal
Fabric suggestion: mauve and green organdy
Thread: machine embroidery thread to match
Accessories: spring hoop; vanishing marker
Stabilizer: water-soluble type

Place a layer of water-soluble stabilizer between two layers of mauve organdy. Clip this into the spring hoop. Draw the design in Fig. 4.17 on it with a water-erasable marker. You will copy the petal design twice. The small sample is done in pieces and combined later (Fig. 4.18).

Set the machine on moderate speed for accuracy. Stitch three times around the edges with a straight stitch. Lines should be close together but not on top of each other. Use a colored thread that matches or is a shade darker than the fabric. Cut out the petals close to the stitching, but not too close.

The leaves should be worked in the same way on green organdy. Stitch only straight stitches as you follow the pattern. Go into the centers and stitch the veins as well. Cut out the leaves.

Place the flower petals on top of each other—stagger them so the petals underneath are not hidden by the top layer. Place this over the leaves and stitch them together with mauve thread by following the stitching in the center of the petals. You may go a step further and fringe the center. Using the tailor tacking foot, green thread, stitch width 2 and stitch length almost 0, stitch in several places in the center of the flower. Finish by holding the flower under the faucet and rinsing out some, but not all, of the stabilizer. Shape the flower and leaves carefully and let

Fig. 4.17 Three-dimensional appliqué design.

them dry. They will be stiff, as if heavily starched, and will retain their shapes. How can you use these three-dimension appliqués? Add a band of them to a bodice of Carrickmacross lace. Make an utterly fake corsage or a flowered hat. Add the flower to a cord for a necklace.

Helpful Hints for appliqué

If an appliqué bubbles, fix it by taking it out of the hoop and nicking the base fabric beneath the appliqué, which will then allow the base to lay flat.

Or slit the back a bit and fill the appliqué area with cotton. This is called trapunto. Hand whip the slit closed. Machine stitch on top of the appliqué to add to the design and hold the batting in place.

Another way to keep appliqué puckers from showing is to hide them by hand or machine embroidering over the appliqué.

When layering net, there is sometimes a moiré look to it that spoils the effect of your picture. To eliminate it, change the direction of one of the layers.

Don't limit yourself to fabric appliqués; thread appliqués are also effective. Work spider webs in another fabric, cut them out, and apply.

Work lace in space inside a small ring. Apply it to a background by free machining all around the inside edge of the ring. Then cut the ring from the lace.

Check out Lesson 6 on beads, baubles, and shishas.

Do pulled and drawn threads with the machine on one fabric and attach them to another background.

Fig. 4.18 Pattern pieces for floral 3-D appliqué.

CHAPTER 5

Stitching Across Open Spaces

- Lesson 12. Cutwork and eyelets
- Lesson 13. Free-machined needlelace
- Lesson 14. Battenberg lace
- Lesson 15. Hemstitching
- Lesson 16. Stitching in rings
- Lesson 17. Making Alençon lace

People have been stitching in space for a hundred years; you can, too. However, if you are nervous about doing it, stitching on water-soluble stabilizer usually produces the same effects with even better results. Water-soluble stabilizer is so thin and pliable that placing multiple layers of it in a hoop, along with fabric, is no problem. Another reason I am sold on it is that, once the design is drawn on the stabilizer, it can be stitched exactly, as if stitching on fabric. That isn't possible when actually stitching in space. I use it for cutwork because it holds the cut edges in place while I stitch them and sometimes I use it on both sides of the fabric to give it even more stability.

I use stabilizer when stitching in rings, too. It keeps threads in place until they are anchored. There is no problem with slipping, as often happens when stitching in space.

In this chapter, I've also included an earring project to stitch on water-soluble stabilizer. Practice on water-soluble stabilizer, then graduate to open space, if the project allows, and try that. There are occasions for both techniques.

This chapter includes cutwork, stitching in rings, creating needlelace, and stitching both Battenberg and Alençon laces. Hemstitching is included, as well. Be sure to keep all your samples in your notebook. You may not use an idea today or tomorrow, but maybe next year you'll refer back to your notebook and find just what you're looking for to make a special gift, or welcome a new baby. My notebook is especially valuable when I want to find machine settings for a technique I haven't used in weeks. No matter how well you know your machine, you can't remember every detail of a method you've tried.

Lesson 12. Cutwork and eyelets

Cutwork

Cutwork is the forerunner of all needlemade laces. It was common as early as the sixteenth century. In handmade cutwork, part of the background fabric is cut away and threads are stretched from one side of the open area to the other. Bars of buttonhole stitches are worked over the stretched threads and the cut edges. Cutwork can be done on most sewing machines, using satin stitches in place of buttonhole stitches.

Project Cutwork Needlecase

When I wanted to do a cutwork project on the machine without dedicating my life to a large, time-consuming sailor collar or tablecloth, I found that the needlecase in Fig. 5.1 was exactly the right size. The single design can be used as a repeat pattern and it can be combined with embroidery, appliqué or shadow work.

I traced the pattern (Fig. 5.2) on paper two different times. On one pattern I added lines where I wanted the thread bars, called "brides," to be.

Before you begin this or any project, practice, using the same fabric, needle and threads, stitch settings and stabilizers you will use on your finished piece. For this design, I practiced turning corners and satin stitching curves, as well as filling spaces with thread bars.

Cutwork is not usually backed by anything, but on this needlecase you can see that it is a necessity. Set the machine for darning.

Stitch width: N–M (0–2)
Stitch length: 0 to satin stitch
Needle position: center
Needle: #80/12
Feed dogs: lowered (covered)
Presser foot: darning foot, transparent zigzag foot N
Tension: *top*, 3 (3); *bobbin*, normal
Fabric suggestion: closely woven linen or kettlecloth
Thread: machine embroidery
Accessories: spring hoop; tracing paper; small, sharp embroidery scissors; pencil, vanishing marker, and permanent white marker
Stabilizer: water-soluble

Place the pattern without the thread bars on the back of the fabric and slip them both into a hoop. The topside of the fabric will be against the machine. Lower or cover the feed dogs and take the presser foot off. Straight stitch around the outlines of the design two times with the same thread you'll use for the satin stitching. (Do not stitch the bars at this time.)

Take the fabric out of the hoop and peel off the pattern. Cut out the larger area.

Fig. 5.1 The cutwork design on this needlecase can be used once, or as a repeat pattern.

Fig. 5.2 Cutwork pattern to copy.

Put a piece of stabilizer over the topside and one underneath the fabric, and place all three layers in the hoop. Slip the second pattern under the hoop. With a permanent white marker, trace the bars on the top stabilizer. Put the pattern aside until later.

With stitch width set to 0, freely stitch in the bars. Do the long, middle branching line first. Anchor the thread at the top by sewing in one place a few stitches, make a pass from top to bottom and then back again. As you sew from the bottom on that second pass, stitch the branches out and back as well.

Go back to stitch width 1 1/2. Stitch the first pass from top to bottom, moving the hoop quite quickly (remember the branches). Then, stitch back up from the bottom: This time move your hoop slowly. The stitches will be closer together. Remember, you control this by how fast you move the hoop. The stitches will look like satin stitches in space. Anchor each branch by sewing at 0 width into the fabric just beyond the stay-stitching. Zigzag to the top and anchor the thread.

Stitch the short bars at each side next. Anchor the threads at the top of the first bar, just beyond the two rows of straight stitching. Sew straight stitches across to the other side, anchor the threads again, and come back on the same line. Then begin zigzagging back across these threads with a 1 1/2 stitch width. When you reach the other side, stop, turn the width to 0 and follow the stay-stitch line to the next bar position. Sew across, back, and then zigzag as you did the first one. Complete all the brides on each side.

Cut out all three smaller shapes that are left in the design. Try to do this without cutting through the stabilizer on the back, but if you clip it, you can always slide another piece of stabilizer underneath. Put another piece of stabilizer on top and place all layers in the hoop. Using your pattern again behind the hoop, draw the bars on the stabilizer. Proceed with these branched bars as you did with the large cutout.

When you have finished all the bars, change the machine settings. Raise the feed dogs and set the machine on stitch width 2. Use the transparent zigzag foot N. Begin sewing at the point of the heart. Anchor the threads and proceed clockwise. As you travel around the curves, stitch very slowly, your machine set on moderate speed. To fill in the curves smoothly, stop with the needle down on the right side, lift the presser-foot lever, pivot the hoop, lower the presser foot, and stitch again. Repeat several times when negotiating curves.

Satin stitch around each cutout. Carefully pull away the stabilizer and rinse out any remaining pieces. Press the embroidery from the back.

Eyelets

I've used eyelets in my embroideries, clumping them together for a center of interest, and one of my teachers uses them to decorate lovely bed linens.

Since there is not an eyelet maker for the Galaxie, I make mine with the buttonhole foot A. I close it completely at the back where the button would normally be placed. I use the one-step rounded buttonhole, the first one when reading left to right. Pull down the buttonhole lever and proceed as if you were doing a buttonhole. It isn't perfectly round, but it works nicely. I use a Japanese flower maker for eyelets on the 940/950.

Lesson 13. Free-machined needlelace

The terms *cutwork, lacy spiderwebs,* and *openwork* all describe a machine stitchery technique far removed from darning holes in socks or shredded elbows. But, like darning, they do entail stitching across open spaces. Set the machine for darning.

Stitch width: 0
Stitch length: 0
Needle position: auto (center)
Needle: #80/12
Feed dogs: lowered (covered)
Presser foot: darning foot or spring, or no presser foot
Tension: *top*, normal; *bobbin*, normal
Fabric suggestions: any weight

Thread: one color, machine embroidery or polyester
Accessories: 6" (15.2cm) wrapped wooden hoop; water-soluble stabilizer (optional)

Openwork is done in a hoop with the fabric stretched tightly. Place the hoop, fabric side down, on the machine bed. Draw a circle on the fabric: Circles are easier to control than the squares, crescents and paisley shapes you may want to try later.

Start stitching at the edge of the circle by bringing the bobbin thread to the top. Anchor the threads by sewing a few stitches in one spot. Guide the hoop slowly as you stitch around the circle three times

(Fig. 5.3A). Take the hoop off the machine and, without removing the fabric from it, cut out the circle close to the stitches. If you have opted to use water-soluble stabilizer, now is the time to slip it into the hoop under your fabric. Replace the hoop and secure the threads once again at the edge of the hole.

Now you will begin to lay in a network of spokelike threads across the space (Fig. 5.3B). To do this, begin by stitching across from one side of the hole to the other side. Move the hoop slowly, but run the machine moderately fast to strengthen and put a tighter twist on the spoke. When your needle enters the fabric again, move along the circle to another spot, secure threads, and sew directly across the hole again. Continue in this manner until you have as many spokes as you wish. On the last pass, go up to the center and backstitch right at the center of the wheel to strengthen the web. Starting at that backstitch, fill in the spokes by sewing in ever-widening circles around the center until the "button" is the size you wish it to be (Fig. 5.3C). Sew a few stitches into the button to lock the thread in place and again move to the outside to anchor the threads and complete that spoke.

Would you like a lacier filling? Sew one backstitch over each spoke after crossing it as you stitch around the center. This keeps the threads from slipping to the center. Travel around and around in wider circles till you reach the edge of the hole.

Although there are as many ways to finish off the edges of the spaces as there are ways to fill them with stitches, one of the softest looks is accomplished by straight

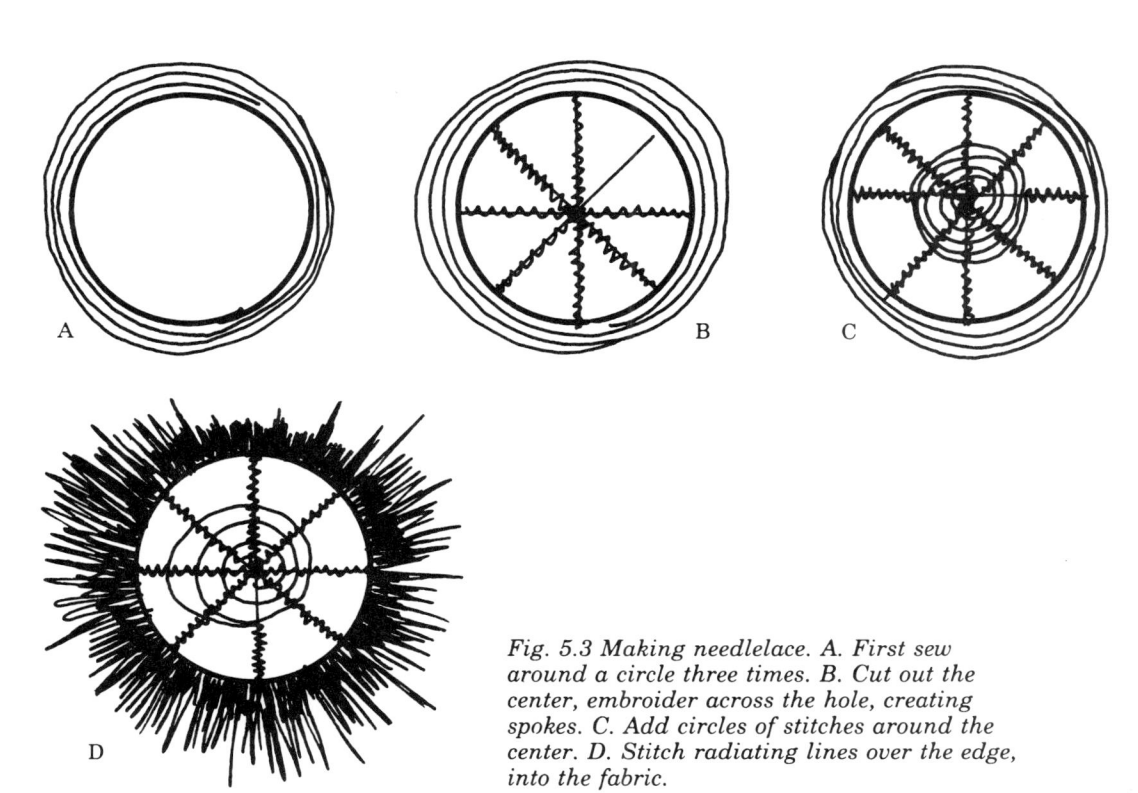

Fig. 5.3 Making needlelace. A. First sew around a circle three times. B. Cut out the center, embroider across the hole, creating spokes. C. Add circles of stitches around the center. D. Stitch radiating lines over the edge, into the fabric.

85

stitching from the edge of the hole, out past it and back again, moving the hoop back and forth as if stitching sun rays (Fig. 5.3D). You can also use the widest zigzag and accomplish the same rays. Or, satin stitch around the edge and combine that with other embroidery. These are only a few ideas; try some of your own.

If you have used stabilizer, place your embroidery under a faucet and wash it out when your work is completed.

Create your own samples by placing a piece of medium-weight cotton in a hoop and drawing several circles on it. Stitch around one circle three times. Cut out the center. Stitch a spider web in the hole and finish it off on the edges. Go to the next circle and stitch both the center and the edges in a different way from your first sample. Then do another and another until you have many needlelace samples for your notebook. If you're pleased with the result and want to show it off, back with another fabric and use as a tote bag square.

Project
Earrings

This project includes directions for stitching three different earring styles, shown in the color section. All three have one thing in common—they're stitched on water-soluble stabilizer.

The first earrings are small, beaded triangles created from layers of gold metallic stitches. I used metallic thread because it doesn't pack down as tightly as rayon or cottons so the earrings are more attractive.

Stitch width: 0 to medium (0–2⁰)
Stitch length: 0
Feed dogs: lowered or covered
Presser foot: darning or spring
Needle: #90/14 sharp
Tension: *top*, loosened; *bobbin*, normal
Thread: gold metallic machine embroidery

Fabric: ¼" (6.4mm) square scraps to match gold thread (cut out 2)
Accessories: permanent white opaque marker; 5" (12.7cm) or 7" (17.8cm) spring hoop, glue stick, epoxy (2-tube type)
Stabilizer: water-soluble
Miscellaneous: small beads to match earrings; earring clips or posts

Place gold metallic thread on the top of the machine and wind a bobbin of the same thread. Cover or lower the feed dogs and set the machine on "0" stitch width and length.

Clip two layers of water-soluble stabilizer into a spring hoop. I use larger spring hoops because then I can make several pairs of earrings at one time.

Draw the outlines for your triangles on the stabilizer with the white marker. The pattern is provided in Fig. 5.4 (1). Slip the hoop under the needle; then dip the needle down to bring up the bobbin thread and hold it to one side. Take a few stitches along the outline; then clip off the thread tail. Stitch around the outline twice, Fig.

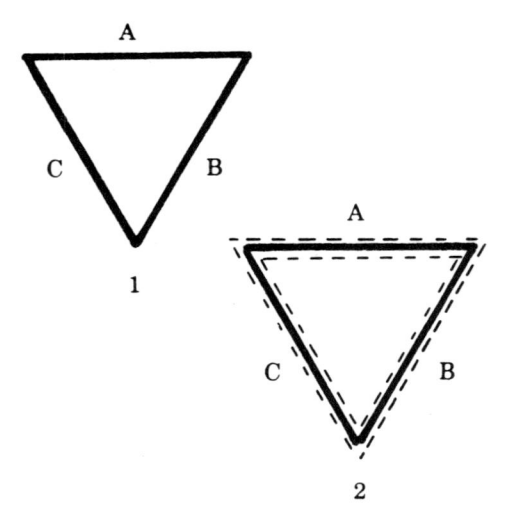

Fig. 5.4 Pattern for earrings. 1. Draw two outlines on water-soluble stabilizer. 2. Stitch twice around the perimeters of the triangles.

5.4 (2). Then, fill in the triangle with one layer of straight stitches. Keep your rows of stitches close together, but not on top of each other, as shown in Fig. 5.5 (1). If the stabilizer tears, slip a small scrap of it under the tear to repair it.

After the triangle is filled in, turn the hoop a quarter turn and straight stitch across the earring as shown in Fig. 5.5 (2). Before the third and final pass, turn the hoop back a quarter turn, and place the tiny scrap of matching fabric underneath the earring where you'll glue the clip or post later. (The fabric prevents the epoxy from soaking into the layers of stitches.) You may want to place a small dot of glue stick between the scrap of fabric and earring to help hold the fabric in place when you stitch. On this final pass, change stitch width to medium before traveling back and forth across the earring; Fig. 5.5 (3). Blend in the stitches evenly to prevent satin stitch ridges. When you reach edges B and C, go slightly beyond them to create a soft fringe. Again, turn the hoop back a quarter turn. With your machine still set on medium stitch width, satin stitch down the edge of side A, Fig. 5.5 (4). Move the hoop so the stitches go off the edge on the left swing, but stitch on the earring on the right swing. Every few stitches, stitch sideways into the earring to anchor the ridge securely. Go back and repeat the last row without side stitching to make a smoothly finished edge. See Fig. 5.5 (5).

Take the stabilizer out of the hoop and cut around the earrings to remove most of the stabilizer. Hold the earrings under a faucet to wash out the rest of it; then place them between two layers of toweling and squeeze out the moisture. Next, use a hand sewing needle and a doubled gold thread to stitch the beads in place (Fig. 5.6).

Mix the epoxy and follow directions on

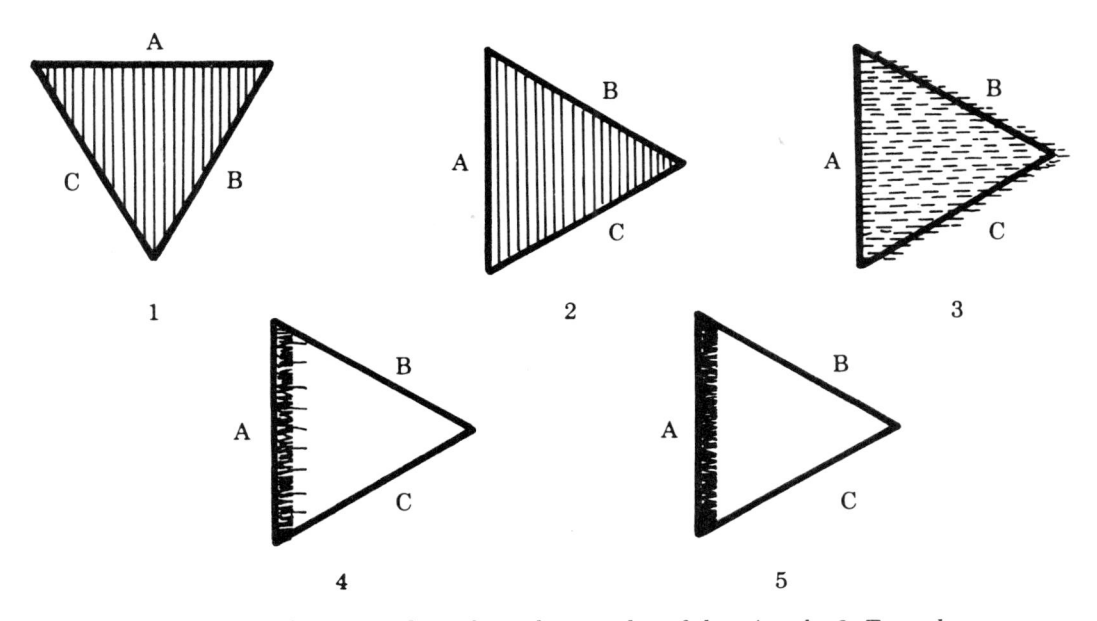

Fig. 5.5 1. Straight stitch in rows down from the top edge of the triangle. 2. Turn the hoop and straight stitch across the triangle, perpendicular to the first pass. 3. Zigzag at a medium width to fill in the triangle and fringe the edge at the same time. 4. Finish edge A with medium satin stitches. 5. Satin stitch over the edge again.

Fig. 5.6 Hand sew beads to earrings.

the package to glue the backings to the earrings. Let the glue dry thoroughly before wearing.

The second pair of earrings is made with gold ribbon thread or narrow gold braid on the bobbin and gold metallic thread on the top of the machine (see Chapter 3).

- Stitch width: 0
- Stitch length: 0
- Feed dogs: lowered or covered
- Presser foot: darning foot or spring
- Needle: #90/14 sharp
- Tension: *top*, 3 (3); *bobbin*, slightly loosened
- Thread: gold metallic, gold metallic ribbon thread or narrow decorative braid
- Fabric: ¼" (6.4mm) square scraps to match gold thread (cut out 2)
- Accessories: permanent white opaque marker; 5" (12.7cm) or 7" (17.8cm) spring hoop; glue stick; epoxy (2-tube type)
- Stabilizer: water-soluble
- Miscellaneous: small beads to match earrings: earring posts or clips

Prepare the hoop as before, with two layers of water-soluble stabilizer. Draw two small rectangles with the white opaque marker. Fig. 5-7 (1) is the pattern. Slip the hoop under the needle and dip the needle down to bring the ribbon to the top. Hold the ribbon to one side as you stitch around the perimeter of the rectangle and then over the ribbon at the starting point to anchor it. See Fig. 5.7 (2). Clip off the end close to the stabilizer. Continue, stitching up and back to the left across the rectan-

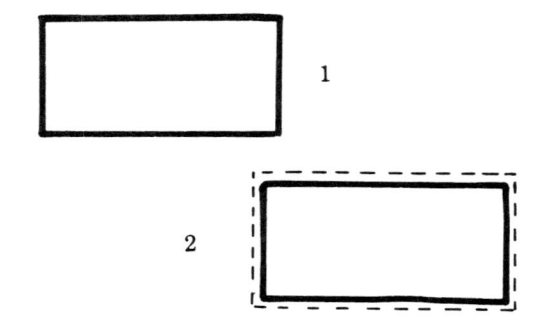

Fig. 5.7 1. Draw two rectangle patterns on water-soluble stabilizer. 2. Stitch once around the perimeter of each of the rectangles.

gle, beginning at A and ending at B in Fig. 5.8 (1). Keep your rows close together. When you reach the lower left corner, turn the hoop a quarter turn to the right and stitch up, down and across the rectangle, perpendicular to the direction you stitched first, as shown in Fig. 5.8 (2). For the last pass, turn your hoop back left a quarter turn.

With the white marker, draw a line across slightly beyond the bottom of the earring to indicate how long you want the fringe to extend; I suggest ¼" (6.4mm) to

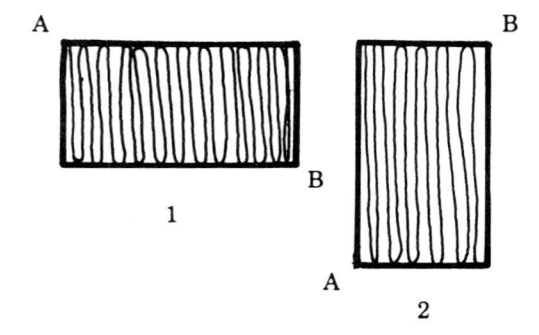

Fig. 5.8 1. Stitch down and back in close rows, beginning at A and ending at B. 2. Turn and stitch in rows perpendicular to the first pass, beginning at B and ending at A.

⅜" (9.5mm). Before you begin stitching the third and final pass, place a tiny scrap of matching fabric over the place where you'll glue the earring back later. (You are working with the underside of the earrings on top; the top or ribbon side is underneath.)

Stitch the last pass slowly. Again you'll stitch up and back as you did on the first layer, but instead of stitching to the bottom edge, *stitch beyond to the fringe line* you've drawn, from A to C in Fig. 5.9. Then stitch back to the top, as close as you can next to the first row without stitching on top of it. Continue to stitch across the rectangle. The last two rows are completed by stitching down and back to the top, leaving a ½" (12.7mm) tail of thread and ribbon to work in underneath later when you sew on the beads. Remove the stabilizer from the hoop, cut around the earrings, then hold them under a faucet to wash out any remaining stabilizer. Place the earrings between two pieces of toweling and squeeze out the moisture. Leave the fringe in loops or clip the ends to fray the ribbon.

Pull the ribbon end to the underside and hold it there, catching it in the stitches as you attach the beads by hand (Fig. 5.10). Glue on the backings, as described previously.

The last earring shape is a long triangle stitched with two layers of variegated, machine embroidery rayon. When completed, the stiffened, gauze-like, plaid earrings are

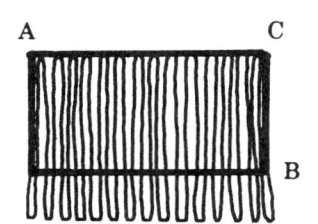

Fig. 5.9 Fringe earrings on the third pass by stitching from A to C.

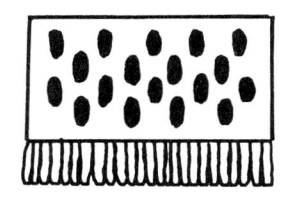

Fig. 5.10 Attach beads to the earrings by hand.

manipulated into three-dimensional shapes.

Stitch width: 0
Stitch length: 0
Feed dogs: lowered or covered
Presser foot: darning foot or spring
Needle: #90/14 sharp
Tension: *top*, normal; *bobbin*, normal
Thread: rayon variegated machine embroidery thread on top and thread of one color found in the variegated on the bobbin
Accessories: white opaque marker; 5" (12.7cm) or 7" (17.8cm) spring hoop
Stabilizer: water-soluble type
Miscellaneous: earring posts or clips

Prepare the hoop as before and draw the pattern provided in Fig. 5.11A on the water-soluble stabilizer. Stitch up and back from the point to what will become the earring fringe. Stitch in the first pass without crossing threads—if you can manage it—but stitching the rows as close together as possible (Fig. 5.11B). When finished, go back across the earrings, traveling from the top point down to a place ¼" (6.4mm) from the bottom fringed edge (Fig. 5.11C).

Remove the stabilizer from the hoop, cut around the earrings, then run water over them to wash out some of the stabilizer. Leave enough residue in the earrings to stiffen them. Roll down the pointed end and hold it in place with a pin, if necessary, until dry (Fig. 5.11D).

Use epoxy to glue backings on when the earring is completely dry.

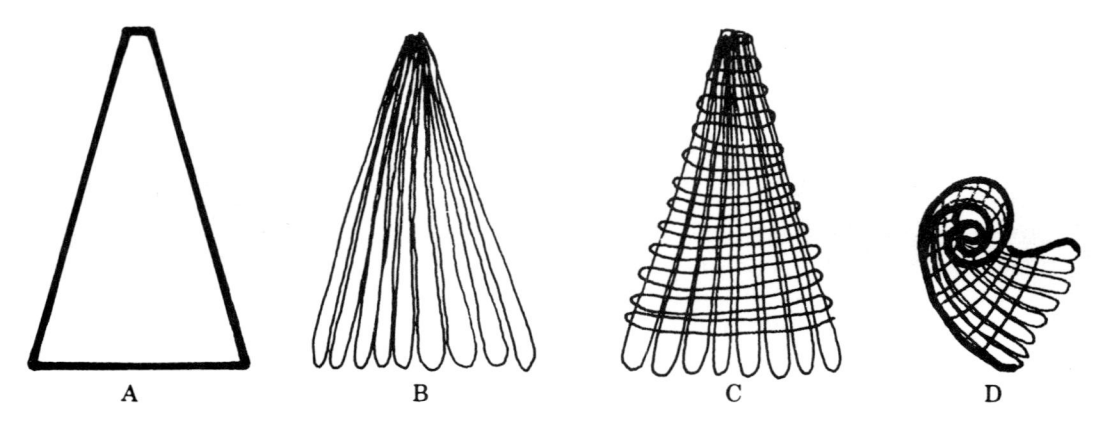

Fig. 5.11 A. Pattern to trace onto water-soluble stabilizer. B. Stitch up and back within the triangle. C. Stitch across and back. D. Roll into three-dimensional earrings.

Another idea? Make the same variegated earrings, but don't roll down the top. Instead, attach a "fish hook" or "kidney" finding to them for pierced ears. Another alternative comes from Jan Saunders of Columbus, Ohio. Jan pokes a plain, small, ball post through her needlelace pieces to eliminate gluing the posts to the earring backs.

Don't limit yourself; try other shapes and styles while experimenting with the many new threads and ribbons available today for machine embroidery.

Lesson 14. Battenberg lace

Battenberg lace was popular in the late 1800s. Straight, machine-made tape was shaped into a design and basted to stiff paper. Then the open spaces were filled with bars and embroidery stitches, which held the tape in shape. After the stitchery was completed, the paper was removed and the Battenberg lace could be used to decorate dresses, curtains or linens.

Project Bird-shaped Lace

This lesson will teach you how to make a small piece of Battenberg (Fig. 5.12). From there, you can go on to bigger projects, but let's see if you like Battenberg lacemaking by machine.

There is a variety of white, off-white, gold, and silver Battenberg tape from which to choose. It's available by mail-order (see Sources of Supplies) and from some needlework shops.

Set your machine for darning.

Stitch width: 0–1 1/2
Stitch length: 0
Needle position: center (center)
Needle: #80/12
Feed dogs: lowered (covered)
Tension: *top*, 5 (4); *bobbin*, normal
Thread: wash-away basting thread; white machine embroidery

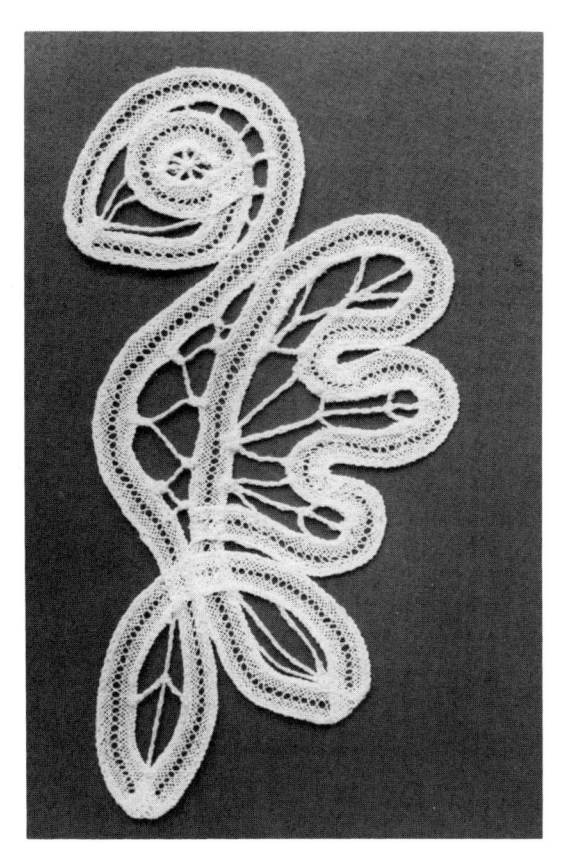

Fig. 5.12 Battenberg is embroidered after narrow tape has been shaped into a design.

Accessories: 7" (17.8cm) spring hoop; vanishing marker and white permanent marker; white Battenberg tape; glue stick; dressmaker's pins

Stabilizer: water-soluble, large enough for double layer in the hoop

On each side of the tape is a thread that is thicker than the others. As you pull the threads, the tape is curved into the shape you want. To estimate the length of tape you will need, hold the tape on its edge, place it around the outer edge of the design in the book, and then add several more inches. This lace piece is done with a single piece of Battenberg tape. After cutting the tape, knot the two thicker threads together at both ends so they won't pull through.

Place two layers of water-soluble stabilizer in the hoop. Then place the hoop over the design in Fig. 5.13 and trace the outline with a white permanent marking pen.

Starting at the bird's eye, pull up the threads on the tape to create the circle, then curve it slightly to the beak. Flip the tape over to create a point and continue on as shown in the illustration. Both loops at the bottom are also flipped into points. The three loops at the left side are formed by pulling one of the threads to create tight curves.

As you lay down the tape, pin it to the water-soluble stabilizer and use gluestick to temporarily hold it in place if necessary. Hide the ends as shown.

Then baste both edges of the tape to the stabilizer. I find it more satisfactory to baste the design by hand than by machine, using wash-away basting thread.

Draw in the stitching lines with the white marking pen. Extend them by drawing dots onto the tape with a vanishing marker. At times the stabilizer may be cut out and these dots can be used for reference.

Set up your machine for darning.

Start by straight stitching around the edges of the tape with machine embroidery thread. When you come to a place where two tape edges meet, stitch across from one edge to the other and back again several times to join the tapes.

Zigzag over the tape edges to secure the tape ends, as seen in Fig. 5.13.

After the design is attached, cut out the stabilizer in the eye circle or, if you are more comfortable stitching on the stabilizer, then leave it in place until the Battenberg is completed. If you stitch the bars without the stabilizer, stitch quickly to put a tighter twist on the threads.

First stitch one long pass from the point at the center bottom of the eye up to the

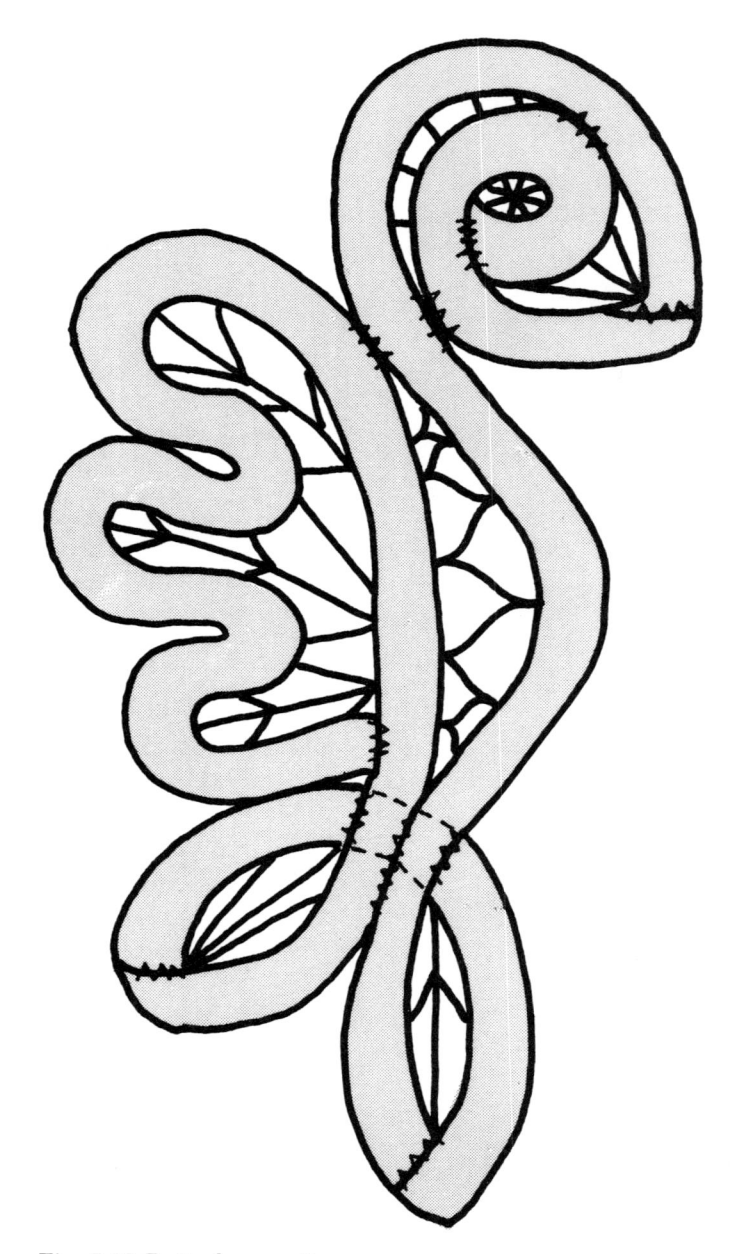

Fig. 5.13 Battenberg pattern.

center top and back again (Fig. 5.14A). Stitch back over these threads with stitch width 2 (1 1/2). Move the hoop quite fast. Don't build up thick bars as in cutwork.

Following the side of the tape, straight stitch to the next mark, stitch to the other side and back again. Then zigzag over the bars. Straight stitch to the next mark, across the opening and back again. Zigzag over the bars. Continue on until the spokes are completed for the bird's eye.

To do the loop at the bottom of the design (Fig. 5.14B), stitch from top center at the crossed tapes to the bottom and back again. Zigzag back over the threads. Follow the tape to one side and straight stitch across to the center bar and over to the other side. Stitch back, then zigzag over the bar as shown.

Using this same method, fill in the wings at the left side of the design (Fig. 5.14C).

The bottom left loop below the wings (Fig. 5.14D) and pointed beak (Fig. 5.14E), are both stitched with three straight bars from top to bottom as shown.

At the right curved area, straight stitch from one side of the tape to the other across the area, then straight stitch back again (Fig. 5.14F). Zigzag back over the threads, always straight stitching to anchor whenever you reach the tape. Then zigzag several stitches over the threads entering and leaving the tape to hold them together. Travel on over the next threads. Stitch down to the tape, then back over both threads with a few stitches before zigzagging over the next bar to the other side of the tape. Complete this area.

Stitch the area above the bird's eye by stitching bars across from one tape to the other as shown in Fig. 5.14G.

After the lace is completed, wash out the stabilizer and basting thread, place the Battenberg on toweling, and gently work the tape and design into shape. Place toweling over the lace and press.

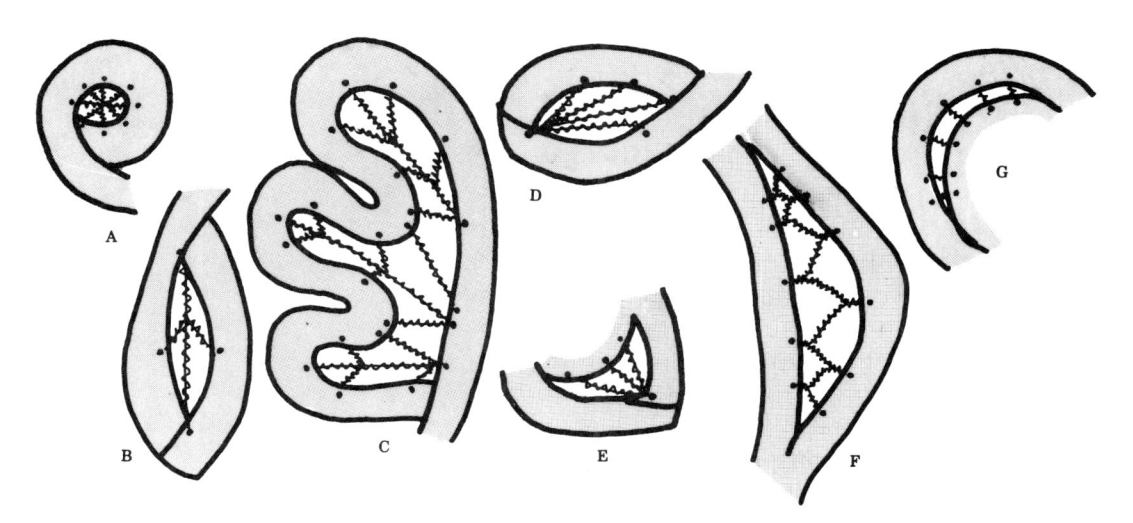

Fig. 5.14 A. Stitch spokes in the circle for bird's eye. B and C. Feather shapes are filled in with veins called Sorrento bars. D and E. Both the beak and bottom left loop contain three bars of zigzagged threads. F. This fill-in stitch is referred to as Point d'Alençon when done by hand. G. The area at the top is filled with six straight zigzagged bars.

Lesson 15. Hemstitching

Hemstitching is used on garments and table linens whenever a delicate, feminine look is desired. The technique looks complicated and difficult, but it is surprisingly easy to accomplish using both double- and single-winged needles.

Before you begin to stitch the bonnet, practice on two layers of cotton organdy.

Set up your machine for zigzag and use the transparent zigzag foot N. Be sure to choose a double needle that is no wider than 2mm. When using it on the Galaxie, press the double needle button, which will automatically set your width.

Stitch width: 0–auto (0 to no wider than the throat plate opening when using a double needle)
Stitch length: varies
Needle position: auto (center)
Needle: single and double wing needles; double needles to match size of pintuck foot
Feed dogs: up
Presser foot: open embroidery foot, pintuck foot
Tension: *top*, normal; *bobbin*, normal
Fabric: crisp fabric, such as organdy or linen
Thread: cotton machine embroidery

To thread two needles, take both threads together through each thread guide and the tension wheel and do not separate them until you reach the needles. Thread each needle separately by hand (the automatic threader will not work with a wing needle). Remember always to thread your machine with the presser foot up.

Start with the wing needle and use the rickrack stitch (#21, width 5). Stitch a row of hemstitching. Set your machine for the triple stretch stitch (#21, stitch width 0, needle position L). Work several parallel rows of stretch stitch using the edge of the presser foot as a guide. Now set up again for the rickrack stitch (width 5) and work one row of rickrack. Move slightly to the right and work a row of #79 (#20, stitch width 5), and #84.

You can make an all-over design, covering a large area with hemstitches. This is usually worked on the bias, then appliquéd to something else.

Now practice with the double wing needle. Set up your machine in this way:

Stitch width: double needle (0–3)
Stitch length: 3 (2)
Needle position: auto (center)
Feed dogs: up
Presser foot: transparent embroidery foot N
Built-in stitch: rickrack stitch (#21)

Make one pass, ending to the left. Lift the presser foot, turn the fabric and stitch the second pass.

Try this blind stitch (#5) using the double needle.

Stitch width: double needle (0–3)
Stitch length: auto (2)
Needle position: auto (center)
Feed dogs: up
Presser foot: transparent embroidery foot N
Built-in stitch: blind stitch (#5)

Project Infant's Bonnet

I've combined hemstitching with built-in stitches and double needles to make the infant's bonnet shown in Fig. 5.15. Also included is a line of ribbon sewing. This can be made in the time it would take you to shop for a baby gift.

Nora Lou Kampe of LaGrange, Illinois, made this bonnet using embroidered eye-

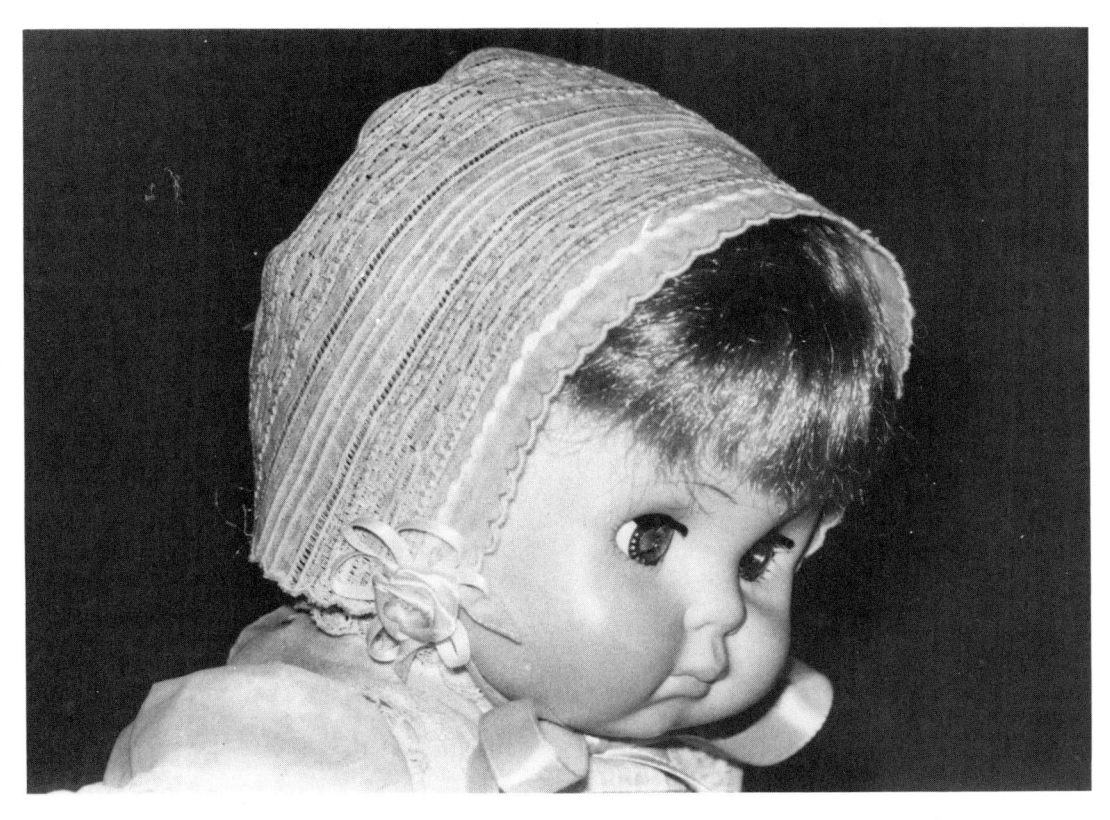

Fig. 5.15 Hemstitching, pintucking, and embroidery decorate the organdy bonnet for an infant or a doll.

let fabric with a scalloped border–a way to make a baby gift in no more than an hour's time. I used her bonnet idea, but took the long-cut and embroidered the bonnet myself; it fits a newborn and you could make one for a christening. A gown can be done in the same hemstitching technique.

The finished bonnet is 13" × 5¾" (33.0cm × 14.6cm). Add to both width and length if you're adapting it for an older baby. Set your machine for zigzag.

- Stitch width: varies
- Stitch length: varies
- Needle position: center, right
- Needle: 1.6mm twin needle; single and double wing needles
- Feed dogs: up
- Presser foot: transparent embroidery foot N
- Tension: *top*, normal; *bobbin*, normal
- Fabric suggestion: white cotton organdy
- Thread: light-blue, fine machine-embroidery thread; #5 light-blue pearl cotton; white cordonnet
- Other supplies: pearl bead (optional); ⅛" (3.2mm) double-faced satin ribbon, approximately 1 yard (91.4cm); ¼" (6.3mm) double-faced satin ribbon, ½ yard (45.7cm); ½" (12.7mm) double-faced satin ribbon, approximately 1½ yards (137.2cm)

Begin with two pieces of organdy, each 18" × 9" (45.7cm × 22.9cm). I start with a much larger area than I need because I practice on the margin–running the decorative stitches so they will match when I do a mirror image.

Wash and iron the organdy. Mark the top fabric lengthwise, using a vanishing marker (Fig. 5.16). Start by marking lines 1″ (2.5cm) apart from the front edge. Use a T-square for accuracy. Draw six lines. Then mark a line ½″ (12.7mm) from the last line, and another ½″ (12.7mm) from that one; 7″ × 13″ (17.8cm × 33.0cm) is marked. Pin the two pieces of fabric together at the top of the lines.

Once you have learned how to hemstitch, the decoration is up to you. The following is only a suggestion: Thread the double-wing needle with light-blue thread. The first line of blind hemstitches are stitched 1″ (2.5cm) from the front edge. Set the machine for rickrack stitch (#21, width 4). Use the blue line as your guide and stitch on top of it.

Spread the fabric apart. The pintucking is done between the blue lines on the top piece only.

Change to the 1.6mm double needle. Place light blue #5 pearl cotton between the needles under the fabric (needle in left position), feed dogs up, stitch length 4 (2).

There are three lines of pintucking, so stitch the first line exactly in the middle, between the blue marker lines. Stitch the others on either side of this one, using the edge of the zigzag foot as a guide.

If you wish, stitch all four groups of pintucks between the blue lines at one time. Then go back, cut the pearl cotton and remove, change to the wing needle, and continue to hemstitch on the blue lines with the blind stitch. Remember, when you pintuck, work on one layer of fabric, but hemstitch on both layers.

Complete 4½″ (11.4cm) of the bonnet (shaded area on Fig. 5.16) by filling in the empty spaces between the hemstitched blind hem pattern and the pintucks. Use the open effect of the single-wing needle, sewing in a straight line with the triple stretch stitch at left position (#21, width 0).

Should you want still more decoration, use a built-in stitch of your choice. Sew down the sides of the lines of blind hemstitches. When you have decorated the fabric enough, straight stitch around the edge of the bonnet rectangle. Cut back to the stitching line. Put the piece you've practiced on into your notebook.

Fold the bonnet rectangle in half (Fig. 5.17). The fold will be the top of the bonnet. Pin the fabric together, matching decorative stitches so it is exact. Round off the front corners where the rosettes will be

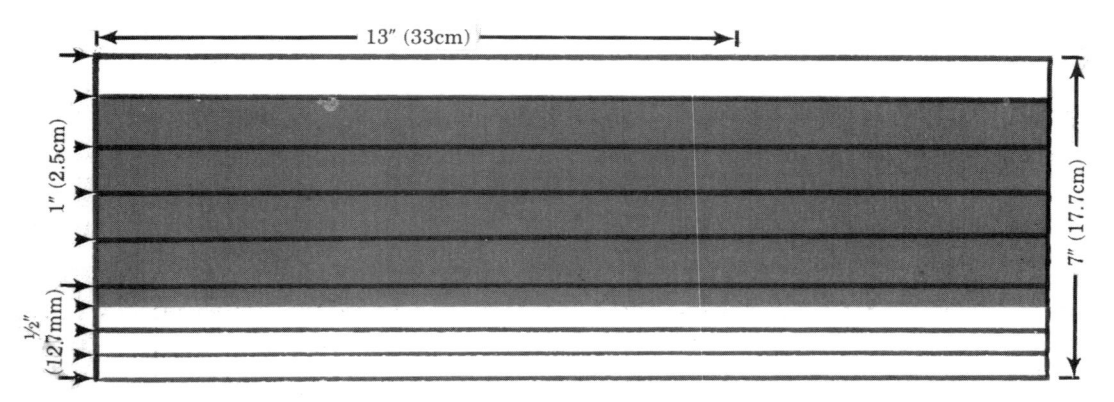

Fig. 5.16 The shaded area of the diagram indicates the portions to be embroidered.

sewn (see Fig. 5.17). Open up and stitch ⅛" (3.2mm) in from the edges of the bottom and front.

Change to a scallop design or satin stitch to stitch the front edge and the sides of the bonnet. Use a cording foot, size #80 needle, stitch width 4, stitch length 1/2 (or whatever works best for you to cover cord smoothly). Do a sample first.

Thread cordonnet through the hole in the foot. Place the foot with the thread hole on the line of stitching. Hold the cord up slightly as you cover it with stitches. When the scallops are completed, clip fabric back from the edge to the stitching, but not too close to the scallops.

Stitch down on the line ½" (12.7mm) from the edge (back of bonnet) and stitch another ½" (12.7mm) from that line. Fold the back under ½" (12.7mm), then again another ½" (12.7mm). Stitch across the first fold to make the ribbon casing.

Next, wind the bobbin with ⅛" (3.2mm) double-faced satin ribbon. Tape the end onto the bobbin and begin winding by hand. Finish by winding slowly on the machine. Don't thread it through the spring when full. Instead, if you are working on the Galaxie, bypass the tension spring by taking the ribbon directly through the rectangular opening on the top of the bobbin case. My 950 balks when I put ribbon in the bobbin case. Insert the bobbin into the machine and bring the ribbon to the top. Pull out at least 8" (20.3cm) of ribbon before beginning to sew. Use the longest stitch length 7 (5).

Use the zigzag foot, tension turned up to 10, and needle position to the right. Place the bonnet front on the bed of the machine. The ribbon will be stitched from underneath, ½" (12.7mm) from the front edge. When you finish stitching, pull out 8" (20.3cm) of ribbon and cut off.

On the 950 attach the ribbon by hand as follows: Leave 8' of ribbon for a bow and begin tying overhand knots every inch until you have enough knotted ribbon to stretch from one rounded corner to the next across the top front of the bonnet. Then, attach each knot by invisibly stitching it to the bonnet by hand.

Cut two ½" (12.7mm) satin ribbons, each 12" (30.5cm) long, for the bonnet ties and attach by stitching several zigzag stitches in one place at the rounded corners under the ⅛" (3.2mm) ribbon.

Make six loops from the 8" (20.3cm) of ⅛" (3.2mm) ribbon. Tack them by hand at the center on top of the ribbon ties. Make ribbon roses as shown in Fig. 5.18A, or tiny bows from the ½" (12.7mm) ribbon and attach these over the loops by hand (Fig. 5.18B). Use double thread. Poke the needle up from the inside of the bonnet, through the ribbon ties, loops, and the center of the flower and a pearl bead. Then poke the needle back through the flower, loops, ribbon tie and bonnet. Do this several times. It's not necessary to go through the bead each time. Anchor the thread underneath.

Thread 18" (45.7cm) of ¼" (6.3mm) ribbon through the back casing on the bonnet and pull up to tie into a bow at the back (Fig. 5.19). Cut off at the length you prefer. There you have it—a priceless gift.

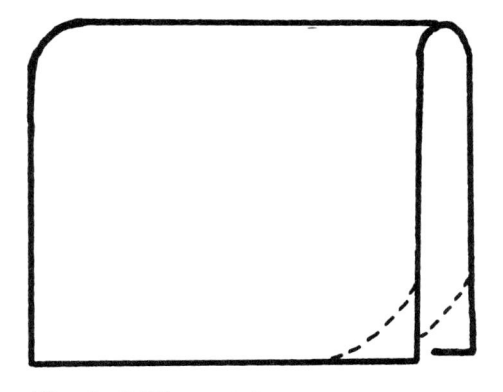

Fig. 5.17 When stitching is completed, fold the rectangle in half and round off the front corners, as shown.

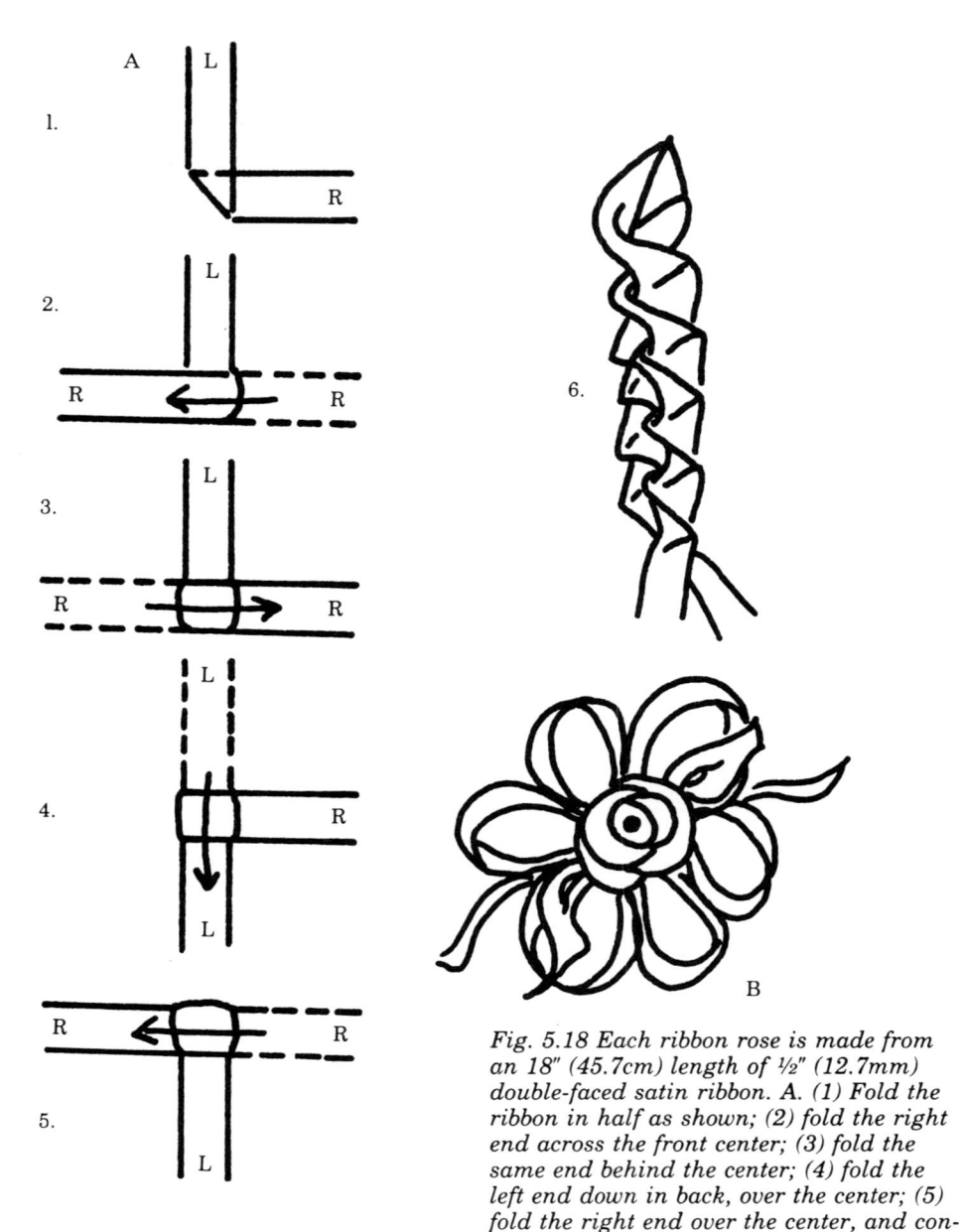

Fig. 5.18 Each ribbon rose is made from an 18" (45.7cm) length of ½" (12.7mm) double-faced satin ribbon. A. (1) Fold the ribbon in half as shown; (2) fold the right end across the front center; (3) fold the same end behind the center; (4) fold the left end down in back, over the center; (5) fold the right end over the center, and continue folding over the center until there are 30 folds between your fingers; (6) holding the last fold between your thumb and forefinger, release the rest of the ribbon, then pull on the ribbon end under the last fold to create the rose. B. By hand, stitch from the back to the center and back again to keep the rose from unwinding. Leave ½" (12.7mm) ends and cut each on a slant. Hold the loops in place with a small ribbon rose or tie small bows at the centers.

Fig. 5.19 Pull on each end of the back ribbon and tie into a bow to shape the crown of the bonnet.

Lesson 16. Stitching in rings

Stitching in rings is like making needlelace (Fig. 5.20). Instead of fabric surrounding a space, in this lesson the thread is attached to narrow gold rings. I selected rings about 2½" (6.4cm) in diameter as an appropriate size for tree ornaments. See Sources of Supplies for ordering these rings.

Project Christmas Ornaments

A stabilizer isn't always needed when you sew in space, but you may want to use it. I used to make these Christmas ornaments without a stabilizer and it worked beautifully. But with water-soluble stabilizer underneath, you can stitch more intricate designs, and the thread will stay in one place, as if you were stitching on fabric.

Set your machine for darning.

Stitch width: N–W; 0–5
Stitch length: 0
Needle position: auto (center)
Needle: #80/12
Feed dogs: lowered
Presser foot: none
Tension: *top*, 3 (3); *bobbin*, normal
Thread: gold metallic on top and bobbin
Accessories: 2½" (6.4cm) gold ring; 7" (17.8cm) spring hoop; permanent white marker
Stabilizer: water-soluble

Double the stabilizer and put it into the hoop. Place the gold ring in the center. Draw a design in the ring.

Dip the needle down at the side of the ring and bring the bobbin thread to the top. Hold the threads to one side. Anchor the ring by hand-walking the needle from the outside to the inside of it. Stitch from one side to the other several times. Hold onto the ring and stitch across to the other

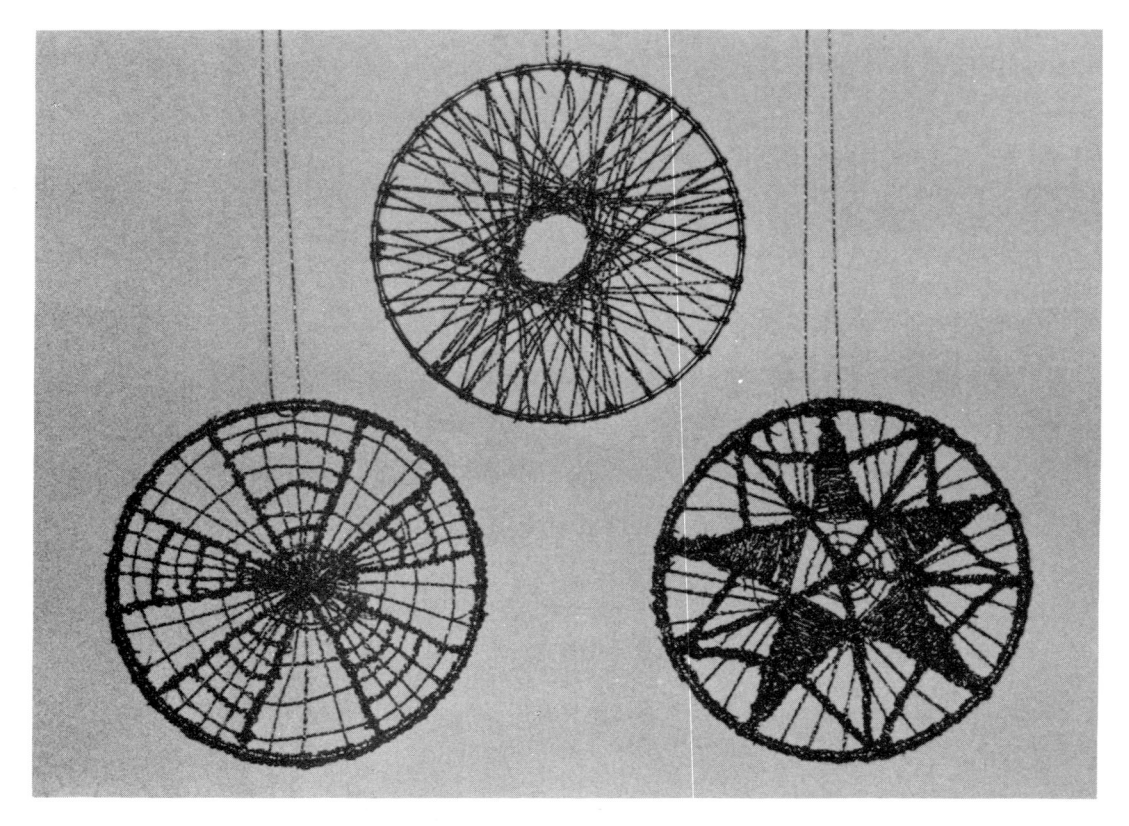

Fig. 5.20 Christmas ornaments stitched in gold rings.

side. The chain of stitches will be tighter if you sew fast but move the hoop slowly. Anchor the thread on the other side by sewing over and back on the ring as you did at first.

Work back across and anchor on the other side. Keep doing this until you have laid in the spokes of the design. Remember, with water-soluble stabilizer you can change direction when stitching in open spaces. After the last anchoring stitches, go back into the ring and finish the piece. It can be symmetrical or not. I feel that the lighter the look, the better. Stitching it too thickly will be a detraction, but you may want to zigzag over threads, as in cutwork, to add variety to the design.

Anchor the last stitches and take the ring out of the hoop. Cut back the stabilizer, then dissolve it by holding the ring under running water. Hang it from your Christmas tree with a cord.

Lesson 17. Making Alençon lace

Alençon lace took its name from the French town. The lace was developed there and was so expensive it was rarely seen, except in shops with a wealthy clientele, where it was sold as yardage and used as trimming for lingerie, dresses, and household items.

On the fine, mesh net background is a heavy design, so closely woven it is almost clothlike. Characteristic of Alençon lace is the heavy thread that outlines the design.

Project Alençon Pincushion

Our Alençon is made on a single layer of bridal veiling. The design is freely embroidered by machine, then outlined with pearl cotton or cordonnet (Fig. 5.21). Set your machine for darning.

Stitch width: 0
Stitch length: 0
Needle position: auto (center)
Needle: #80/12
Feed dogs: lowered (covered)
Presser feet: darning foot or spring
Tension: *top*, 3 (3); *bobbin*, normal
Fabric suggestion: bridal veil, 36" × 5" (91.4cm × 12.7cm); pink satin, 4½" × 11" (11.4cm × 28.0cm)
Thread: #100 or #120 fine white sewing thread; #8 pearl cotton or cordonnet on bobbin to match
Accessories: 7" (17.8cm) spring hoop; permanent white marker; 2 cups of sawdust
Stabilizer: tear-away and water-soluble

Prepare a sample of your stitching to be sure it looks like you want it to. I like a slight bubbly look to the pearl cotton, but you may want a tighter or even looser stitch. If so, tighten or loosen the top tension.

Put the water-soluble stabilizer in the hoop. Place it over the design and copy it with the permanent marker (Fig. 5.22). Then place the veiling over the stabilizer in the hoop.

Thread with fine thread in the top and bobbin. Bring the bobbin thread to the top

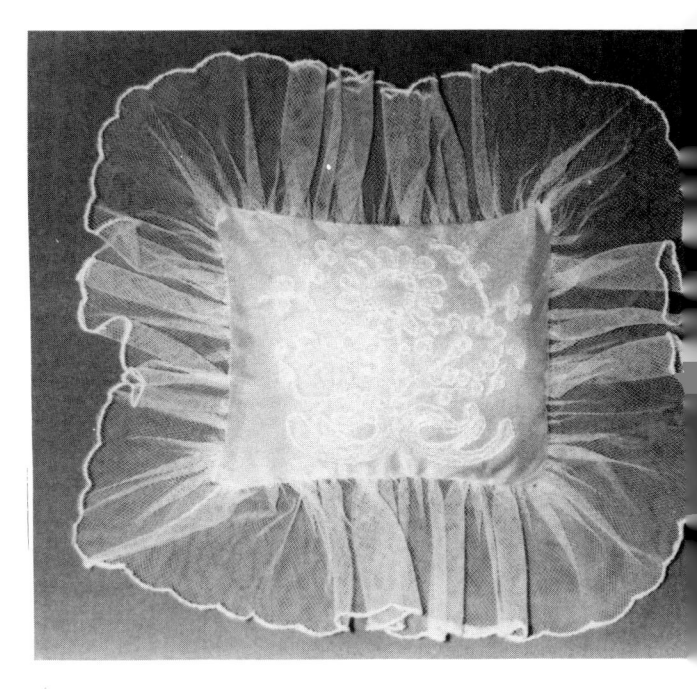

Fig. 5.21 Alençon lace pincushion.

and hold both threads to one side. After stitching a few stitches, clip these ends off. I don't anchor the threads as they will be sewn in anyway. Outline the design first with straight stitches.

When completed, go back and stitch in the petals and leaves. Sew a line next to the outline, then another within that and another, and so on until you have filled it in. If some of the lines overlap, don't despair, as this will happen. Just try to keep from building up heavy stitching lines.

It's not necessary to cut the thread as you complete one section and start another. Loosen the top thread by lifting up on the presser foot and turning the handwheel if necessary. Slowly pull or push the hoop to the next place. There's no need to bring up the bobbin thread again, as long as it is still connected to the fabric.

When finished stitching, go back and clip threads between motifs. Bring long threads to the back to be clipped and dot-

Fig. 5.22 Lace pincushion design.

ted with a drop of No-Fray or Fray-Check. Use tweezers to pull out loose threads on the back.

Change the bobbin to the one containing pearl cotton. Take the veiling out of the hoop and turn it over. The topside of the lace will be underneath. Double check the tensions by sewing on another piece of veiling in another hoop. The pearl cotton should lay flat underneath without pulling; yet it should not be so loose it looks loopy.

Dip the needle into the veil and bring the pearl to the top. Hold it to one side as you begin: Don't anchor it. Outline the design. It is very important to keep from going over lines too many times. You want it to be thick, but not ugly.

When you complete outlining, cut off the pearl cotton, bringing any long ends to the back. Work those under a few stitches on back by hand and clip them off. Put your lace, still in the hoop, under the faucet to wash out the stabilizer.

Measure the top of the pincushion. The finished size will be 4" × 5" (10.2cm × 12.7cm) so add ½" (12.7mm) to each measurement; 4½" × 5½" (12.7cm × 14.0cm). Cut two pieces of pink satin this size. Stitch the lace to one of the rectangles. Seam allowance is ¼" (6.3mm).

Cut a piece of veiling 36" (91.4cm) long (twice the perimeter of the pincushion), and 5" (12.7cm) wide. Cut a piece of tear-away stabilizer the same length and 2" (5.1cm) wide. Pin the cut edges of the veiling together to hold it in place. Slip tear-away under the fold. Set your machine to satin stitch or the scallop stitch (refer to your manual).

Turn feed dogs up. With the right edge of the embroidery foot placed just within the edge of the fold, stitch width 4, length at 1/2 (or whatever would give you an attractive stitch), sew down the length of the veiling and cut back to the stitching. Wash out the stabilizer.

To gather the ruffle, zigzag over cordonnet (see Lesson 4). Stitch the length of the cut edges—stitch length medium (2), stitch width narrow (1). Use the cord to gather the ruffle.

Join the two ends of the ruffle by placing one end over the other about ½" (12.7mm). Using a 2 stitch width, and 1/2 length, satin stitch down the width of the piece of veiling. Cut back to the line of stitching on both sides.

Gather the ruffle, placing the seam at a corner. Corners should be heavily gathered to make sure they lay beautifully when completed. Distribute the ruffles around the edge of the pincushion. Remember that the embroidered edge will be toward the *center* of the pincushion. Stitch in place. It's not necessary to remove the cordonnet.

The last step is to sew the back of the pincushion to the lace. Place right sides together, and work all the net ruffles inside as you pin around the edge.

Sew within the stitching line on front. Leave a large enough opening so you can turn the pincushion to the outside. When turned, fill it very tightly with sawdust (or use another filler, if you prefer). Stitch the opening shut by hand.

Do you like making lace? Try other variations by using built-in stitches, satin-stitch star flowers, or bands of intertwined cordonnet at the edges.

CHAPTER **6**

Drawing Threads Out of Your Fabric

■ **Lesson 18. Needleweaving**

To create an area of free, lacy openwork called needleweaving, first draw threads out of a fabric, then stitch over the remaining threads. On this long-cut, I used exactly the same color thread on the top and bobbin as that of the dress; I'm constantly being asked how it was stitched. The solution to the mystery follows.

Lesson 18. Needleweaving

Because needleweaving is worked in a straight line, I chose to decorate the sleeves of a summer dress (Fig. 6.1). I knew this dress would be washed many times, so I chose a polyester sewing thread for durability. I matched it perfectly, both spool and bobbin, with the fabric.

First do a small sample of needleweaving for your notebook. The openwork is 1" (2.5cm) wide. Pull out a horizontal thread at the top and the bottom where the openwork will be. Straight stitch across those lines. Then pull out the horizontal or weft threads in that space.

Project
Openwork on Sleeves

You will machine stitch over the vertical or warp threads, drawing them together as you zigzag (Fig. 6.2). Set your machine for darning.

Stitch width: N–W
Stitch length: 2 (0–1/2)
Needle position: auto (center)
Needle: #80/12
Feed dogs: lowered (covered), up
Presser foot: transparent embroidery foot N, darning, or no presser foot
Tension: *top*, normal, loosened; *bobbin*, normal
Fabric suggestion: loosely woven
Thread: Metrosene polyester
Stabilizer: tear-away, or construction paper to match thread; water-soluble (optional)

Take off the regular presser foot and use a bare needle or darning foot. Try working without a hoop on this project. The stitching goes fast and a hoop would only slow you down.

You may stitch with water-soluble stabilizer behind your work, but that is optional. Prepare your machine for embroidery by lowering (covering) the feed dogs. Be sure the presser bar is down before you start to stitch. Dip the needle down and bring the bobbin thread to the top. Anchor

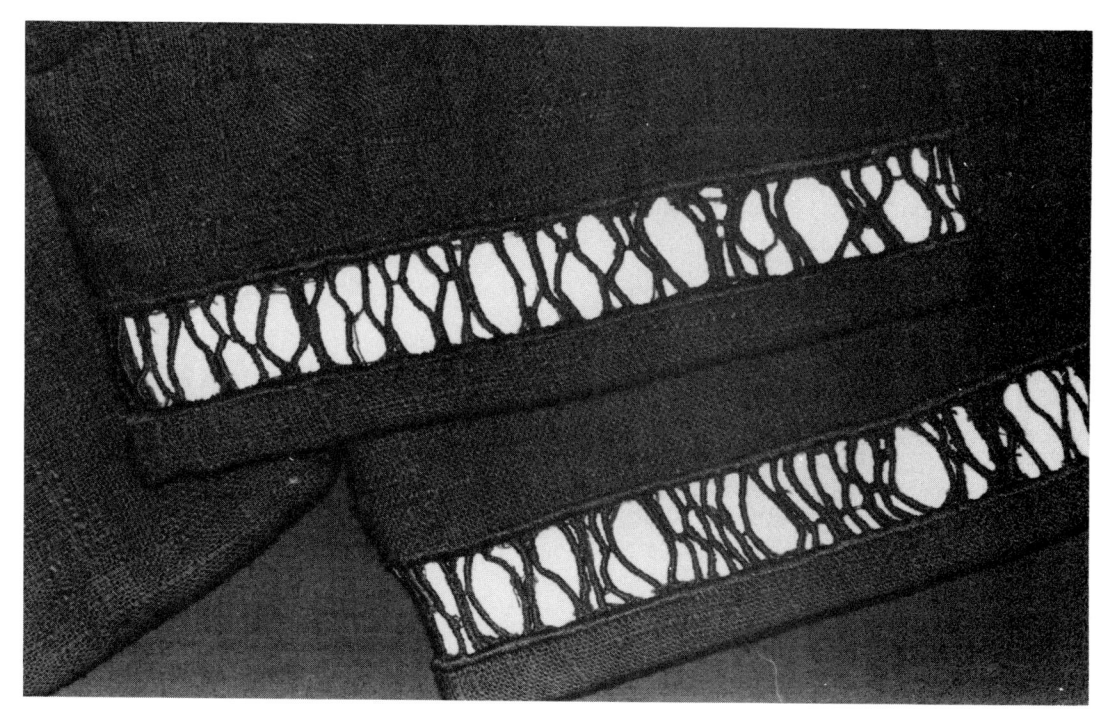

Fig. 6.1 Needleweaving decorates the sleeves on a summer dress.

Fig. 6.2 Pull out warp threads from the fabric and zigzag freely over the remaining wefts. Then finish the edges on each side with satin stitching.

the threads. Set the machine on stitch width 4 and normal tension.

Using both hands, grasp the top and bottom of the fabric between your fingers, stretching it slightly as you stitch. Keep the fabric as close as you can to the needleplate, and keep tension on the warp threads.

Begin to move from just below the stitched line at the bottom to just over the stitched line on top. Move the fabric slowly, but sew at a comfortable speed, catching several warp threads together as you zigzag to the top.

When you reach the top, move sideways to the next several warp threads and begin stitching those together. About halfway down, move the fabric to the side and catch a few stitches into the previous group of zigzagged threads. Then move back and continue to the bottom of the threads. Finish all the warp threads in the same manner, satin stitching up and down, while at the same time catching threads from the previous run in one or two places. This adds interest and strength to your openwork and is an integral part of your needleweaving.

After finishing, remove water-soluble stabilizer and pull the piece back into shape while damp. Press.

If you did not use stabilizer, then spray with water to enable you to pull it into shape. Press.

Draw two horizontal lines (one inch apart and as long as your needleweaving) across a piece of construction paper or tear-away stabilizer. Place your needleweaving on top of this, using the drawn lines as guides to keep the open area straight.

Set up your machine for straight stitching with feed dogs up and the transparent zigzag foot N. Sew a line of straight stitches across the top and bottom on the same guidelines you stitched at the beginning. This will hold the needleweaving in place and stabilize it for the final stitching.

Set the machine to a wide zigzag, feed dogs still up, stitch length 2 (1/2) (or whatever will result in a perfect satin stitch). Loosen tension slightly and satin stitch over those lines, covering the edges in two passes—the first narrower and more open than the second. This takes longer, but the results are more professional-looking. The stitching will fall just to one side of the fabric and will catch the fabric on the other side to neatly finish the edge of the needlelace. Tear off the stabilizer and steam press the embroidery carefully.

If the stabilizer can still be seen behind the stitches, it may be possible to remove it by dampening it, then using a tweezers to remove it. Or use this trick: if you can find a permanent marker the same color as the thread, dab in the color where necessary.

Try needleweaving across the yoke or pocket of a blouse, or down the middle of sleeves, or combine two rows of this with lacy spiderweb circles scattered between.

If you don't like the see-through look, or if you want to add another color, back the open area with another fabric.

You are more than halfway through *Know Your Brother Sewing Machine.* Do you know your sewing machine?

CHAPTER 7

Layering Fabrics: Quilting

- **Lesson 19. Quilting with feed dogs up**
- **Lesson 20. Quilting with feed dogs lowered**
- **Lesson 21. Trapunto**
- **Lesson 22. Italian cording**

I've always taken time to make handmade gifts for special people. But if I make a crib quilt, for example, I'd like to know that the baby won't be twice as long as the quilt by the time the gift is presented. If I'm sewing clothes, I'm realistic: I want the garment to be in style when the recipient opens the box.

So, although I love hand quilting and hand sewing, they often take too long. Machine quilting, on the other hand, is speedy and sturdy. You can use heavy fabrics like corduroy, as well as thick batts, and you will have no trouble stitching them together. If machine quilting is done properly, it can be as fine as handwork.

In this chapter I've included quilting with the feed dogs lowered and in place, trapunto, and Italian cording.

Remember several things when doing any type of quilting. The first is to preshrink all fabrics. I usually use cotton polyester blends for my quilts so they stay new-looking for a long time. Sheets are excellent backing materials. They come in a myriad of colors and prints, can be of excellent quality, and they won't have to be pieced. When I make a quilt, I use a sheet that is larger than the top.

I usually quilt with a polyester sewing thread. Most brands come in a wealth of colors. Should I want to emphasize the stitching line, I will double the thread. But when I sew on a patterned material or a fabric that changes color throughout, I choose a monofilament. I may or may not use monofilament on the bobbin, depending upon the samples I do first.

Using safety pins instead of hand basting is my favorite method of holding the fabrics and batt together before I quilt. I don't use dressmaker's pins because many of them fall out before the quilt is completed—and those that don't usually stab me.

Lesson 19. Quilting with feed dogs up

Instead of a regular presser foot, I use an even-feed or walking foot when I sew lines of straight quilting stitches. It minimizes puckering on the backing fabric, as the top and bottom fabrics are fed through at the same speed with no slipping.

Before I had one of those helpful attachments, I grasped the quilt in both hands and kept it taut as it fed through the machine. As I progressed, I stopped and looked underneath to be sure I had a smooth lining. I must admit I became an expert at sewing without puckers. It may take a little longer, but the lack of a walking foot should not deter you from starting your first quilt experiment.

Can you imagine how fast you could make a quilt using striped fabric or a striped sheet for the top? Use the stripes as quilting lines. If you use stripes for garments, keep in mind that the more rows of quilting, the smaller the piece becomes. I either quilt the fabric first and then cut out the pattern, or I cut my pattern larger than necessary, do the quilting and then lay the pattern back on it when finished. I recut the pattern where necessary.

If you piece a quilt and decide to machine quilt it by using stitch-in-a-ditch, you may prefer using the zipper foot I or the blind hemming foot L with the white bar extension. Stitch-in-a-ditch is done on top of the quilt by stitching in the seam lines (the ditches). On the Galaxie you will need to set the machine for zigzag, activate the manual-stitch-width-release lever and push it all the way to the left to get a center position. Adjust the white extension to exactly match the needle and begin stitching with the guide riding in the ditch.

Project
Tote Bag Square (Appliqué and Quilting)

This quilted sample can be used as a square for the tote bag in Chapter 12. It includes appliqué, satin stitches, and sewing with feed dogs up and lowered (Fig. 7.1).

Stitch width: N–W (0–5)
Stitch length: 0–4 (0–2)
Needle position: auto (center)
Feed dogs: up and lowered (covered)
Presser foot: transparent zigzag N, darning
Needle: #80/12

Tension: *top*, 3 (3); *bobbin*, normal
Thread: green cotton machine embroidery
Fabric: one 9" (23cm) square of green lightweight cotton; scraps of pin-dot fabric in blue, green, red, yellow and orange; 10" (25.4cm) squares of fleece and nylon tulle
Accessories: vanishing marker; fusible webbing; ruler; Teflon pressing sheet; tracing paper and pencil
Stabilizer: freezer paper

There are five fabrics used in this quilted square. Iron on the freezer paper to the back of the 9" (23cm) square, which will be used as the backing. Iron fusible webbing onto each of the pin-dot scraps, using the Teflon sheet.

Trace the design in Fig. 7.1 and cut apart. Place each piece on fabric and draw around it with the vanishing marker. Have you noticed how butting pieces of appliqué next to each other usually leaves gaping areas, no matter how careful you are? To prevent this, plan to overlap adjacent pieces by ¼" (6.4mm) so you don't have to sew over two raw edges. Decide ahead of time which piece will have a seam allowance that can be slipped under the edge of the fabric next to it. If you use this method, you'll have only one edge to cover with satin stitches.

Using green machine-embroidery thread, dial down the satin stitch to a hair narrower and shorter than the numbers you will use on the second and final pass. On the second pass, use a medium stitch width (2 1/2) and a close satin stitch length. Sew at a moderate speed. Remove the freezer paper.

Now make a sandwich with the appliquéd piece on top, the fleece in the middle and the tulle on the bottom. The tulle serves a dual purpose: it helps push the loft of the quilting to the top and keeps bits of batt from getting into the feed dogs or bobbin case. Set your machine for straight stitching, with a stitch length 6 (4) and

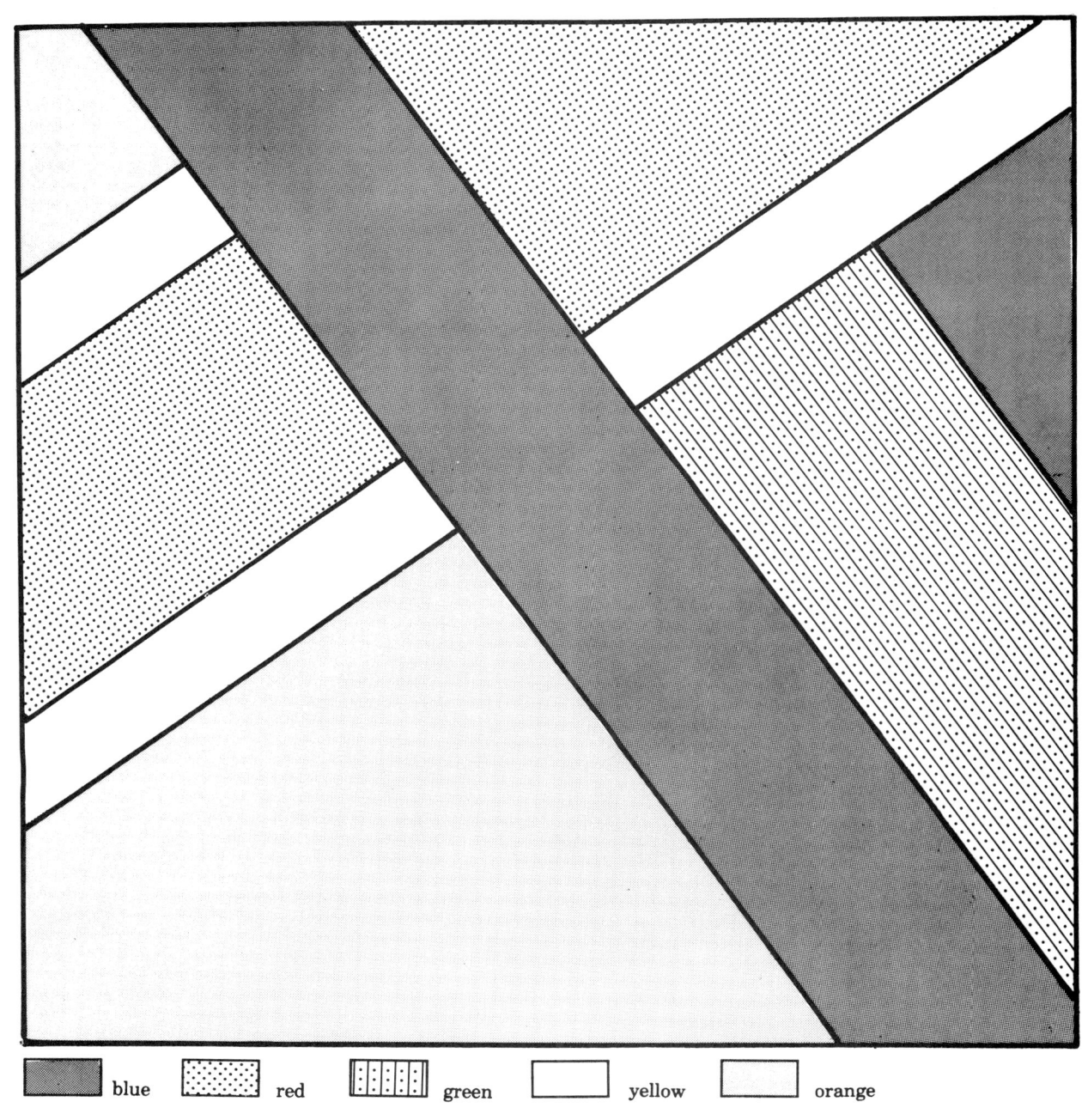

Fig. 7.1 Pattern for appliquéd and quilted tote bag square.

stitch down *each* side of the satin stitches. This not only quilts the fabric, but it gives the satin stitches a clean finish.

Finish quilting the square as described in Chapter 12.

Lesson 20. Quilting with feed dogs lowered

As you can tell from the lesson title, this will be free-machine quilting. The machine setting will not control the length of the stitches; you will. If you move the fabric fast, the stitches will be longer than if you move it slowly. Not working in a hoop, you must use a darning foot to prevent skipped stitches. And no hoop means you must hold the fabric taut while stitching. Set the machine for darning.

Stitch width: 0
Stitch length: 0
Needle position: auto (0)
Needle: #90/14
Feed dogs: lowered (covered)
Presser foot: darning foot or spring
Tension: *top*, 3 (3); *bottom*, normal
Fabric suggestion: medium-weight cotton; fleece or quilt batting
Thread: machine embroidery
Accessories: water-erasable marker

One of the easiest ways to learn free quilting and to practice control at the same time is to quilt around the motifs of a printed fabric as shown in Fig. 7.2. Even the underside looks terrific: you may like the looks of the lining better than the printed side. If so, it makes for a stunning reversible jacket.

When quilting any fabrics with feed dogs lowered, don't place the stitching lines too closely together, unless you want to emphasize the area that *isn't* stitched. Closely stitched, it will be too stiff and you'll lose the contrast of light and dark shadowing that makes this type of machining so effective.

Fig. 7.2 Cotton print, batting and velveteen are quilted together by stitching the butterfly design.

Lesson 21. Trapunto

In trapunto, two pieces of fabric are stitched together, following a design. Then the quilter selects the areas of the design to be stuffed with fiberfill. Usually trapunto is done from underneath the fabrics.

Layer two pieces of material together. Transfer the design of your choice to the top fabric. Place both fabrics in a hoop. Stitch in the design, using machine embroidery thread the same color as the fabric, with your machine set up for free-machine embroidery or feed dogs up and embroidery foot on. Stitch in the design.

Make small slits in the backing fabric behind the petals, leaves, or stamens—or all three. Add fiberfill, poking it in with a tool that is not sharply pointed. Whip stitch the slits closed by hand.

You can trapunto from the top by appliquéing on top of a base fabric. Slip filling inside the appliqué before you've attached it all the way around. You may want to add stitches over the surface of the appliqué to hold the stuffing firmly and to embellish the design.

Lesson 22. Italian cording

Italian cording is often mistaken for trapunto. The difference is that the area to be stuffed in Italian cording will be the space between two stitching lines. Instead of using fiberfill, thread a cord of appropriate size through the double lines of stitching.

It's also possible to create the look of Italian cording in one pass of the machine, on one layer of fabric when stitching with a double needle.

Project
Tote Bag Square (Italian Cording)

This square (see color section) was done using a single needle. I doubled the thread and used a longer than normal straight stitch. Usually the thread color matches the fabric, but I used red thread with green fabric to emphasize the design and to make a more decorative square. You may use the zigzag presser foot J for this square, but the transparent zigzag foot N will give you more visibility for greater accuracy. Stitch slowly and turn exactly where the tracing indicates (contrasting thread emphasizes any errors or overstitching). Set your machine for straight stitch.

Stitch width: auto (0)
Stitch length: 7 (4)
Needle position: auto (center)
Needle: #100
Feed dogs: up
Presser foot: transparent embroidery foot N
Tension: *top*, 5 (4); *bobbin*, normal
Fabric suggestions: green lightweight cotton for top; stiffer cotton for backing
Thread: red machine embroidery cotton (use two strands)
Cord: appropriate-size acrylic yarn or cable cord
Accessories: hand-sewing needle; large-eyed hand-sewing tapestry needle to thread cord through the design; tracing paper; pencil; ruler; dressmaker's carbon and empty ballpoint pen

Fig. 7.3 Italian cording tote bag square.

Use tracing paper, ruler, and pencil to trace the cording pattern in Fig. 7.3. Transfer your design onto the fabric with dressmaker's carbon and empty ballpoint pen, indicating where the lines will cross and which ones cross over, which under. When you are stitching the lines, don't anchor threads when the lines cross. Instead, pull several inches of thread out of the needle. Hold the thread to one side. Skip over the intersection; then begin stitching again. When finished, go back and clip the threads in the middle. Thread up a sewing needle and poke all the top threads through to the back and work them in. Finish up by working the cord through the design by hand.

It's difficult to turn corners with cording and make those corners look sharp. Poke the needle out of the back fabric at a corner, and then back in again in the same place, leaving a small loop of the cord out in back.

When working with a double needle, turn corners in three steps. Stitch to the corner. Stop. Needles should be grazing the fabric. Lift the presser foot. Half-turn the fabric. Lower the presser foot and turn the wheel by hand to make one stitch. Raise the needles and again bring the needle points down to barely touch the top of the fabric. Lift the presser foot again and complete the turn. Lower the presser foot and continue stitching.

Directions for finishing the square are in Chapter 12.

Look for inspirations for Italian cording in books on Celtic designs or bargello borders.

CHAPTER 8

Adding Interesting Seams to Your Fabric

- Lesson 23. Heirloom sewing by machine
- Lesson 24. Seaming with feed dogs up and lowered

In previous chapters, the emphasis was on decorative stitchery. In Chapters 8 and 9, the focus is on sewing. The chapters are so closely related that at times they even overlap. Included in Chapters 8 and 9 are many of the sewing long-cuts I mentioned in the Preface and Chapter 1. But now, instead of decorating a garment by embroidering or appliquéing on it, you'll learn to make the garment unique by changing the seams, hems and edges.

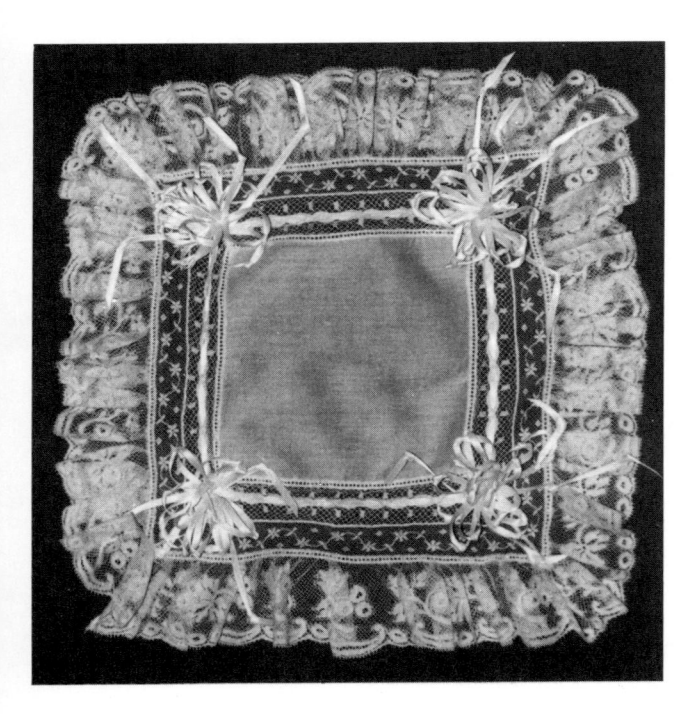

Let's face it: seams are not always interesting. Most of them are hidden and it's not necessary that they do anything but hold two pieces of fabric together. On the other hand, seams can be the focal point of your creation. This chapter includes seams for the finest lace to the heaviest canvas — seams purely practical and those that combine decoration with practicality. Stitch up samples of all of them for your notebook. You'll discover that knowing your sewing machine is a joy.

The project in this chapter is a wedding handkerchief (Fig. 8.1). After learning how to accomplish heirloom sewing on the machine, work this project. It can also be used as a pillow top.

Fig. 8.1 Heirloom-sewn wedding handkerchief.

Lesson 23. Heirloom sewing by machine

When I first heard about the type of clothing construction called French handsewing, I thought it was something new — until Marcia Strickland, a friend from Birmingham, Alabama, showed me her daughters' dresses. They were made of laces, with pintucks and embroidery, entredeux and hemstitching, and looked like our family's christening gown. I knew French handsewing; I just hadn't been acquainted with the term. We'd always called it "sewing by hand" and I had agonized over it years ago, when I was sure I'd be struck blind by the tiny stitches before I made it through junior high school. It was hard for me to believe that I could accomplish the perfection of Marcia's clothing on my sewing machine (called "heirloom sewing" or "French machine sewing").

It's possible to find lace and tucked blouses, skirts and dresses in any department store today. Because this feminine look is expensive in ready-to-wear, if you learn the following hand-sewing techniques by machine and sew them yourself, you will save money and have a lot of fun besides.

First, I had to learn basics before I could stitch collars or dresses. Marcia taught me that if I apply fabric to lace, one of the rules of French handsewing is that I must always have entredeux between.

Entredeux literally means "between two." It is purchased by the yard in fabric shops. The fabric on either side of the ladderlike strip down the center is trimmed off before it is attached. I also learned that the holes in entredeux are never evenly spaced, no matter how expensive it is.

Marcia suggested size 100 pure cotton thread and #70 needle for sewing. She uses an extra-fine thread because the batiste fabric used is extremely lightweight, and stitches are visible when attaching lace and entredeux or stitching pintucks. And she suggests using cotton thread for heirlooms because it will last a long time.

When handsewing, Marcia chooses cotton batiste because it is easier to roll and whip the edges of cotton. Polyester or cotton/polyester blends have minds of their own. It's hard to roll them as they keep unrolling while you try to whip them in place.

But heirloom sewing can easily be done on blends, so I often choose a cotton/polyester for fabric (and thread), as it doesn't wrinkle like pure cotton.

I learned so much from Marcia, I filled a notebook with samples, ideas, and shortcuts. When you stitch up samples for your own notebook, if a technique can be done several ways, do them all and then decide which works best for you. The following techniques are all you need to learn for heirloom sewing.

Sewing French seams

French seams are used on lightweight, transparent fabrics to finish the seams beautifully, disguising raw edges. They are also found on smocked garments as a fine finish.

The seams are accomplished in two different operations (Fig. 8.2). Begin with fabric pieces, wrong sides facing. Stitch the seam, using a #70 needle and fine sewing thread. Open and press seam to one side. Cut back the seam allowance evenly, to ⅛" (3.2mm). Turn the fabric back over the raw edges, press again (the seam will be at the edge), pin, and stitch again, enclosing the ⅛" (3.2mm) seam allowance.

The side-cutter accessory produces an exceptionally clean French seam. As you sew the seam on the first pass, the fabric is also trimmed to ⅛" (3.2mm), without the uneven edge that sometimes occurs when you cut by hand. When the fabric is folded back over the seam allowance, no maddening wispy threads poke out to ruin the perfect French seam.

Stitching rolled and whipped edges

Rolled and whipped edges (Fig. 8.3) are always used in conjunction with heirloom sewing because each piece of fabric must have a finished edge before it is attached to lace or to entredeux. When working by machine, sometimes you can finish the edge at the same time you attach it to the lace. These edges can be worked several ways and everyone seems to have her own favorite.

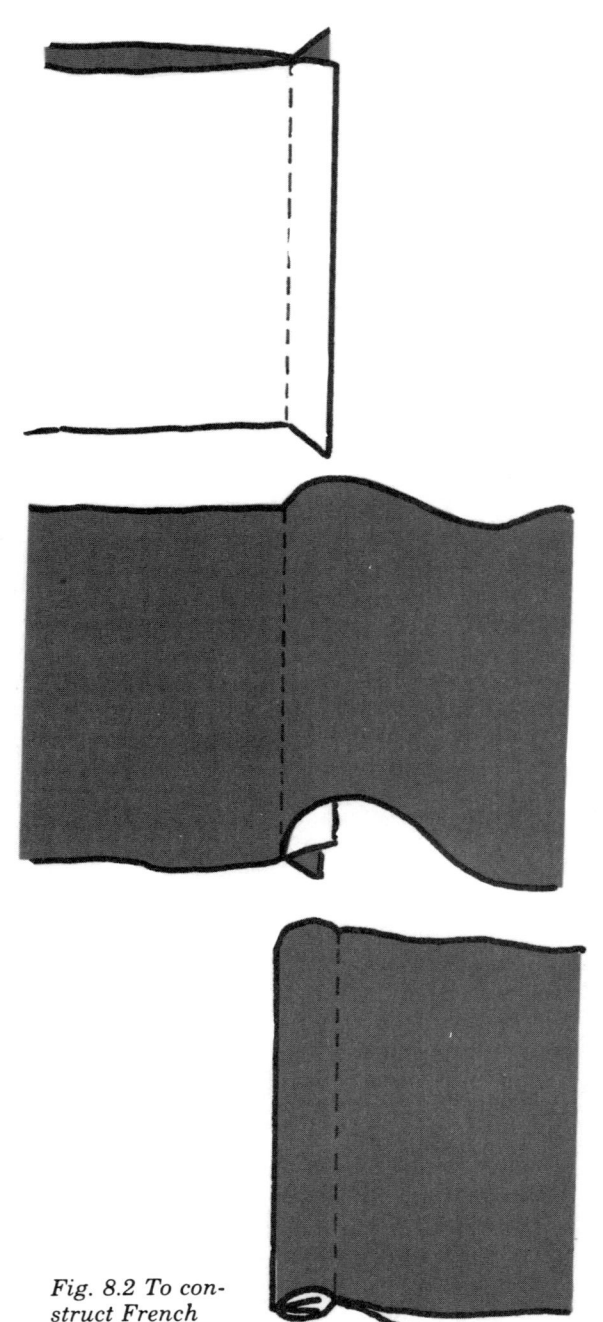

Set your machine for zigzag.

Stitch width: auto (2 1/2)
Stitch length: 3 (1 1/2)
Needle position: auto (left)
Needle: #70/10
Feed dogs: up
Presser foot: transparent zigzag foot N
Tension: *top*, 6 (5); *bobbin*, normal
Fabric: batiste
Thread: #100 cotton

Start the edge so even the first thread in the fabric will be rolled and whipped: Feed a small piece of scrap fabric—about 2"

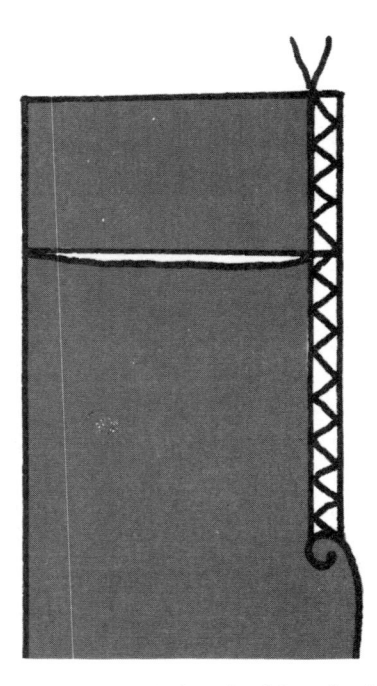

Fig. 8.2 To construct French seams, place fabrics wrong sides together, stitch the seam, trim to 1/8" (3.2mm), then fold the fabric back over the seam allowance and stitch down outside the allowance.

Fig. 8.3 Rolled and whipped edges, started by stitching first on a piece of scrap fabric, then placing the good fabric directly in front of the scrap to begin the roll and whip at the edge.

(5.1cm) long—under the foot. Use the same fabric you will be sewing on. The edge should be placed a hair to the right of the presser foot.

Stitch, holding the threads from the top and bobbin until the fabric begins to roll. As it rolls and as you approach the end of the scrap fabric, butt the good fabric up to it (see Fig. 8.3). It will also roll, beginning exactly at the edge. Later you will cut off the scrap fabric.

Gathering rolled and whipped edges

Before you roll and whip, straight stitch [stitch length 4 (2)] along the edge of the fabric. Instead of anchoring your threads, leave several inches of thread at the beginning and end of the stitching. Starting at the top again, overcast the edge as you did before rolling and whipping (Fig. 8.4A). The straight stitching must not be caught in these zigzags.

Hold the thread ends at the beginning of your line of straight stitching to keep them from slipping through as you gather. Pull on the top thread at the other end of the line of straight stitches and evenly distribute the ruffling (Fig. 8.4B).

Applying insertion

Insertion is lace with two straight sides. It is easily applied by machine (Fig. 8.5). Draw two lines the width of the lace on the fabric. Pin the lace inside the lines. Machine straight stitch down both sides of the lace to hold it in place. Cut straight down the fabric behind the lace. Fold the seam allowances back and press.

Then zigzag over the edges of the lace and the straight stitching to attach the lace and finish the edges simultaneously. Cut the seam allowances back to the stitching.

Apply scalloped lace as an insertion by placing it on the fabric and basting it down both sides. Zigzag closely over the edge, following the scallop. Cut away the fabric underneath. This method can also be used for straight-edge insertion, but the join will not be as strong as folding back the seam allowance and stitching over the doubled fabric.

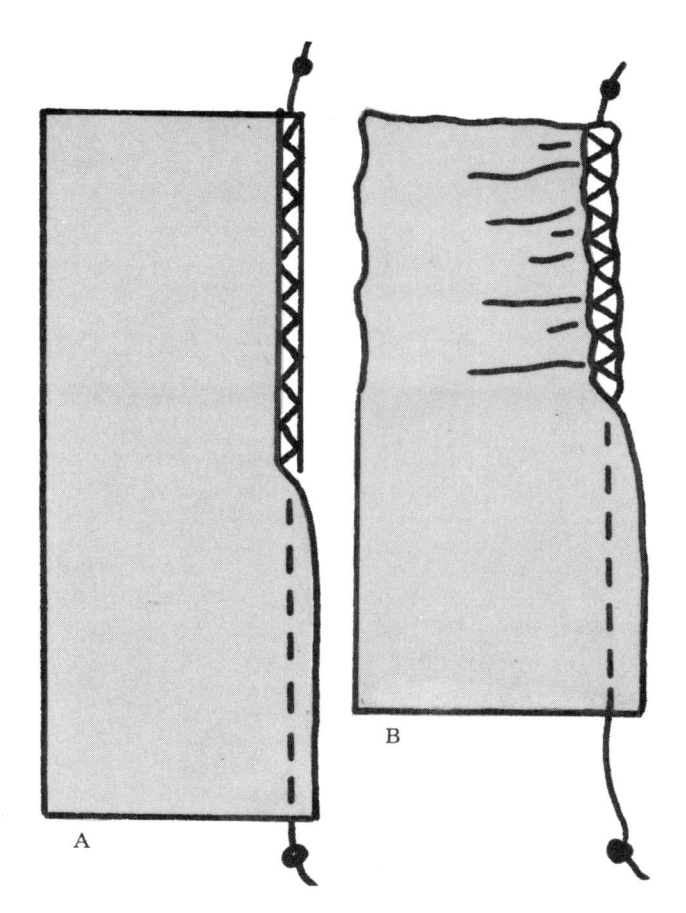

Fig. 8.4 Gathering a rolled and whipped edge. A. Sew a line of straight stitches along the edge of the fabric, then roll and whip over the line of stitching. B. Gather the material by pulling on the top thread from the line of straight stitches.

Joining scalloped lace

Find the most heavily patterned place in the design to join scalloped lace. Overlap two identical patterns, and stitch a fine zigzag [stitch width N–M (1 1/2), stitch

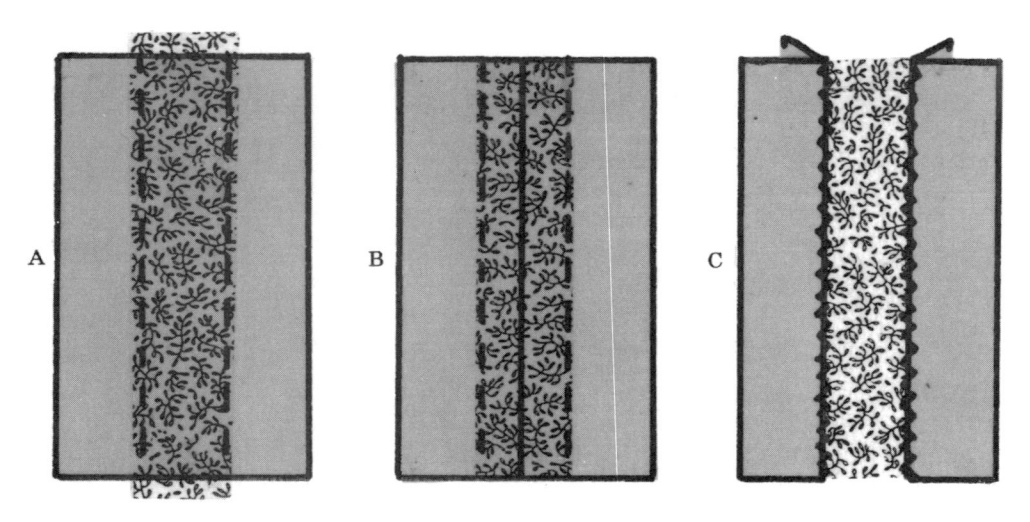

Fig. 8.5 A. Sew lace insert to fabric by straight stitching down each side of the lace. B. Cut through the fabric behind the lace from top to bottom. C. Turn back the seam allowances on both sides and zigzag down the edges of the insertion. Trim the seam allowances back to the stitching.

length 2 (3/4)] with feed dogs up. Follow the edge of the design as shown in Fig. 8.6. Trim back to the line of stitching.

Using entredeux

Entredeux is used between fabric and lace. Only the ladderlike strip of stitching down the center of the entredeux is attached. Set the machine for zigzag.

Stitch width: medium (2)
Stitch length: 2–3 (1 – 1 1/4)
Needle position: auto (center)
Needle: #70/10
Feed dogs: up

Fig. 8.6 Join two pieces of lace together by overlapping the design at each end, zigzagging the "seam," then cutting back the surplus lace to the stitches.

Presser foot: transparent zigzag foot N
Tension: *top*, normal; *bobbin*, normal
Fabric suggestions: batiste
Thread: #100

Measure the length of entredeux you will need and cut off the fabric on only one side. Attach that side. Place the topside of the entredeux to the topside of the rolled and whipped edge, the entredeux on top, as shown at left in Fig. 8.7. Be sure the edges touch. Hand walk the machine through the first couple of stitches to be sure the needle is clearing the edge on the right side and falls into the holes of the entredeux on the left (Fig. 8.7). Don't worry if the needle skips a hole in the entredeux once in awhile, because it won't show. Sew with the machine set on moderate speed. When finished, pull the entredeux to the side away from the fabric and press (at right in Fig. 8.7). Repeat for the other side.

Gathering lace edging

There are several threads at the edges of lace. Use a pin to find the one that gathers the lace and then pull up the thread. Hold onto both ends of this thread, or you might pull it all the way through when gathering the lace. Evenly space the gathers.

Attaching straight-edged lace to rolled and whipped edges

Place the topside of the lace against the topside of the fabric (Fig. 8.8). Be sure the edges are even. Use a zigzag at a setting of stitch width medium (2 1/2) and length 2–3 (1). The needle should stitch within the edges of lace and fabric on the left, and stitch off of them on the right swing (Fig. 8.8). Flatten out and press.

Attaching entredeux to lace insertion

Stitch width: medium (2)
Stitch length: 2–3 (1)
Presser foot: transparent zigzag foot N

Trim fabric from one side of the entredeux. With topsides up, place the trimmed edge of the entredeux up next to the edge of the lace.

Zigzag the edges together so the needle

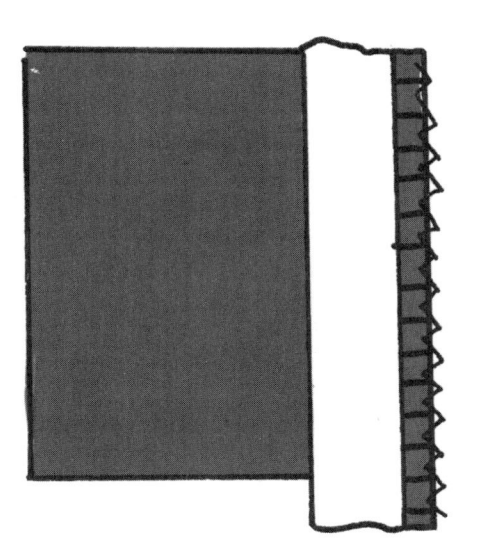

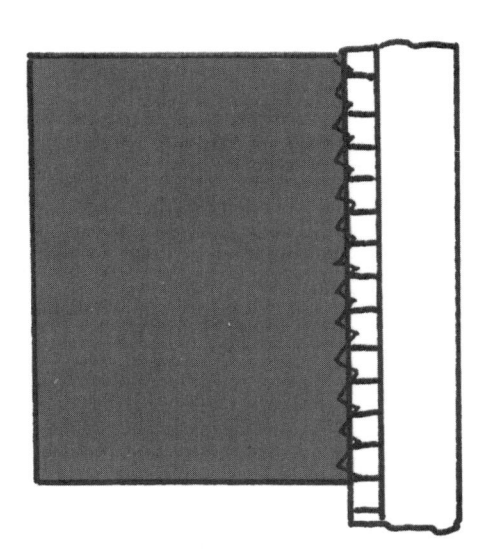

Fig. 8.7 To apply entredeux to rolled and whipped edges, place it on the fabric, right sides together. Zigzag into each hole and off the edges. Then press open.

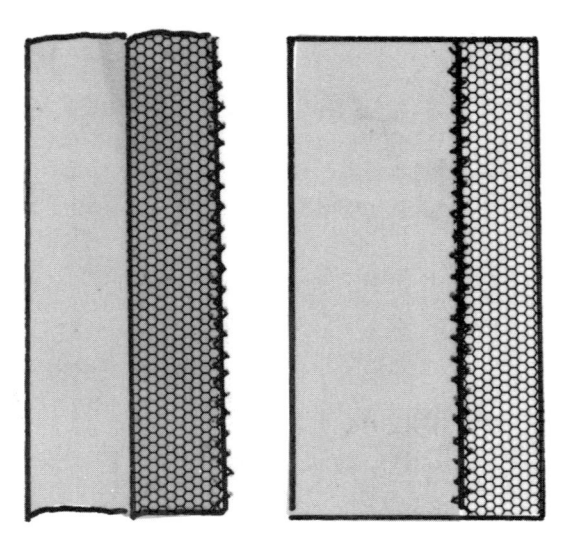

Fig. 8.8 Place insertion on top of a rolled and whipped edge; zigzag to attach. Press open.

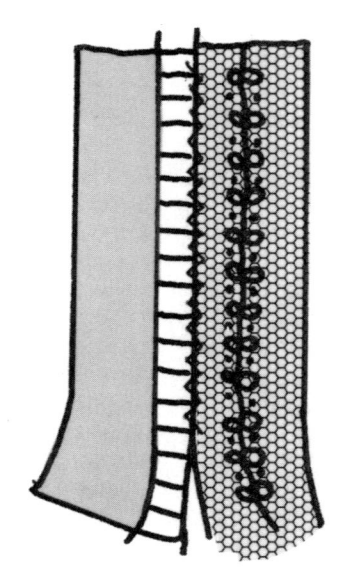

Fig. 8.9 To attach entredeux to lace insertion, place edges next to each other and zigzag together.

barely catches the lace and goes into each hole of the entredeux (Fig. 8.9). Start by using a medium (2) stitch width and 2-3 (1) stitch length, but make adjustments in these figures if you find they are needed.

Sewing lace to lace

Set your machine for zigzag.

Stitch width: medium (3)
Stitch length: auto (1)
Presser foot: transparent zigzag foot N

To sew two strips of straight-edged lace together, butt the edges. Hold one lace in each hand and sew the length of the lace, keeping them from overlapping.

Fagoting

There are times when we need different detailing on a bodice, sleeve or skirt. It may not be called for in the pattern, but it's a way to make that garment our own, so we choose to take a long-cut and add a creative touch of our choosing to the original pattern.

Fagoting is one way to change a seam or add one. With your machine, you need only a tailor tacking foot, since it's like making fringe.

Stitch width: 2
Stitch length: 1/2
Presser foot: tailor tacking

Make a sample first. Set up your machine; try loosening the top tension to 1.

Place two pieces of fabric together, with right sides facing. Stitch along the seam line. When the line is completed, pull the seam open to reveal the stitches. Change to an embroidery foot and put stabilizer underneath your work. Choose a decorative stitch or straight stitch to sew each side of the fabric close to the fold.

Go even further with fagoting and bundle the stitches: Sew down the center of the openwork over four stitches with a free-machine straight stitch, back up, and go forward again, stitching past the first bundle and four more stitches (Fig. 8.10).

Fig. 8.10 Fagoting and bundling stitches for an open seam.

Back up over those four stitches, then stitch forward and over four more stitches. Continue like this until you finish bundling all the stitches.

Use the triple-stretch stitch (#21) at the automatic (left) position. The backward-forward motion will bundle the middle section automatically.

Use fagoting above the hem of a skirt or around a sleeve or square collar.

Project
Wedding Handkerchief

Many of the techniques you have learned for heirloom sewing will be used to make the handkerchief (see Fig. 8.1). You will need: 5" (12.7cm) square of fine batiste; ½" (12.7mm) lace insertion; 1" (2.5cm) beading; entredeux; lace edging; ⅛" (3.2mm) double-face satin ribbon, about 6 yards (5.5m); a ruler and vanishing marker.

How to figure exact amounts of lace and entredeux is included in the directions below; the width of your lace will determine the length you will need. Use a #70 needle and #100 sewing thread.

For the center of this handkerchief (Fig. 8.11), I rolled and whipped a 5" (12.7cm) square of batiste. Use the method you prefer. Entredeux was added to the edges; do one side of entredeux at a time, cut and overlap the openings of the entredeux at the corners.

Stitch the beading (the lace with holes for threaded ribbon) and lace strip together before attaching them to the entredeux. Together, the strip of lace is 1½" (3.8cm) wide.

Estimate how much lace you'll need for your wedding handkerchief by first measuring around the center square of batiste and entredeux; the example is approximately 20" (50.8cm).

Double the width measurement of the strip of lace you've made when you stitched the beading to the lace insertion: 1½" × 2 = 3" (3.8cm × 2 = 7.6cm).

Multiply 3" × 4 = 12" (7.6cm × 4 = 30.5cm) to arrive at the number of inches (cm) needed for the corner miters.

Add the distance around the center square (20" or 50.8cm) to the corner miters (12" or 30.5cm). Exact measurement of the lace needed is 32" (81.3cm). Add 2" (5.1cm) more for safety.

Leave 2" (5.1cm) of lace at the corner before you begin attaching lace to the entredeux (Fig. 8.12). Trim the entredeux. Place the edge of the lace strip next to the entredeux so the edges touch (see Fig. 8.12A). Stitch along the first side, ending with needle down at the corner, extending the lace 1½" (3.8cm) beyond the corner (this is the width measurement of the strip

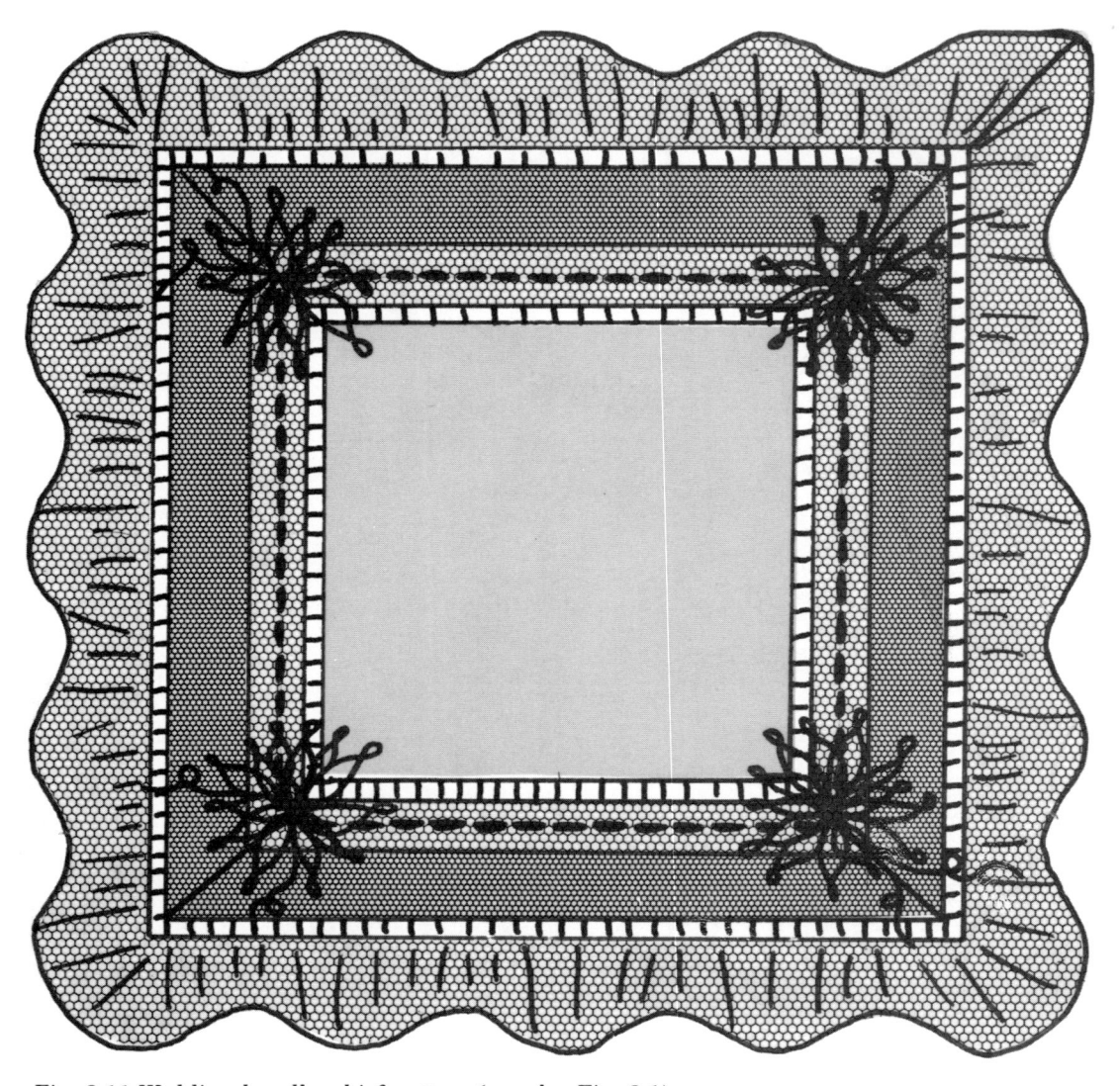

Fig. 8.11 Wedding handkerchief pattern (see also Fig. 8.1)

of lace I used). Raise the presser foot. Fold the lace back on itself by the same measurement, 1½″ (3.8cm) or the width of your lace. Pin the lace together at the corner and then fold the lace so it will lie at the edge of the entredeux on the next side you will stitch (Fig. 8.12B). Turn your work to continue stitching, and put the

presser foot down. Hand-walk the first stitch to be sure it catches the lace. Continue stitching slowly to the next corner. Attach lace to the other sides as you did the first.

After the strip of lace has been attached, go back to each corner and fold the lace diagonally to miter it. Check carefully that

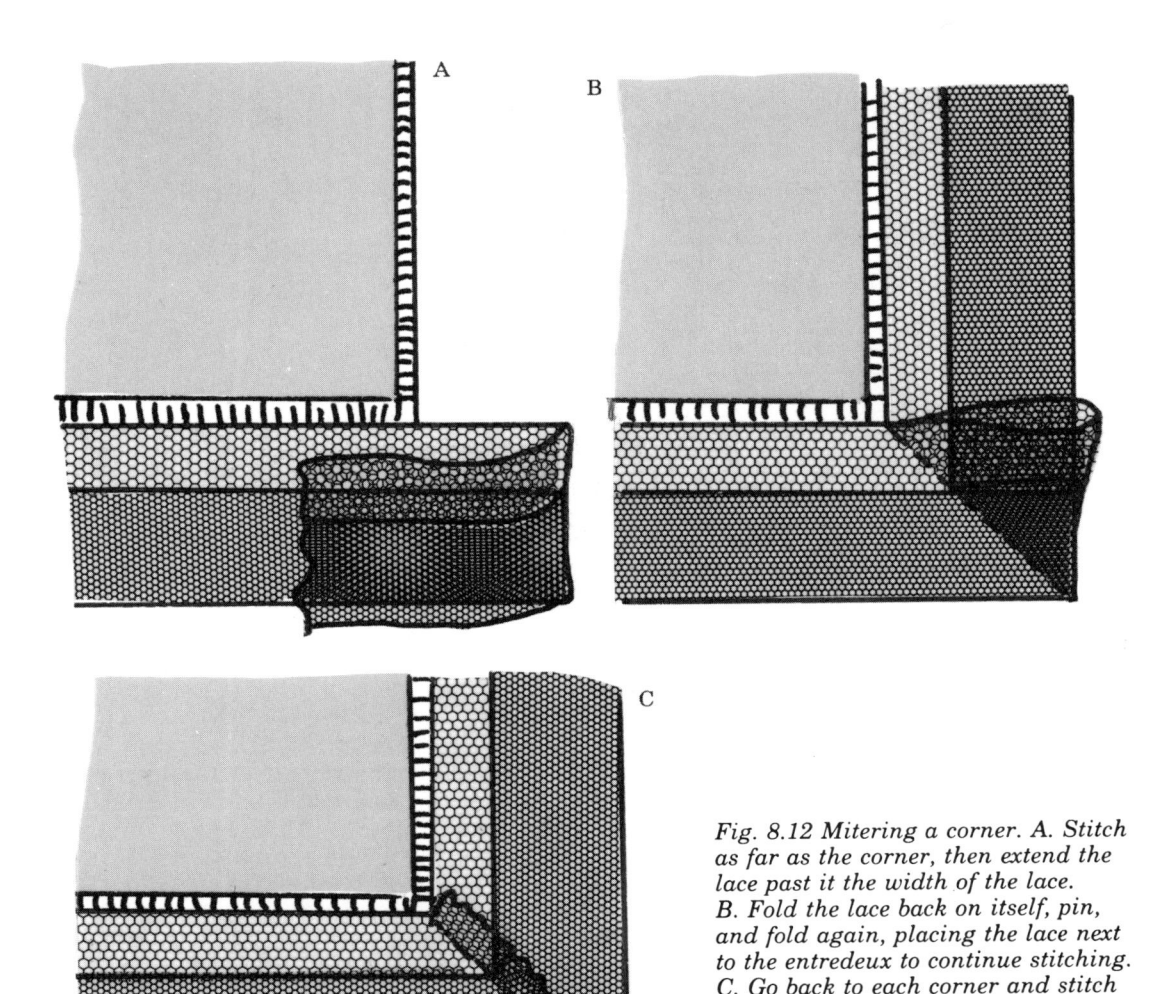

Fig. 8.12 Mitering a corner. A. Stitch as far as the corner, then extend the lace past it the width of the lace. B. Fold the lace back on itself, pin, and fold again, placing the lace next to the entredeux to continue stitching. C. Go back to each corner and stitch diagonally, then cut off the extra fabric, leaving enough to roll and whip. Finish by rolling and whipping each corner.

the corners will lie flat. Pin each one. Mark with a ruler and vanishing marker where the line of stitching will be (Fig. 8.12B). Sew down the line with a straight stitch before cutting back, leaving enough lace to roll and whip by machine (Fig. 8.12C).

Attach entredeux to the edge of the lace, overlapping the holes of each piece at the corners, as done previously.

Measure around the outside edge. Double this for the gathered lace measurement. Sew the ends of the lace together by overlapping and at the same time, matching the designs top and bottom. Sew a narrow zigzag along the design and cut back to the line. Place this seam in a corner.

Gather the lace edging by pulling the correct thread and attaching it to the

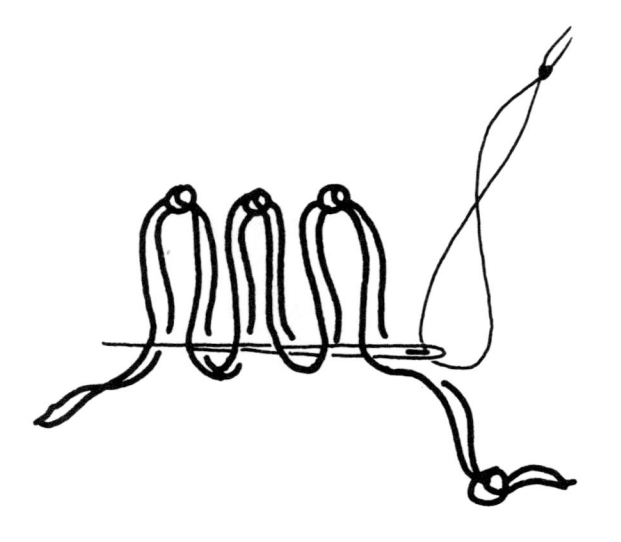

Fig. 8.13 To make a rosette, tie overhand knots in the ribbon every 2½" (6.4cm). Fold the ribbon into loops with knots at the tops. Sew through each loop, then pull into a rosette.

entredeux. Pin the gathered lace to the entredeux first to adjust the gathers. Keep the corners of the lace ruffle quite full. Next, stitch the lace to the entredeux. This can be done in two ways: (1) Place entredeux on top of the gathered lace, topsides together. Line up the edges and proceed as if attaching the entredeux to rolled and whipped edges; or (2) Place gathered lace next to the entredeux, topsides up, and zigzag stitch as you did in "Attaching Entredeux to Lace Insertion."

Thread ⅛" (3.2mm) double-faced satin ribbon through each of the four sides. Leave 3" (7.6cm) tails at each end. Tie overhand knots at the ends. Stitch the tails in place by hand to keep the ribbon in place.

Make rosettes for each corner (Fig. 8.13): First tie an overhand knot every 2½" (6.4cm) along a length of ribbon until you have 16 knots. Leave long ends. Use a double-threaded needle. Make loops on the needle by arranging the ribbon with knots at the top (Fig. 8.13). Sew back through all of the loops again. Pull up and attach the rosettes to the corners of the handkerchief. Tie knots at the ends of the ribbons.

Lesson 24. Seaming with feed dogs up and lowered

Sewing a fake lapped hem

There is no felling foot available for the Brother sewing machines, so we will make a fake lapped hem by sewing a ⅝" (15.9mm) seam and pressing the fabric to the left (Fig. 8.14A, B).

Using the blind hemming foot with the white extension, place the white guide in the ditch or seam line, the needle position at the left. Move the guide so the needle is about ⅛" (3.2mm) from the ditch. Stitch.

For the second run, move the guide about ⅛" (3.2mm) to the right, place the guide on the first stitched line, and with the needle to the far left, sew a fake-felled seam (Fig. 8.14C).

Of course, you can stitch fake lapped

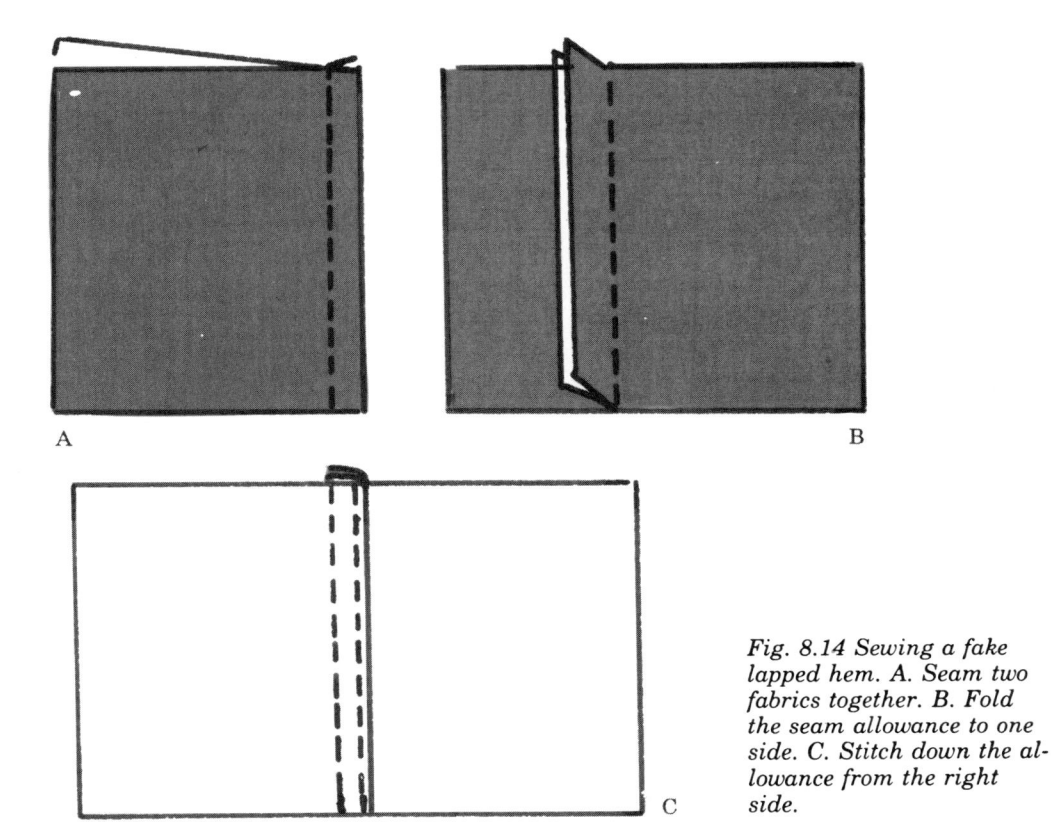

Fig. 8.14 Sewing a fake lapped hem. A. Seam two fabrics together. B. Fold the seam allowance to one side. C. Stitch down the allowance from the right side.

hems with just the zigzag or straight stitch foot. It's possible to use the edges of some presser feet as a measure. Or, mark the stitching lines with a water-erasable marker.

Seaming with the side-cutter

The side-cutter is wonderful for cutting fabric and overcasting it in one operation (it's a little like turning your sewing machine into a serger). I didn't think I needed one until it was given to me as a gift. Now I use it constantly. You'll want to use it with many of the practical stitches, such as overlock, double overlock and zigzag. One limitation is the type of fabric it will accept. I could not sew the canvas tote bag with it — it doesn't like tough, tightly woven fabrics.

Stitching over thread on knits

No more stretched-out seams on knits and jerseys when you use this method. Set the machine for zigzag.

Stitch width: N–M (2)
Stitch length: 2–3 (1)
Needle position: auto
Needle: #80/12
Feed dogs: up
Presser foot: cording foot
Tension: *top*, normal; *bobbin*, normal
Thread: polyester sewing

With a separate spool of thread, thread polyester through the hole or in the groove

125

in the presser foot from front to back and tie a knot at the end. Zigzag stitch over the thread, pulling on it gently as you stitch.

Imitating hand piecing on quilts

Here is a seam shown to me by a quilter. After stitching two quilt pieces together, run a narrow zigzag over this line of straight stitches (Fig. 8.15). When the seam is pressed open, it gives the impression of perfect hand piecing. Why not skip the first step of straight stitching? Because the two passes will make the quilt seams sturdier, and the line of straight stitching is an excellent guideline for the zigzagging.

English piecing by machine

English piecing is the most precise type of hand piecing and is generally used for hexagons, diamonds, and other oddly shaped pieces. Pieces in the finished size are cut from paper; fabric pieces — finished

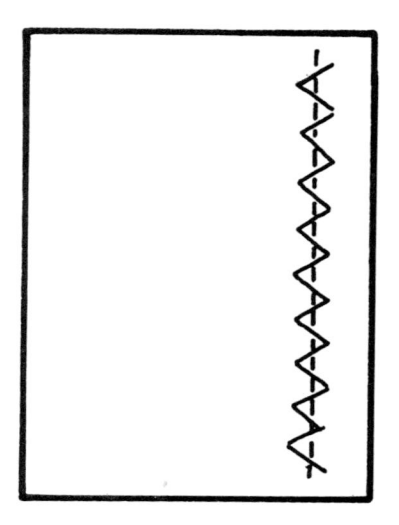

Fig. 8.15 To create the look of hand piecing, zigzag over a seam of straight stitches. Then press the seam open.

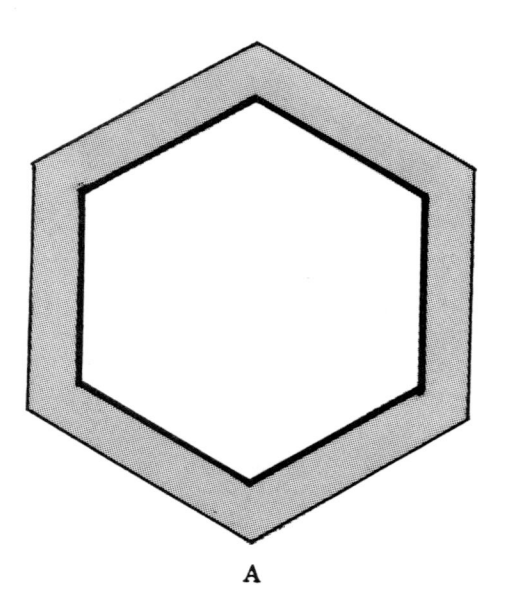

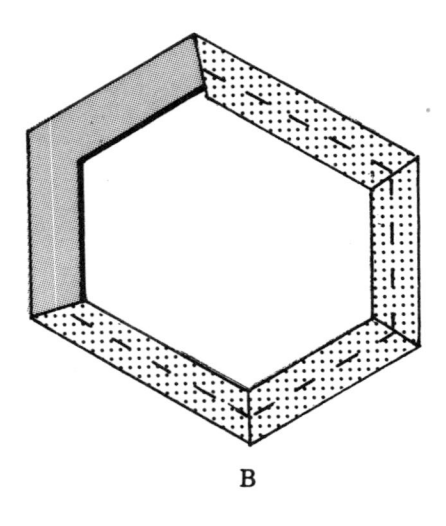

Fig. 8.16 English piecing. A. Prepare pieces by cutting fabric slightly larger than template, then pressing down the seam allowance around the paper. B. Basting fabric to paper by machine.

size *plus* seam allowance—are basted to the paper (Fig. 8.16A). Prepare as many pieces as required by first pressing the seam allowance down around the paper and then basting with the longest length straight stitch on the machine. See Fig. 8.16B.

Place two pieces, right sides together, and stitch with a zigzag stitch, width 3 (3) and length 2 (1 1/2). The left swing of the needle will barely catch the folds and the right swing will stitch in space. Tie off your threads at the beginning and end of each seam by stitching in place. When you have finished with all the seams, remove the basting and the paper and carefully press the pieced area.

Joining veiling with a scallop stitch

What kind of a seam can be used on veiling? In Lesson 17, a straight seam is stitched on Alençon lace, using a close zigzag stitch. A more decorative seam is stitched with the built-in scallop stitch. Overlap the edges, stitch, then cut back excess material on each side to the scallop.

Using built-in stitches

Built-in stitches can be sewn between two pieces of fabric to create an open, interesting seam (Fig. 8.17). Built-in stitch #78 (#19) is one that works beautifully, as do #77 and #79 (#20), the feather stitches. The feather stitch is one of my favorites. I use it on quilt tops to stitch the layers together.

I also used #78 (#19) on a Bermuda bag I made from Ultrasuede scraps. Using a commercial kit, I cut the scraps into squares and rectangles—enough to cover the pattern. I used the Teflon presser foot and polyester thread to stitch the scraps together. To do this, I lifted them in pairs from the pattern and sewed the horizontal seams first. Then I went back and sewed the vertical seams. When the stitching was completed, I placed the pattern over the Ultrasuede and cut off fabric projecting beyond the edges. After that, I was able to finish the bag according to the kit directions.

Creating seams with feed dogs lowered

If you use a similar seam with fabric instead of Ultrasuede, fold under seam allowances at least 5/8" (15.9mm) and press. Move the two pieces of fabric about 1/8" (3.2mm) apart, topsides down. If the fabric is washable, you may want to slip water-soluble stabilizer under it and baste the fabric 1/8" apart. Use thick cord in the bob-

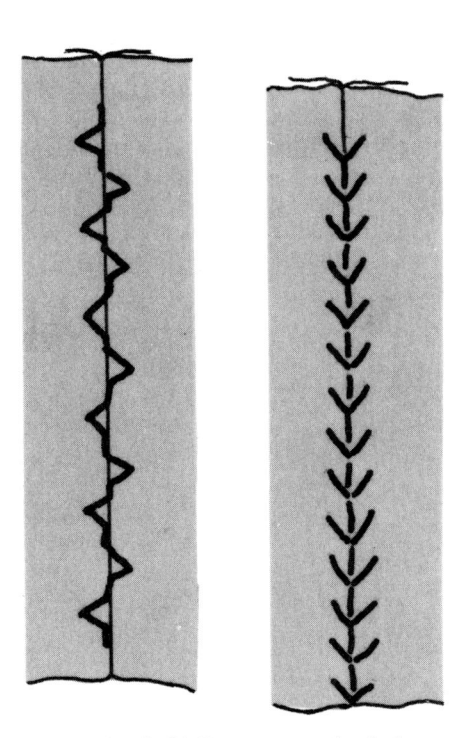

Fig. 8.17 (left) Decorate and stitch a seam with either the gathering stitch (left) or feather stitch.

127

bin. Set your machine for darning and use a darning foot. Sew freely from one side of the fabric to the other, making loops as you enter and leave it (Fig. 8.18). When you finish, change to regular bobbin thread, turn your fabric over, and stitch down along the folds again. Then cut back underneath to the stitching.

These techniques only scratch the surface of interesting seams for your fabric. New finishes are introduced every time a different utility or decorative stitch is incorporated into a garment.

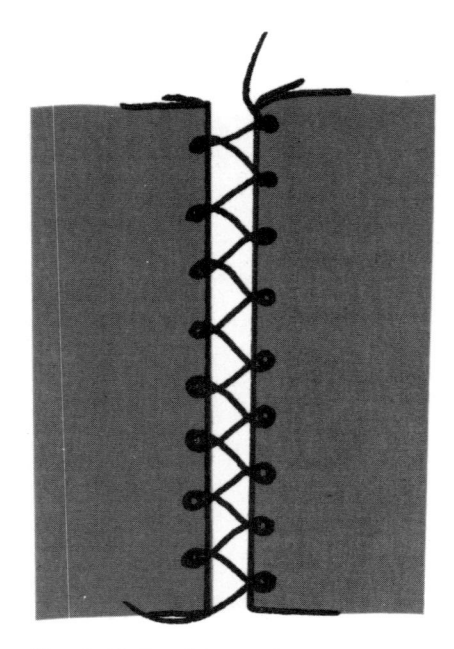

Fig. 8.18 Stitching a decorative seam using free machining.

CHAPTER 9

Adding Hems and Edges

- Lesson 25. Turning hems once
- Lesson 26. Blind hemming
- Lesson 27. Sewing narrow hems
- Lesson 28. Using bias tape
- Lesson 29. Zigzagging a narrow edge
- Lesson 30. Covering wire for shaped edge
- Lesson 31. Cording edges
- Lesson 32. Making thread fringe
- Lesson 33. Piping edges
- Lesson 34. Topstitching

I remember when "good clothes" didn't mean "clean jeans." There were puffed sleeves, sweetheart necklines—always braided, piped, or embroidered in some way. We wanted to dress like movie stars. Dresses were molded to them and then decorated creatively. Designers always took many long-cuts.

The more you know about your machine, the more inventive you can become: no more boring clothes! You may not think you'll ever use all the decorative hems and edgings in this chapter, but make samples for your notebook anyway. You may be surprised.

With the range of fabrics and styles now available, and the variety of effects we want to achieve, choosing the appropriate hem or edge is not always easy. Before sewing a hem or decorative edge on anything, ask yourself these questions: What type of fabric? What type of garment? Who is the garment for? Will it be worn forever? How decorative is it to be?

I have my favorite ways to hem and finish edges. I've also learned hems and edges I will never do again. What makes the difference? Appearance, of course, and ease of stitching. I think I have tried every imaginable variation, and those that follow are the ones I prefer because they are useful and good-looking.

Stitch samples of each and put the results in your notebook for reference. Include your own favorites as well. Write the machine settings on each one, along with comments such as what fabrics work well, where you would use them, whether they were long-cuts with happy endings or more trouble than they were worth.

Lesson 25. Turning hems once

I used to cringe at the thought of hems turned only once—all those raw edges! But I have changed my way of thinking.

Using double needles on knits

My favorite hem for T-shirts and other casual knits is turned once and stitched in place with a double needle. The two stitching lines share one bobbin thread, giving the stitches the stretch they need. Set the machine for straight stitching with a double needle.

Stitch width: auto (0)
Stitch length: auto (2)
Needle position: auto (center)
Needle: double, at least 2mm
Tension: *top, normal*; bobbin, normal
Fabric: knit
Presser foot: transparent zigzag foot N
Thread: polyester
Stabilizer: tear-away

It is simple to fold up the hem and sew with a double needle from the topside of the fabric.

When finished, trim the fabric back to the stitching underneath. The multi-zigzag can be used for variation. On the 950, handwalk the needle through the first few stitches to be sure the zigzag will clear the needle plate opening.

Hemming with a double needle on sheers

Use a double needle for sheer fabrics, too. When a narrow hem would be neither suitable nor attractive, fold up a 4" (10.2cm) hem on lightweight fabrics and sew across. Lightweight garments hang better with the weight of a deep hem and it's also more attractive when the hem of the underskirt isn't visible underneath.

Of course you can add more rows of stitching, evenly spaced from the first. Cut back to the top of the stitching.

Hemming with built-in stitches on front

The next hem for delicate fabrics is much the same, but uses a single needle and either built-in scallop stitch. Set the machine for zigzag.

Stitch width: auto (5)
Stitch length: auto (1/2)
Needle position: left (center)
Presser foot: transparent zigzag foot N

To hem heavy, canvas-type fabrics use the triple stretch stitch (#21) at the left position or the rickrack stitch (#21, stitch width 5). First find the correct width and length by practicing on a piece of the same fabric you will use for the finished article. Set up the machine for either the triple stretch stitch (#21) or the rickrack stitch (#21, stitch width 5).

Stitch width: varies
Stitch length: varies
Needle position: center
Needle: #110 jeans
Presser foot: transparent zigzag foot N

This is an extremely strong stitch. Use it for anything from deck furniture canvas to jeans.

Refer back to the stitch samples you did in Chapter 2. You may prefer other decorative built-in stitches to those mentioned here. Experiment with different fabrics and built-in stitches, keeping all your samples in your notebook.

Quilting a hem

Another single-fold hem can be done on heavy materials such as wool or velveteen. Use a walking foot. Allow about 8" (20.3cm) for the hem of the skirt. Put light batting, such as flannel sheeting, inside and pin in place. Sew four or five rows of straight stitches, one line at a time, to quilt the hem (Fig. 9.1). Space the lines of stitching as you wish. Try quilting a long Christmas skirt or an evening skirt using metallic thread.

Or turn the skirt inside out and put pearl cotton on the bobbin to contrast with the skirt. The topside will be against the bed of the machine. Stitch rows, then cut back to the last line of stitching. This can be done around sleeve bands or down jacket facings as well.

Fig. 9.1 Use light flannel between hem and skirt, then quilt the hem with lines of straight stitching.

Lesson 26. Blind hemming

I remember when most of the hems I put in garments were blind hems worked by hand. Times have changed, but that doesn't mean I've given up blind hems. The only difference is that I do them more quickly now — by machine.

To begin the hem, decide first if you can live with a raw edge. If you can, then leave it as it is, but if you hate that unfinished edge, then attach a lace edging over it or stitch around the edge with the multi-zig-zag stitch before you proceed.

Turn up the hem 1½″ to 2″ (3.8cm to 5.1cm) and pin very closely around it, about an inch from the top. If the fabric slips, the hem will be a mess, so don't try to save time by not pinning a lot.

Or use Tami Durand's method. Baste the hem and skirt together, by machine, ¼″ from the edge of the turned-up hem. There will definitely be no slipping. Fold back and proceed as you do with the pinned hem. When finished, pull out the basting.

Set your machine for blind stitching.

Stitch width: auto (2–2 1/2)
Stitch length: auto (2)
Needle position: auto (right)
Feed dogs: up
Presser foot: blind hemming foot L
Built-in stitch: blind stitch
Tension: *top*, loosened; *bobbin*, normal
Thread: sewing
Accessories: dressmakers' pins

Fold the garment back on itself, leaving

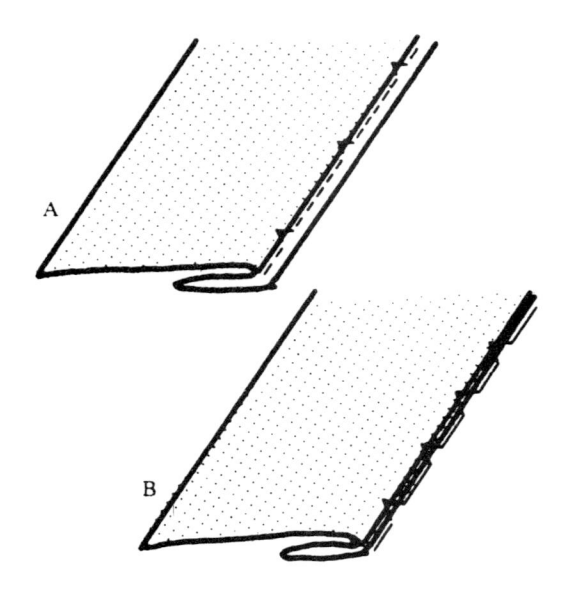

Fig. 9.2 Blind hemming. A. Fold over the hem, then fold the skirt back, letting ⅛" (3.2mm) show beyond the edge; stitch on the edge of the fabric. B. Or fold the garment back even with the edge, and stitch off the fabric, the left swing stitching the fold.

⅛" (3.2mm) of hem at the edge to stitch on (Fig. 9.2A). Put the fold of the fabric against the left side of the white extension and adjust so the bite of the needle barely enters the fold. Stitch on the edge of the fabric with the needle catching about two threads of the fold. Check the settings on scrap fabric first to determine the correct stitch width and length. Thick fabrics will require different settings than lightweight fabrics.

I made a fine batiste bishop dress with yards of blind hemming, but the stitching pulled too tightly. Despite the fine thread, loosened tension, and a #60 needle, I didn't like the looks of it. The answer? I sewed from off the fabric. I folded the fabric back so the fold met the edge exactly. Then I stitched outside the fabric and the left bite held it together with no pulling (Fig. 9.2B). I've tried it on several heavier weights of fabric as well, and it works beautifully.

Still hesitant about stitching in space? Then place water-soluble stabilizer under your stitching.

Lesson 27. Sewing narrow hems

Next to wing needles, the most unused accessories are the hemming presser feet. I think I know why: few stitchers ever take time to practice with them. They're great time savers, but I had to learn to use them, too. Now after yards of hem samples, I can't do without them.

Set up your machine, read the directions, and reread as you work. Before you begin to hem a garment with one of the hemmers, cut back the seam allowances that have to be sewn over. Then learn to start the fabric. I hated starting a hem because of those first problem inches until I tried Gail Brown's method, which follows.

Straight stitching

Practice with a medium-width hemmer at first, because it is easier to use when learning. Also needed are lightweight cotton to hem and a 3" (7.6cm) square of tear-away stabilizer.

Overlap the piece of tear-away stabilizer with the fabric about ¼" (6.3mm) and sew them together. Start rolling the stabilizer into the scroll of the hemming foot. By the time the fabric is introduced into the hemmer, the hem is being sewn down starting on the first thread of the fabric.

Guide the fabric by holding it taut and lifting it slightly as it rolls through the foot. The edge of the fabric must be vertical. As long as you pay attention, guiding and holding the fabric correctly, the machine does the rest.

Sewing on lace

This method is simple and it does save time. Set the machine for zigzag.

    Stitch width: M–W (3–5)
    Stitch length: 3 (1–1 1/2)
    Needle position: left
    Presser foot: transparent zigzag N
    Fabric: lightweight cotton, lace edging
    Thread: fine sewing thread to match

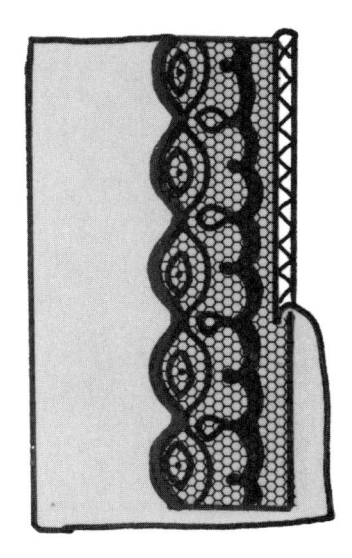

Fig. 9.3 Lace is attached with a finished edge in one step.

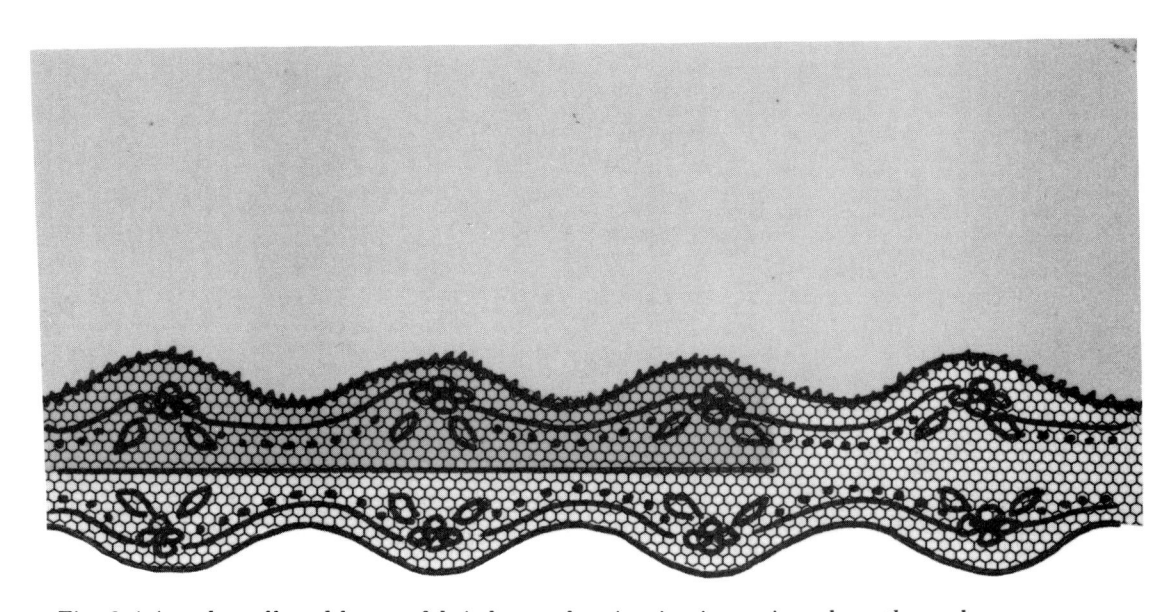

Fig. 9.4 Attach scalloped lace to fabric by overlapping it, zigzagging along the scalloped edge, then cutting the fabric back to the stitching line.

Place the lace on top of the fabric, topsides together, the edge of the lace ⅛" (3.2mm) from the edge of the fabric.

The fabric is usually placed to the right of the middle of the presser foot but practice first. As you sew, it will roll and be whipped over the heading of the lace (Fig. 9.3).

See other methods of sewing lace to fabric in Lesson 23, "Heirloom sewing."

Attaching scalloped lace

Apply scalloped lace to fabric, topsides up, by overlapping it to make a hem (Fig. 9.4). Let the fabric extend well past the curve on top of the lace. Baste lace to fabric. Zigzag along the edge, following the scallop. Cut back the fabric underneath to the stitching line.

Stitching shell edging

This is a good hem and edging for lingerie (Fig. 9.5). Or use it to decorate ribbon and tucks. Set your machine for blind stitching.

Stitch width: auto (5)
Stitch length: auto (1)
Needle position: auto (center)
Feed dogs: up
Presser foot: transparent zigzag N
Built-in stitch: blind stitch (#5)

If you are going to cross a seam when hemming, then cut back the seam allowances that will be sewn over.

The foot rests on the fabric for this one; you do not feed fabric into the foot. Fold the fabric under ½" (12.7mm) and place the folded edge to the left. Stitch, letting the left swing of the needle sew over the edge, creating the shell pattern. At the end, cut back to the stitching underneath.

Roll and shell hemming

The narrow hemmer (accommodates a zigzag stitch) not only makes a narrow, straight-stitch hem, but it also rolls and shells as shown in Fig. 9.6, if the machine is set on zigzag. Usually it's the finish of choice when hemming tricot, as it decorates and hems in one operation. It's impossible to turn square corners on these hems, so round off any corners before you begin to stitch. Because tricot rolls to one side, hem with the right side up. If you will stitch over a seam while hemming, first cut back the seam allowances you'll cross so the fabric will feed in without a problem. As the fabric is rolled into the foot, it will curl and be sewn into a narrow, puffy roll. Set the machine for zigzag.

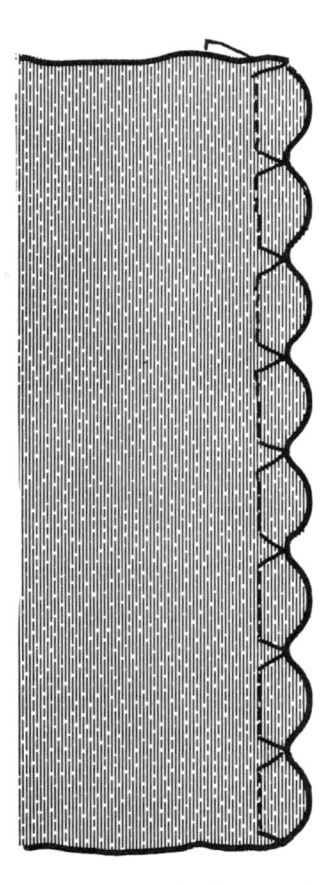

Fig. 9.5 A shell edge on tricot, stitched with the blind-hem stitch.

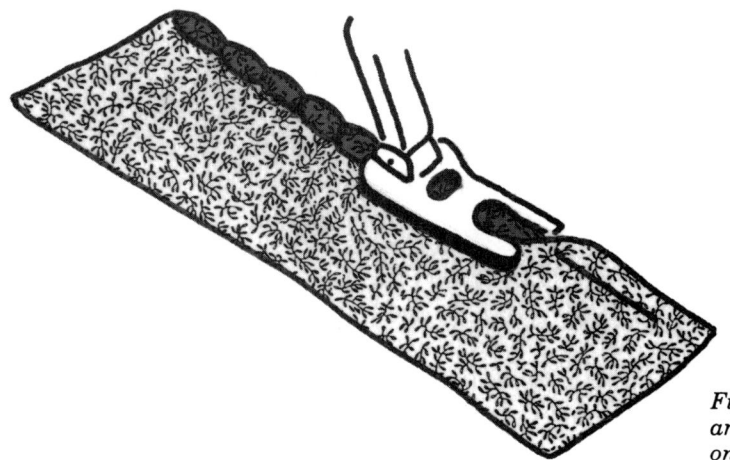

Fig. 9.6 Roll and shell edges are used for decorative hems on lingerie fabrics.

Stitch width: auto (5)
Stitch length: auto (2 1/2)
Needle position: auto (center)
Feed dogs: up
Presser foot: narrow hemmer

It's important to keep the fabric straight ahead of the presser foot and raise it a bit to keep it feeding easily. The needle goes into the fabric at the left, then off the edge of the fabric at the right.

Lesson 28. Using bias tape

I must admit, I equate bias tape with the edges of Grandma's apron, but now that I can apply it so easily, I'm finding new ways to use it. I especially like it for toddlers' sunsuits and dresses.

This is the only method I use; what I like best about it is that the tape is sewn on almost invisibly. You don't need the bias binder accessory. Set the machine for straight stitch.

Stitch width: auto (0)
Stitch length: auto (2)
Feed dogs: up
Presser foot: transparent zigzag foot N or blind hem foot L
Needle: #80/12
Needle position: auto (center)
Thread: monofilament

Fabric: lightweight cotton, double-fold bias tape
Accessories: glue stick, pins

Look at the bias tape: One side is wider than the other. The wide side will be on the back of your work. Open the bias tape and place the narrow side on top, the cut edge of the tape along the cut edge of the fabric. If there is a 5/8" (15.9mm) seam, cut it back to fit the width of the bias. Pin in place.

Adjust the foot or needle position — it will depend upon the foot you use — and the fabric will either be held against the side of the foot or a middle extension will ride on the crease to ensure a perfect stitch-in-the-ditch. Stitch along the crease.

Fold the tape over the edge. I sometimes dab the underside with glue stick between

135

tape and fabric. Pin if you wish, or baste by hand.

Press the bias and check that the underside of the bias extends slightly beyond the seam line on the topside.

From the topside, stitch in the ditch of the seam. Again, adjust the foot to enable you to sew exactly in the ditch. The stitching catches the edge of the bias underneath.

Lesson 29. Zigzagging a narrow edge

This is only one of several methods to produce a strong, finished hem or edge of tiny, tight zigzag stitches. Use it to finish ruffles, napkins and scarves. Set the machine for zigzag.

Stitch width: M (1 1/2–2 1/2)
Stitch length: 2–3 (1/2)
Needle position: auto (center)
Presser foot: transparent zigzag foot N

Fold the fabric under about ½" (12.7mm) and guide the fold of the fabric exactly in the middle of the transparent zigzag foot N.

Stitch on the fabric with the left swing of the needle, the right swing stitching just off the right side of it (Fig. 9.7). After stitching is completed, cut the fabric back to the stitched edge.

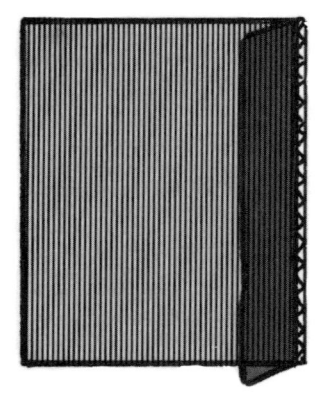

Fig. 9.7 From the top of the fabric, sew a narrow, close zigzag down the folded edge (left). Cut back the fabric underneath to the stitching line.

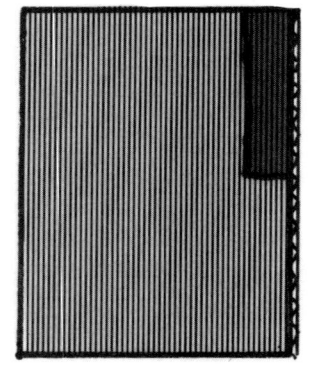

Lesson 30. Covering wire for shaped edges

In a bridal shop I saw yard goods that included nylon filament at the edges of chiffon and organdy ruffles. It was an attractive finish for the ruffles that can be applied to skirt and sleeve hems or across the drop-shoulders of wedding gowns and formal wear.

A case displayed dozens of headpieces using the same nylon filament to keep bows perky and ribbons from wilting. You are invited to create your own, combining filament and sheer fabrics, beads and silk flowers.

I could also see many Halloween costume possibilities here. Use the filament at the bottom edge of a long, filmy skirt or, if you want to make an angel costume, use heavy gauge filament for floppy wings.

Nylon filament is available by the yard at stores that sell bridal lace and fabrics. But I found that it is much easier to buy 25-pound-test fishing line in a sporting goods store. Cheaper, too. I've used both and I don't think there's a difference. There are different weights to fishing lines, which means they come in different thicknesses.

For super-thick costume fabric, you can use weed-trimmer line. It comes in a 50-foot length and the diameter to use is .05mm. This fits in the groove of the cording foot. Use the same method to apply any of the nylon filament mentioned. Set the machine for zigzag.

Stitch width: M (3)
Stitch length: 2–3 (1)
Presser foot: cording foot

I placed the filament about ¼" (6.3mm) from the edge of the fabric (the needle should stitch off the edge of the material on the right swing). As you sew, the edge of the fabric will roll over and enclose the line (Fig. 9.8).

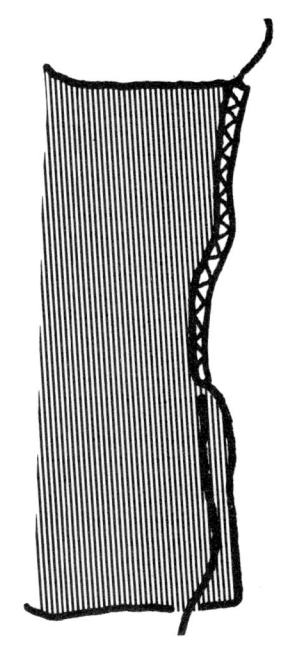

Fig. 9.8 Rolling fabric over nylon filament or wire creates a rigid, finished edge.

Milliner's wire or florist's wire is available already covered with thread. Both of these can be stitched into the edge of fabric in the same way as nylon filament. They both come in different gauges. Unlike the nylon edge, the wire can be bent into any shape you might want. Buy milliner's wire at bridal shops and florist's wire at craft shops. Make flower petals and leaves using wire.

Lesson 31. Cording edges

Covering cords

Covered cord produces one of the finest, prettiest edges to use on table linens, on scarves, collars, wherever you want a delicate but very strong edge. Set the machine for zigzag.

Stitch width: N–M (2–4)
Stitch length: 2–3 (1/2)
Needle position: auto (center)
Presser foot: cording foot
Thread: machine-embroidery or sewing thread; #5 pearl cotton

Fold the fabric under about ½" (12.7mm) and press. Thread pearl cotton through the hole in the cording foot. Place the hole at the edge of the fabric and stitch (Fig. 9.9). Cut back to the stitching underneath when it's completed.

To create a thicker edge, go back over the first line of stitching with the buttonhole foot A. Place the edge you've completed in the slot to the left and another cord of pearl cotton between the toes of the presser foot to hold it in place. Change to stitch width 4.

If you use this method to finish the edge of a collar, you won't need to turn the collar. Instead, sew with wrong sides of upper and under collar together to eliminate the bulk of a turned-in seam allowance.

To make a delicate edging for a bridal veil, cord the edge. Set the machine for zigzag.

Stitch width: N–M (2)
Stitch length: 2–3 (1/2–3/4) not too tight
Needle position: auto (center)
Presser foot: cording foot
Thread: fine sewing thread to match veil; #8 pearl cotton to match veil

Without folding the veiling, place it so the edge extends past the presser foot on the right. Slip #8 pearl cotton in the hole of the cording foot. Sew over the pearl. Cut back to the pearl for a fine finished edge. (Try a corded scallop stitch, too.)

Fig. 9.9 Zigzagging over cord produces a strong corded edge.

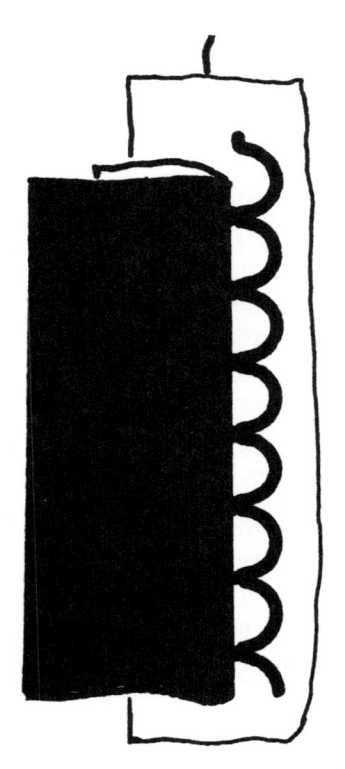

Fig. 9.10 Make a crocheted edge with the built-in scallop stitch.

Creating crocheted edges

This decorative edge is used to finish shirt plackets and collars. It's a delicate, lacelike finish that lends itself to feminine clothes and baby items.

Set the machine for the satin stitch scallop (#9).

Stitch width: auto (4–5)
Stitch length: auto (1/2)
Presser foot: transparent zigzag foot N
Built-in stitch: scallop (#9)
Fabric: medium-weight cotton
Thread: color to contrast with fabric
Accessories: 2 layers of water-soluble stabilizer

Use the transparent zigzag foot N to simulate a crocheted edge while using the scallop stitch. Place stabilizer underneath and far enough to the right to be under the stitches, as shown in Fig. 9.10. The fabric should be doubled; the fold is placed just to the left of the hole in front of the presser foot. Stitch at the edge. The scallops will catch the fabric, but most of the stitches will be off the edge onto the stabilizer (Fig. 9.10). Rinse out the stabilizer when you finish.

Try decorative stitch #69 (#8) at the edges of fabrics. Use it on the edges of plackets or sleeves and decorate collars with it. Sew on doubled fabric, then cut back to the stitching. The edge of the baby bonnet in Fig. 5.15 was worked this way.

Reshaping knits with elastic

Elastic can be used to keep stretchy edges in shape, or to reshape them. Set the machine for zigzag.

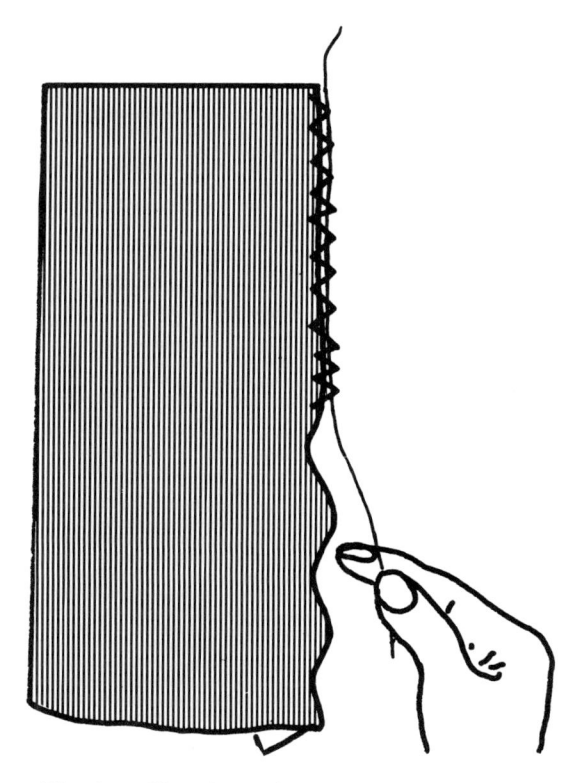

Fig. 9.11 Keep knits from stretching by stitching in an elastic thread.

Stitch width: auto (2)
Stitch length: auto (2)
Presser foot: cording foot

Thread the elastic though the hole in the cording foot. Keep the elastic at the edge of the knit and sew down the fold (Fig. 9.11).

Lesson 32. Making thread fringe

How many machine owners use a tailor-tacking foot for tailor tacking? I can't find one. Most of the time the tailor tacking foot is used for fringing, fagoting, or for sewing on buttons.

To make thread fringe, you'll need one

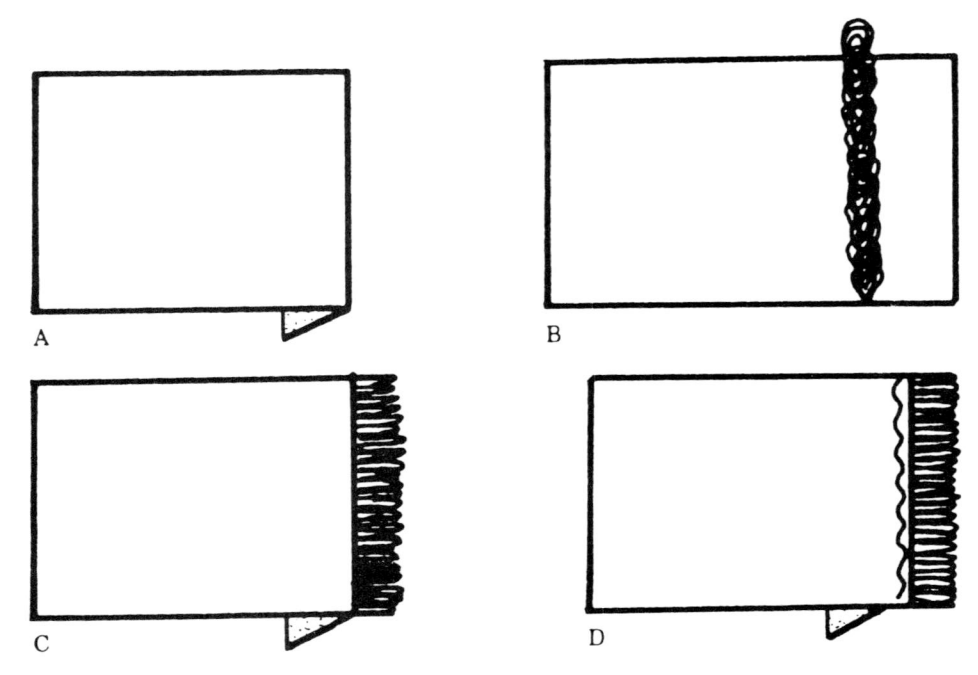

Fig. 9.12 Making thread fringe. A. Fold under fabric edge 1" (2.5cm). B. Open fabric and use closely stitched tailor tacking along the crease. C. Fold fabric edge under again and smooth down fringe. D. Stitch close to fold to hold fringe in place.

piece of fabric, folded over at least 1" (2.5cm) at the edge where you want the fringe to be sewn (Fig. 9.12A). Press the fold line; then open up the fabric so you can stitch on the right side of that pressed line. Set the machine for zigzag.

Stitch width: 3 (2)
Stitch length: 2 (1)
Presser foot: tailor tacking, transparent embroidery foot N
Needle: #80/12
Needle position: auto (center)
Tension: *top*, 2 (2); *bobbin*, normal
Stabilizer: tear-away

Stitch on a single thickness of fabric using the tailor tacking foot—no stabilizer is needed for this (Fig. 9.12B). Be sure the stitches are as close together as you can make them and still have the fabric move easily under the presser foot.

When the stitching is complete, refold on the line and smooth the fringe in place (Fig. 9.12C). Press, then choose a decorative stitch such as #79 (#20) or use a straight stitch to hold the fringe in place (Fig. 9.12D). Return your upper tension to normal, slip stabilizer under your work, and use the embroidery foot as you stitch. Sometimes I place a strip of paper over the fringe as I stitch so it can't possibly get tangled up in the presser foot. Cut back underneath to your stitching, if you wish.

If you look closely at the eyelashes of the denim doll in Fig. 3.17, you will see thread fringe. As you get to know your machine, you'll see more and more ways to use it to make the simplest tasks even simpler. On to the next lesson.

Lesson 33. Piping edges

Miniature piping is especially pretty and colorful on the edges of children's clothing. Use a #3 or #5 pearl cotton and a piece of bias fabric twice the width of the seam allowance. I may not use bias fabric at all. Piping cut on the straight grain seems to make little difference, and though considered sacrilegious, you can save fabric by cutting on the straight or anywhere between the straight and the true bias, so try it for yourself. Or cover the pearl with purchased bias tape. Use the blind hemming foot L and set the Galaxie for straight stitching, the 950 for straight stitching with the left needle position. Adjust the white guide so the needle sews at the edge of the cord.

Cover thick cord for upholstery in the same way. Forget what you've learned about always using a zipper foot for this procedure. The wrapped cord fits between the needle and the white guide of the blind hemming foot and never slips. I sewed over 100 yards of that one day and it couldn't have been easier. Attaching covered cording to a pillow is also a breeze with this foot.

Lesson 34. Topstitching

There is nothing richer-looking on a coat or suit than an even line of topstitching.

When you need a narrowly spaced double line, use a double needle. For topstitching a heavy fabric, I use a topstitching needle with two sewing threads, eliminating the fraying of buttonhole twist. Sew the second line of stitching in the same direction as the first.

When topstitching on lapels, the roll line indicates where the top threads will go to the underside. For this reason, if you use two threads on top, you must use two threads on the bobbin as well. Wind the bobbin with two threads at one time instead of using only one. Then treat the threads as if they were one.

Instead of anchoring threads, leave a long enough thread at the beginning and the end to work in later invisibly by hand.

Use the triple-stretch stitch (#21, stitch width 0); experiment. Use orange thread to stitch on denim seams to duplicate the look of commercial topstitching on jeans.

How can you keep topstitching straight? You have several choices. Use tape along the edge of the fabric and sew next to it. Use the side-cutter accessory (width is limited). Again, using the blind hem foot L is my first choice because the width can be set with the white guide.

If using lightweight material, set the machine for 10–12 stitches per inch. If using medium-weight fabric, a longer stitch looks better. Stitch samples on scraps of the same material to see what stitch length setting you prefer.

I think there is hope for more decorative dressing. Have you noticed how Joan Crawford's clothes don't look so funny anymore?

CHAPTER **10**

Machine Tricks: Adding Threads to Threads

- Lesson 35. Making cord
- Lesson 36. Making tassels

For nine chapters, we've used fabric and thread for sewing and embroidering. I'll bet you know your sewing machine pretty well by now, but there's more: In this chapter, I'll show you how to make cords using your machine. Some will be used for practical purposes, such as belt loops and hangers for pendants, but we'll make other cords for decoration, bunching them together into tassels.

Lesson 35. Making cord

Twisting monk's cord

Monk's cord is made from several strands of thread or yarn held together and twisted to make a thick cord. The cord may be used in many ways—as a finish around pillows, as a handle for handbags, and as thick fringe in tassels.

On the machine, monk's cord is made using the bobbin winder. Purchase a bobbin with holes in the top of it. Slip the ends of the cord through one of the holes and tie the ends together. Take the loop formed at the other end and pull the end with the knot through this loop until the loop is snug against the bobbin.

Next, push the bobbin down into place on the pin; release the hand wheel on the 940/950; when clicked into place for bobbin winding, the bobbin will hold the cord securely (Fig. 10.1).

Or thread one end through one of the bobbin holes, bring the two ends together,

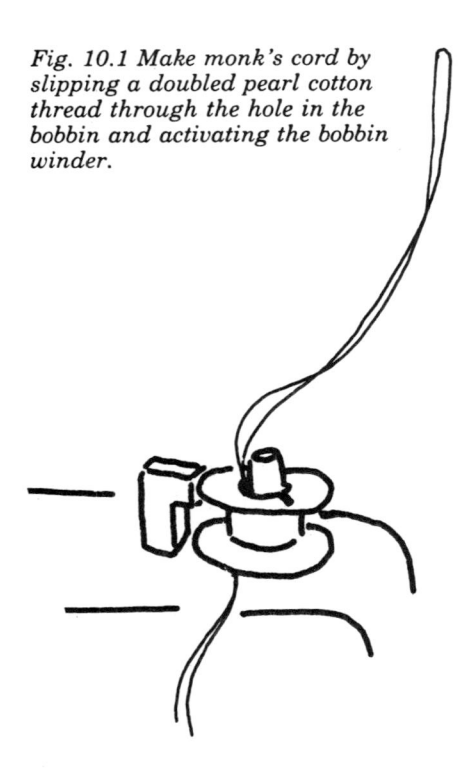

Fig. 10.1 Make monk's cord by slipping a doubled pearl cotton thread through the hole in the bobbin and activating the bobbin winder.

and tie. Of course you can tie the cord onto the bobbin through one of the holes and work with one cord, not two. If you do work with one cord, tie a loop at the end of the cord to slip your finger through before you begin to twist the cord.

If you are working alone on the 940/950, you will be limited by the length of cord you can use and still reach the machine's foot pedal. Pull the foot feed out from under the machine as far as it will reach. This will allow you to use a bit longer cord. Of course, if you have long legs too, start with a 2-yard (1.7m) length. On the Galaxie, however, you are not limited to a certain distance. Remove the foot controller and set the machine to run at medium speed. Tie the cord to the bobbin as explained and put your index finger in the loop of the cord at the other end, stretching the cord to keep tension on it. Push the yellow start/stop button and move quickly away from the machine (across the room if necessary). Keep winding the cord until it is so tight the blood supply to your finger is threatened. Turn off the machine.

Work your finger out of the loop and, still holding it tightly, find the middle of the cord with your other hand. Hold onto that spot while you place the loop from your finger over the thread holder pin, if it is close enough. Otherwise, keeping tension on the cord, bring both ends together and very carefully let it twist to make a monk's cord. Work down the twists with both hands to keep the cord smooth.

When the cord is twisted as tightly as it will go, take it out of the bobbin and off the

Fig. 10.2 Machine-made monk's cord is used to make this tassel.

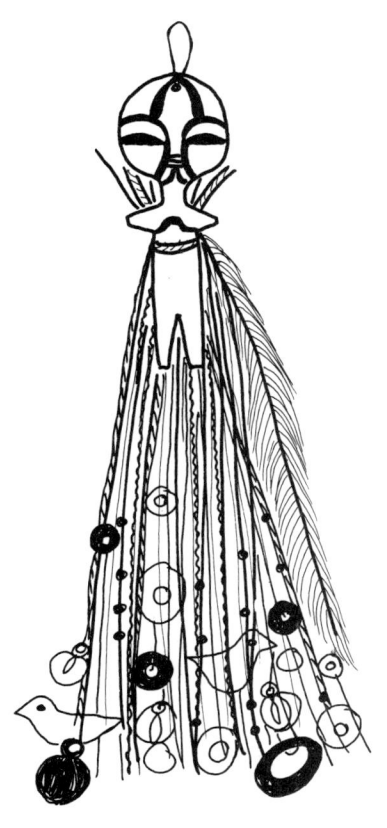

Fig. 10.3 A doll tassel made with monk's cord.

143

thread-holder spool pin. Tie an overhand knot to hold the ends together until you actually use it. I always make a small sample of each cord when I'm twisting one and put it in my notebook, making a note of the kind of thread and the number of strands used. This is a valuable reference when I need a cord. I can look at the sheet and see how each thread looks (shiny, dull, thick, thin, etc.), so I don't waste time twisting up a cord that doesn't work.

I use this cord to make thick fringe for tassels, sometimes slipping washers, bells, beads or a spacer to the middle of the cord after I have twisted it and before I double it and make the final twists (Figs. 10.2 and 10.3).

These quick cords can be used for belt loops, button loops, ties for clothing. Or twist up a batch to tie small packages.

Stitching belt and button loops

Belt loop cords can be made by pulling out the bobbin and top threads and folding them over to make about six strands. Use a wide stitch width (5) and water-soluble stabilizer underneath if desired. Set your machine for free machining, with feed dogs down or covered. Use a darning foot or no presser foot at all. Hold the threads tightly, front and back, as you stitch. You will feed the threads under the needle and determine the stitch length. These tiny cords work well for corded buttonholes.

You can also zigzag over thicker cords and hold them together. If you add a contrasting thread color, you can make interesting tassels (see the next lesson).

Lesson 36. Making tassels

I'm drawn to tassels. I sketch them when I see them in museums or books, and I have a notebook full of ideas cut from magazines. I've labored over a few myself, using hand embroidery, even tiny macramé knots. Sometimes they look like fetish dolls — another weakness — and so I let them evolve that way.

How can my sewing machine help me make tassels? First of all, I make monk's cord using the bobbin winder. I combine those with other cords, sometimes stringing beads or bells on them (Figs. 10.4 and 10.5).

I can also use a braiding foot or open embroidery foot to make colorful cord. Holding several pearl cotton cords together, I place them in the groove on the bottom of the presser foot and zigzag stitch over the pearl with a contrasting color. I choose a medium-wide stitch width (4–5) to enclose the cords, and a stitch length 2–3 (1) to let some of the cord show through.

Project
Tassel Collar

Several ways to make tassels by machine involve using water-soluble stabilizer. The first method is for a collar of stitched cords to wrap around the main tassel cords. Set the machine for zigzag.

Stitch width: M–W (4–5)
Stitch length: 2–3 (1/2)
Needle position: auto (center)
Needle: #80/12
Presser foot: transparent zigzag foot N
Feed dogs: up
Tension: *top*, normal; *bobbin*, normal
Cord: 16 yards (14m) rayon cord (available at fabric shops) for the collar; #5 pearl cotton to match cord; many yards of string, thread or yarn for main part of tassel (the more yarn used, the plumper and more attractive the tassel), cut into 16" (40.6cm) lengths

Fig. 10.4 Monk's cord is used for the tassels at left and center. A collar, stitched by machine, was used for the one at right.

Fig. 10.5 More tassels stitched by machine.

Thread: rayon embroidery to match rayon cord
Accessories: water-soluble stabilizer

First fold the 16" (40.6cm) lengths of yarn in half to find their centers. Use one yarn piece to tie the lengths together there. Knot tightly. Then tie an overhand knot with the ends of that cord to make a hanger for the tassel.

Cut six dozen 8" (20.3cm) lengths of purchased rayon cord. Place a piece of water-soluble stabilizer on the bed of the machine and lay these cords next to each other across the stabilizer (in horizontal rows as you are looking at them). Starting ½" (12.7mm) in from the right side, place a

145

strand of #5 pearl cotton perpendicular to and crossing all the cords (Fig. 10.6). Satin stitch over the pearl cotton and the rayon cords. Sew down several more rows of pearl, lining up each pearl cord next to the one stitched before it. When completed, cut off the ½" (12.7mm) rayon threads protruding from the top of the collar. Zigzag over the edge, which will give the top a smooth finish.

Wrap the collar, inside-out, 1½" (3.8cm) down from the fold of the tassel cords. Pin the collar tightly around the cords. Remove it from the tassel and machine stitch the ends of the collar together. Cut back to the stitching line and zigzag over the edge. Turn right side out, then pull the yarn tassel cords from the bottom through the collar to complete it. The collar should fit snugly.

You could embroider the same basic collar in an almost endless variety of ways for your tassel collection.

Project
Covered Wire Tassel

Cover 18" (45.7cm) of milliner's wire with stitches for the next tassel (Fig. 10.7). Set the machine for zigzag.

Stitch width: M–W (4–5)
Stitch length: 2–3 (1/2)
Needle position: auto (center)
Needle: #80/12
Feed dogs: up
Presser foot: transparent embroidery foot N
Tension: *top*, normal; *bobbin*, normal
Thread: rayon embroidery
Accessories: tweezers
Stabilizer: water-soluble (optional), cut into long strips 1" wide

Set up your machine and place water-soluble stabilizer under the wire if you wish. Sew over the wire. If the wire doesn't feed well, then use a longer length stitch and go over it twice. The milliner's wire is covered with thread and this keeps the rayon stitches from slipping.

Make 45 thick cords for the tassel by zig-zagging over two 12" (30.5cm) strands of #5 pearl cotton for each one. *Hint:* Stitch two 15-yard-long (14m-long) cords together and cut them into 12" (30.5cm) pieces.

To use the wire for the tassel, first fold the 12" (30.5cm) long cords in half. Slip an end of the wire through the fold, extending it past the cord 2" (5.1cm). Bend the wire back 1" (2.5cm) at the end and twist it around itself to make a loop for hanging (the loop will enclose the cords).

With the other end of the wire, wrap the tassel around and around till you reach halfway down the length of it. Hold the end of the wire with the tweezers. Wrap it

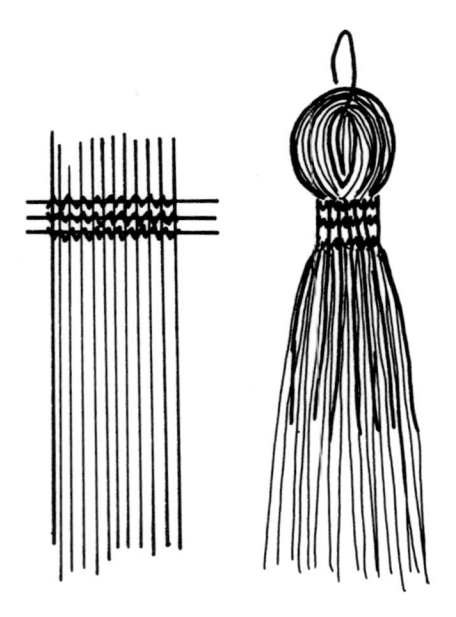

Fig. 10.6 Make a collar for the tassel by placing cords next to each other, then zigzagging over cords laid at right angles across them.

Fig. 10.7 Cover milliner's wire with stitches and twist the wire around cords to make a tassel.

around the point of the tweezers to make a decorative coil at the end (Fig. 10.7).

Project Doll Tassel

The fertility doll tassel is a combination of several dozen 10" (25.4cm) cords, including linen, jute and monk's cords (see Fig. 10.3) all tied to a small African doll. I placed the bundle of cords on the bed of the machine, letting it extend 1" (2.5cm) to the right of the presser foot and flattening it with my fingers to allow me to stitch over the cords. The machine was set up for free-machining, with feed dogs lowered and a darning foot in place. Using the widest zigzag, I stitched forward and back across the cords. When I finished, I spread glue from a glue stick across the stitching on one side of the bundle and placed this at the back of the doll, wrapping and tying it in place with a linen cord.

To decorate the tassel, I slipped a long feather under the linen wrapping cord, and strung some of the tassel cords with beads, brass bells and metal washers. Overhand knots held the objects in place at different heights on the cords. There's a hole in the top of the doll, so I added a loop of cord there to hang the tassel.

Project Making Two Tassel Tops by Machine

For the following tassels shown in Fig. 10.8C and 10.9, the tops are made on the sewing machine. Put a 7" (17.8cm) square of felt in a 5" (12.7cm) spring hoop. Draw half a circle and embroider this using decorative, built-in machine stitches. Take it out of the hoop and cut out the half-circle (Fig. 10.8A). Cut out a wedge from the side of the half-circle (Fig. 10.8B). Fold the larger piece in half, topsides together. Straight stitch the cut edges. Turn to the right side.

Cut six tassel cords, each 18" (45.7cm) in length, from rayon cord or machine-made monk's cord. Find the center and tie them together at the middle with a cord 8" (20.3cm) long. Thread that cord through a large-eyed needle and push it up from inside through the top of the cone. Tie a knot at the end and hang the tassel.

The second tassel is also made of felt, with a machine-stitched top (Fig. 10.9). Set the machine for zigzag.

Stitch width: W (5)
Stitch length: varies
Needle position: auto (center)

Thread: rayon machine embroidery—I chose red, yellow and blue; #8 red pearl cotton; #5 blue pearl cotton (optional)
Accessories: 7" (17.8cm) spring hoop, small bells, glue stick, fine-point marker
Stabilizer: tear-away

The finished size of the tassel top is 2" × 2" (5.1cm × 5.1cm). I worked with a 9" (22.9cm) piece of felt so it would fit in the

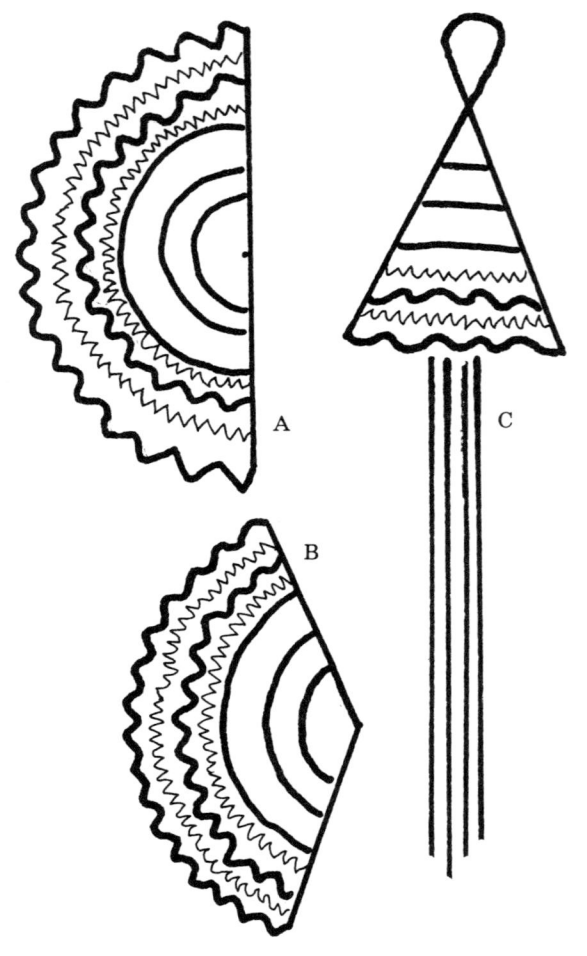

Fig. 10.8 Making a machined tassel. A. Embroider a half-circle of felt. B. Cut a wedge from it, and sew up the sides to form a cone. C. The cone becomes the top of the tassel.

Needle: #90/14, topstitch
Feed dogs: up
Presser foot: cording or transparent zigzag foot N
Tension: *top,* loosened; *bobbin,* normal
Fabric suggestion: 9" (22.9cm) square of felt (tassel top will be completely covered with stitches)

Fig. 10.9 A tassel made of satin stitches on felt.

148

7" (17.8cm) spring hoop. This allows enough room for the presser foot without hitting the edge of the hoop, as you will stitch both sides of the tassel top – 2" × 4" (30.5cm × 10.2cm) area – at once.

Trace the pattern from Fig. 10.9. Cut around the tracing and lay this on the felt. Draw around the pattern with a marker (it won't show when tassel is completed).

Begin by carefully stretching the felt in the hoop. Use corded (#5 pearl cotton) satin stitches made with the cording foot. Starting on the right side, place one line of close, smooth satin stitches. Add another row next to the first, and continue, changing colors as you wish. Now sew between the satin stitches, using a contrasting color and the triple-stretch stitch (#21, stitch width 0).

Cut out the stitched design; then cut it in half. Place wrong sides together.

Cut about five dozen lengths of pearl cotton, each 12" (30.5cm) long. Fold them in half. Place the folds inside the felt pieces along the straight edge. Pin the felt together or use a dot of glue stick to hold everything in place as you stitch. Zigzag across the straight edge of the felt to keep the pearl cotton in place. Zigzag around the curve as well. Then go back with a satin stitch and stitch around it again with stitch width at the widest, stitch length 2–3 (1/2). Add bells to each side and a hanger at the top. Clay or metal found objects also work well as ornaments.

I agree, making tassels is a nutty thing to do (but it's fun). Use them to decorate your tote bag, for key chains, zipper pulls, decorations on clothing, curtain tiebacks. I confess that I hang them all over my sewing room.

CHAPTER 11

Decorative Stitches

by JANE WARNICK

- **Lesson 37. Highlighting structural details**
- **Lesson 38. Coordinating separate elements**
- **Lesson 39. Guiding the eye**

That first zigzag sewing machine I received upon graduation from high school in the mid-fifties also had several decorative stitches. I remember the first outfit I made: it was a brown six-gore skirt with a pink, scoop-neck, sleeveless blouse. I stitched horizontal pink decorative lines on the center back and center front gores. I then stitched the same pattern in brown around the neckline of the blouse, which served the dual purpose of decorating and holding down the facing. I had an *outfit*.

I'd make the same garment today because it is as legitimate a use of the stitches now as it was then. I would, however, make some changes. Rather than placing the rows evenly apart, I would place them close together at the hem and gradually move them farther apart as they neared the waist. By doing so I could create the illusion that the lines were receding into space to make the waistline appear smaller. (Oh, how I would want you to believe that my waist was smaller!)

Then just as your eye reached the waist, I'd want it to suddenly spy the matching line in the opposite color at the neck and have you skip the waist altogether. (Am I telling you something about my waistline?) If I found that one row of stitching at the neck wasn't enough to entice the eye, I'd add another.

In this chapter we will explore how you can best use the Brother decorative stitches. Although you could use the same principles to stitch directly on garments, I've designed a series of accessories for the popular modular knits sold under the names of Units, Multiples, Modulars, etc. (each chain seems to have its own pseudonym). The major pattern companies (including Stretch and Sew) all sell patterns for these modular units if you want to make your own. The accessories within this chapter are a collar, belt ornament, scarf, shoe ornament, and purse. There is also a square for your tote bag.

The modular knits serve as an ideal blank canvas on which we can add stitched accessories to make our own fashion statements. To stitch directly on these garments would limit, rather than enhance, their versatility.

We will also explore the linear nature of decorative stitches through several exercises. Then, by knowing why you are placing decorative stitches in an area and how to group the stitches to achieve your purpose, you can sew something unique and flattering.

The key is to understand why you choose to decorate with stitches. Just having 100 stitches available is not a legitimate reason. The lines may end up looking like an afterthought.

Or worse, they may lead the viewer's eye

directly to a spot you want them to skip altogether. I once saw a woman wearing a long skirt decorated with lace doilies growing up from the hem like flowers. When she turned around, I could see that two of the flowers were growing right on her ample backside. That is a classic example of decorating an area, the skirt, without the least thought as to where the decoration will fall on the body.

To highlight a structural detail, to create an edge, to coordinate two separate elements, to guide the viewer's eye to what you want it to see and away from what you don't want it to see — these are all appropriate uses for decorative stitches.

But before we delve into these uses, let's examine the nature of line itself. What is its place in the design process in general and with decorative machine stitches particularly?

Learning about line

Machine embroidery is a linear form of decoration, even though the lines are often

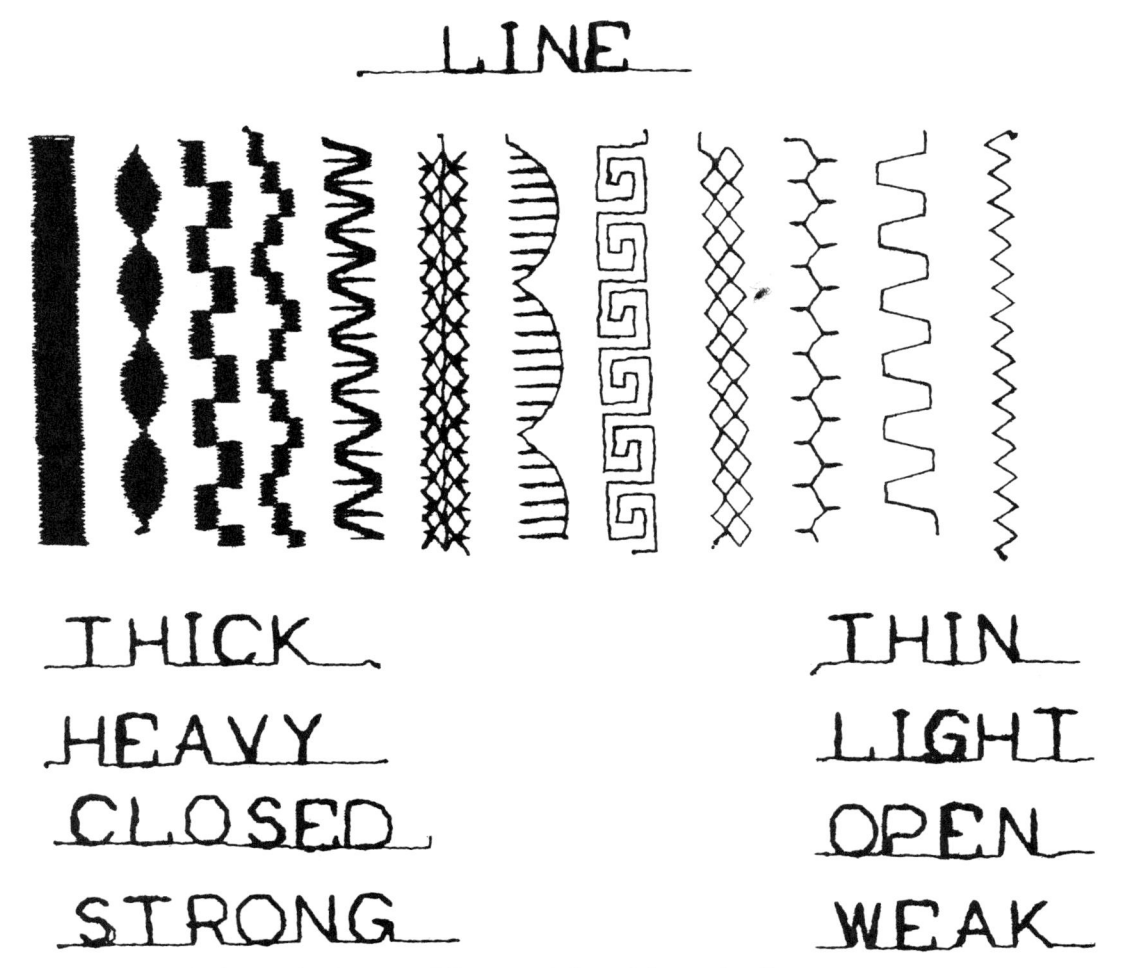

Fig. 11.1 Stitched sample showing different weights of decorative lines.

151

used to fill, create, or outline a shape. Satin stitch is merely thin straight lines laid side by side to create a thick line. Open satin or zigzag is composed of thin diagonal lines. Many decorative stitches lie between these two extremes. They can be closed, combinations of closed and open, curvilinear, open, spiky, pictorial, letters, etc. (Fig. 11.1).

Lines have direction, texture, value, color, and size and can be used to create a shape—thus they embody all the elements of design. Lines are straight or curved. Rhythmic, calligraphic lines are created by varying the width or by using decorative stitches composed of curved lines (for example, the scallop stitches and decorative stitches 94 through 98) [Fig. 11.2]). A line can be as sensitive as a straight stitch freely stitched in a frame to a rigid, unbending, full-width zigzag stitched in a straight line with feed dogs up and a presser foot in place.

An infinite variety is available. The decorative stitches (and the utility stitches used in a decorative way) form a huge body of line-making possibilities. Some stitches can be worked freely; those with a reverse action (letters, pictorial stitches, most stretch stitches) cannot.

Line width can be varied. You can change the weight of the thread, the length of the stitch—packed closely or spread way out—and completely alter the visual impact of a line. Lines can be packed on top of each other, crossed, worked back and forth—scribbled any way you wish. But in the final analysis you still have a line.

Paul Klee, a painter and teacher, said that to make a line, you must take a dot for a walk. To make a line in machine embroidery, you must take the stitch for a walk—whether the line is wide or narrow, long or short, you will make a continuous line until you stop stitching and start another line. You can design a short line or a long line; you can make the line look broken; but you will still be creating a linear path.

Exercise: To help you become familiar with and sensitive to the kinds of lines available on your sewing machine, we are going to take some of them for a walk. Start with a straight stitch and a piece of fabric 8" (20.3cm) x 10" (25.4cm) and head out on an imaginary walk—perhaps your route to school as a child. Every time you turn a corner, change the stitch. Think about where you're walking, and choose your stitch to reflect your thoughts. Maybe you were scared every time you had to pass a certain house. Don't forget how you always enjoyed the flowers in Miss Betty's garden. And here's where you have to cross the river. When you've finished your walk and taken the fabric from the machine, write what you were feeling (happy, sad, scared) or thinking or where you were on each line and put the piece in your notebook (Fig. 11.3). This exercise can be used as a lead-in to a day of stitching. I use it as a meditation to center myself and to focus my attention on the quality of each line. What line says happy? Scared? Love?

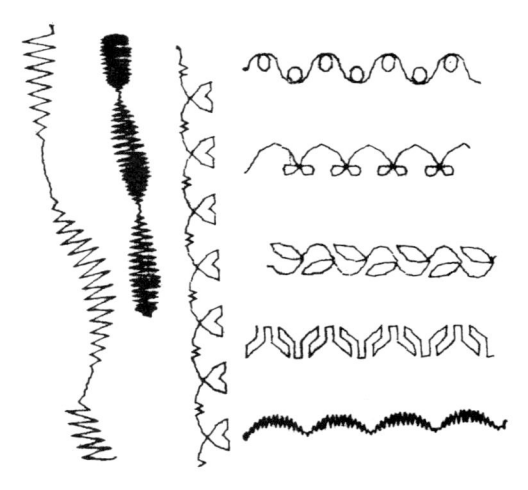

Fig. 11.2 Sample of decorative stitches built of curved lines.

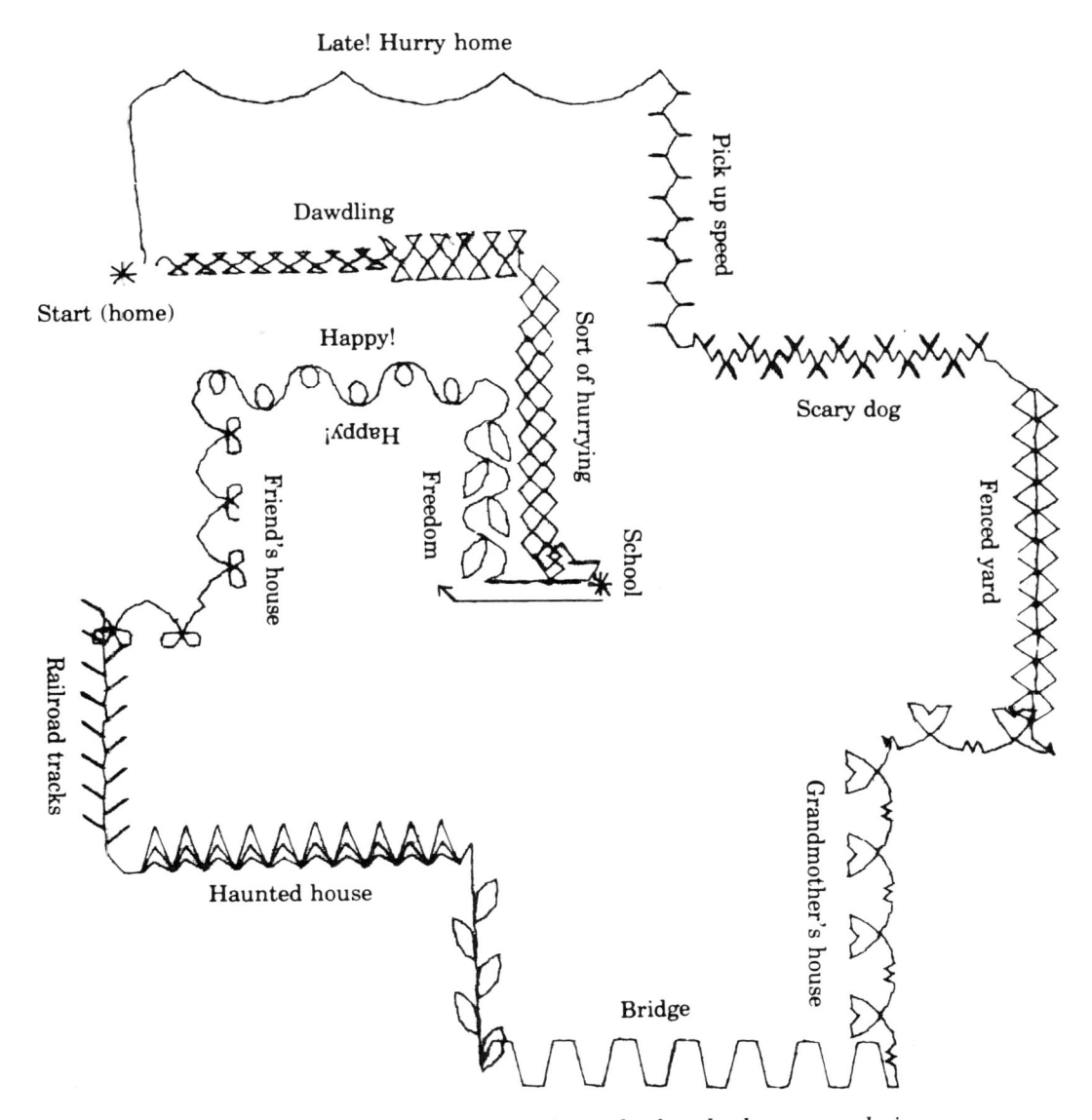

Fig. 11.3 One line that went for a reluctant walk to school and a happy wandering trip home.

The *texture* of a line runs from a single stitch to the heavily packed satin stitch. Look back at Fig. 11.1 and you will see several textures running between the two outside lines. The lines to the left are smooth, satiny, heavy in weight. Then there are the transitional stitches in the middle, busier in texture with many light visible threads, leading to the simple open zigzag on the right. Though not shown, the straight stitch would be the logical final line on the right.

153

You can alter the texture within a stitch by changing its length. This can be done at random or in a planned pattern. You can also use two threads or a heavy thread on top with the more open stitches to create a heavier texture. Working these stitches solidly without any open area between will create yet another texture.

Similarly, the *value* (the degree of light and dark) of the line depends on the width and closeness of the stitch. In Fig. 11.1, from left to right, the value runs from dark to light.

The *size* can be varied within the width of the stitch, whether it is the 7mm of the Brother Galaxie or the 5mm of the 950. You can pack lines close together to create wide lines or place different stitches together to build up a new pattern.

You can stitch a line around an area to create a shape; you can fill a shape with lines; or you can use lines of stitches in close proximity to create a visual shape, as shown in the tote bag square (Fig. 11.4).

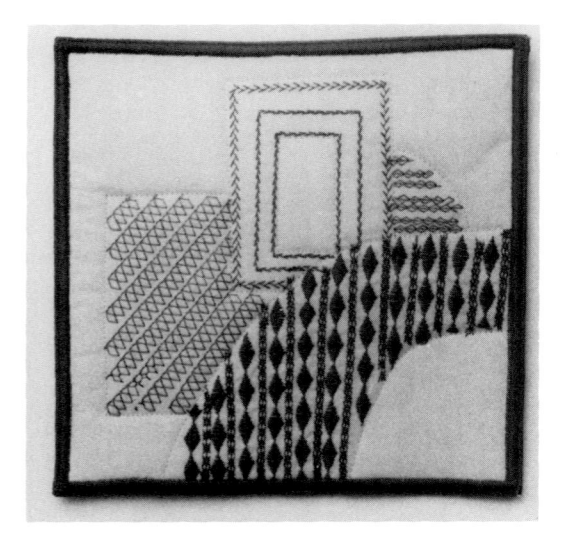

Fig. 11.4 Tote bag square.

Project
Tote Bag Square

The design within the tote bag square is composed entirely of lines of decorative stitching. They are stitched in different directions, close together, a bit apart, in varying widths, open and closed, in various colors, in combination and alone. Notice how the heavier, more textured stitches in the curved shape seem to come forward.

Stitch width: auto (3–5)
Stitch length: auto (1/2)
Needle position: auto (center)
Needle: #90/14
Feed dogs: up
Presser foot: transparent zigzag foot N
Decorative stitches: #74, #79, #82, #83, #87, (#8, #12, #13, #18, #20)
Tension: *top*, 3 (3); *bobbin*, normal
Fabric: 9" (22.9cm) square of yellow fabric; 9" (22.9cm) square of fleece; two 9" (22.9cm) squares of heavyweight fusible interfacing; 9" (22.9cm) square of yellow felt
Thread: red, blue, green, and yellow embroidery thread; bobbin filled with red thread
Accessories: vanishing marker, No-Fray or Fray-Check

Trace the pattern for the square (11.5) directly onto the yellow fabric. Fuse one piece of the heavyweight interfacing to the back of this square, and fuse the other piece to the back of the felt at the same time. Set aside the felt square.

Thread your machine with blue thread. Begin stitching horizontal rows of decorative stitch #87 (#12), medium width, in the designated area. (Test your stitches in the excess area around the square.) Be careful to start and stop directly on the outline of the shape. Then stitch diagonal rows of #82 (#13) where indicated.

Thread your machine with red thread.

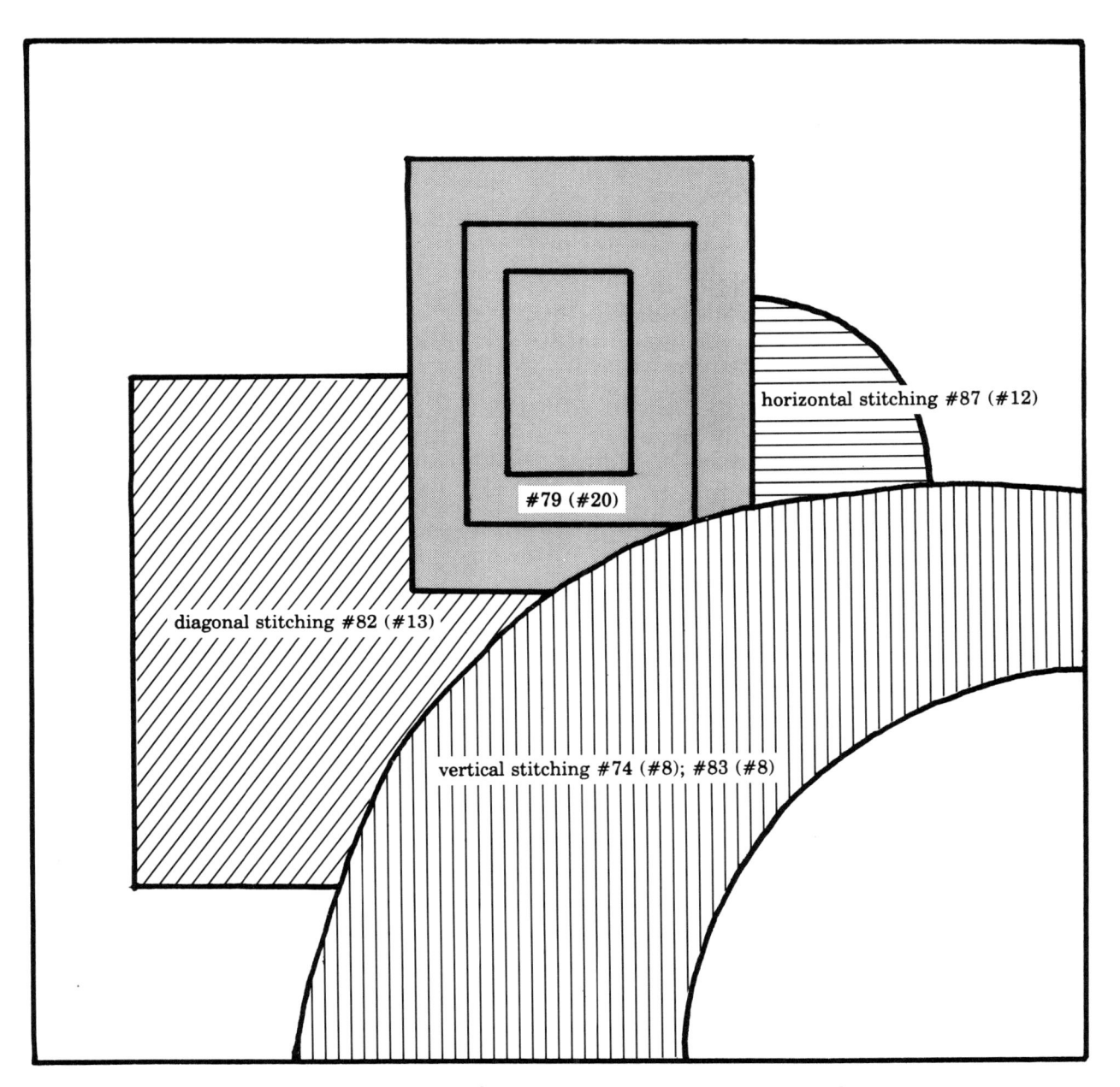

Fig. 11.5 Layout for tote bag square with stitch directions and decorative stitch numbers indicated.

155

Work the three lines of #79 (#20) around the rectangle, working the outside row at a medium width and the two inner rows at a narrow width.

Finally, thread your machine with green thread and work the remaining area, stitching #74 (#8) full width. Use the edge of your presser foot as a guide for the stitching. Stitch #83 (#18) between the rows of #74 (#8), adjusting the width so it just clears the previous stitching.

Clip all threads on the front, removing any stitching that may have strayed into one of the adjacent shapes. Don't clip the thread closely on the back. Place a drop of No-Fray or Fray-Check on the beginning and end of each row of stitching. Press.

Thread your machine with yellow thread and stitch a straight stitch along the outline of each shape if desired. Finish the square as explained in Chapter 12.

You can also fill a shape with closely packed satin or straight stitches (Chapter 2). If you do this, you will begin to understand the linear aspects of a machined line, as you must be careful to preplan in which direction you will fill the area. If you use encroaching zigzag, you will see an area filled with short, packed lines. If you use a straight stitch in a round scribble effect or a bobbin filled with a heavy pearl cotton, you will create the least linear effect.

If you have ever drawn with a computer graphics program, you know that you have within the toolbox a choice of the width of line and whether it is plain or patterned. The same is true with the sewing machine. The needle is your line-making instrument; you can make any of the stitches in any width and length you choose. You can draw with any width of line from 0 to the widest—with straight stitch, plain zigzag, or one of the decorative stitches. Take a few hours and really experiment with the different stitches, different widths and lengths, working with the transparent zigzag foot N and also with the fabric stretched in a frame, to explore some of the many choices you have. Take notes and save your efforts. These will be your most useful reference.

Lesson 37. Highlighting structural details

Before we talk about highlighting structural details, let me define the term. Structural details are any seams or edges used to shape a flat piece of fabric into a final product, whether it is a garment or an accessory. Darts are structural details, as are yokes, collars, gathers, pockets, pleats, tucks, zippers, buttonholes, buttons, hems, etc. A seam is a structural detail that can be decorated or left plain, depending on whether you, the designer, want it to be subtle or eye-catching.

Let's look at how these details can be highlighted. With smocking (Chapter 3, Lesson 7) you highlight gathers by making rows of decorative stitches across the gathers. Stitching lace (Chapter 8, Lesson 23) to the edges of collars, cuffs, bonnets, the wedding handkerchief, etc., directs the viewer's eye to the edge. The needle weaving in Lesson 18 (Chapter 6) calls attention to the edge of the sleeve.

While the primary purpose of the stitching on the scarf and the shoe ornament in Lesson 38 is coordinating separate elements, the lines of stitching also define the edges. Picture the shoe ornament without the fringe and the stitching. You would hardly see it when it was placed on the shoe. The stitching around the edge of the scarf calls attention to that edge as the scarf is pulled through the loop and settles into soft folds.

Sometimes the decorative stitching is

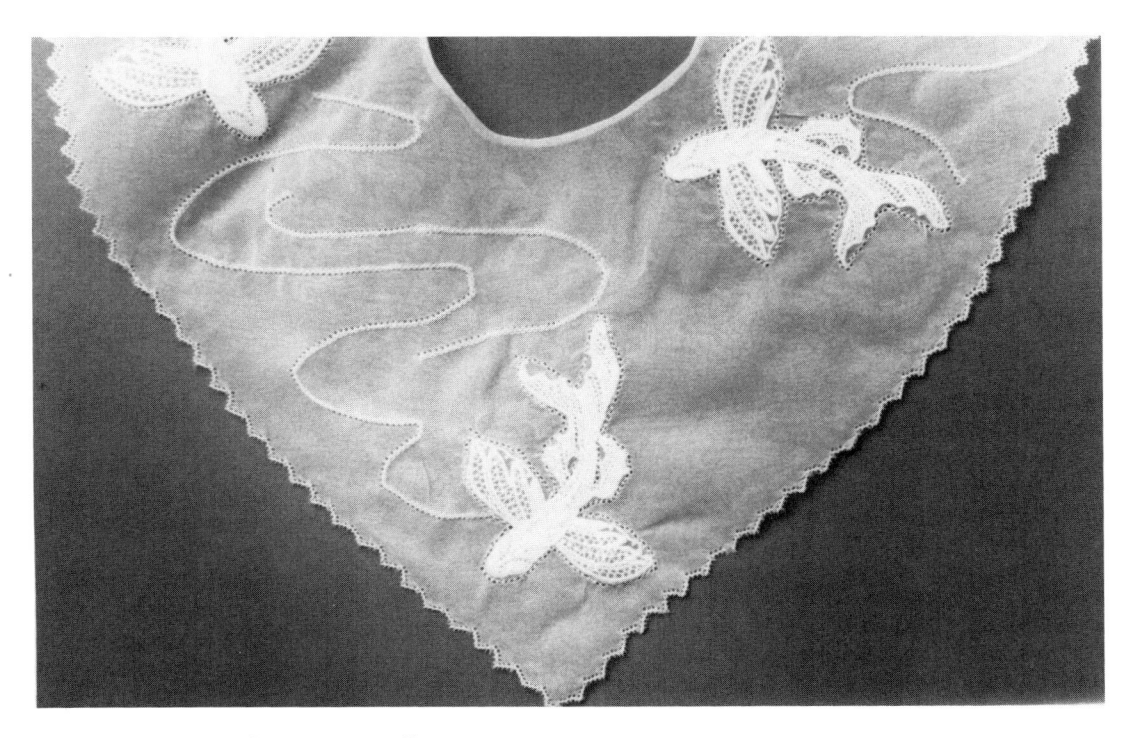

Fig. 11.6 Front of the organza collar.

the structural detail, as in the collar in this lesson (Fig. 11.6). If you join a yoke to a bodice with fagoting, then the fagoting is the structural detail. If you then stitch several rows of decorative stitches on either side of the fagoting, the decorative stitches *highlight* the structural detail.

Project
Shadow-Appliqué Collar

This collar was born because I was playing around with some organza, fancy stitches, and a wing needle one day. I was trying different decorative stitches just to see what they looked like. When I used #84 (a real favorite of mine), I loved the way it looked like an exquisite lace once it was trimmed.

I decided right then to do a collar with this stitched edge. I bought the fish motifs years ago, knowing someday I would have a use for them. If you don't have any treasured motifs on hand, try taking apart some silk flowers and using them. Or cut some shapes from an allover lace, from a print fabric, or from another color of organza.

Do you have a treasure box? If not, start one. Then when you're out shopping (and old clothes from thrift stores often yield the most wonderful trims), you'll have a place to store the wealth until the day you discover a wonderful stitch combination and decide to design something of your own.

Remember when you're planning your collar that less is more; just because you have twelve motifs doesn't mean you have to use them all on one piece. Perhaps you have only one motif and really want to use it. Combine it with others. They don't all have to match; they merely have to have something in common. For example, I wouldn't put silk flowers with my fish, but I might include some shell motifs if I had them.

Stitch width: 0–7 (0–5)
Stitch length: auto (1/2–3)
Needle position: auto (center)
Needle: #70/10, #16 wing needle, double wing needle
Feed dogs: up
Presser foot: transparent zigzag foot N
Tension: 3 (3)
Fabric suggestion: ¾ yd.(68.7cm) of ecru silk or polyester organza, 1 yd. (.9m) ecru 1/8" (3.2mm) ribbon
Thread: ecru sewing thread for seams, ecru rayon thread or light-colored metallic thread (I used Madeira Supertwist color #300) for the decorative stitching
Accessories: lace motifs or silk flowers; pencil; tracing paper; vanishing marker; sewing shears; sharp, pointed embroidery scissors

To make the pattern for the collar, use a favorite bodice pattern with a high, round neck. Put tracing paper over the front bodice pattern twice as wide as the bodice. (You will make a full pattern rather than a half one with a fold because you will cut two collar fronts and two backs. With the full pattern you will have to cut around each piece only once, and it will be easier to place the pattern on the fabric.) Copy the neckline with seam allowance and trace the center front. Place a ruler at the neck seamline at center front and measure down 9" (22.9cm). Move the ruler to the shoulder line and make a mark 5" (12.7cm) from the neck seamline. Draw a straight line between these two points. Now slightly round it out starting about halfway up the line (Fig. 11.7).

Repeat on the back bodice. At the center back make a mark 5½" (14cm) down for the opening. Be sure you include the seam allowances at the shoulder and neck, but don't include one around the lower edge. Fold your tracing paper on the center front and center back to make the full pattern.

Fold the organza on the lengthwise center, place and weight the patterns (I used cans of tuna fish) and cut around each, which yields two fronts and two backs. Mark the back neck opening. After you've cut out the collar, practice all of the following techniques and stitches on the organza scraps until you feel comfortable with the different procedures.

Join the shoulder seams using the triple stretch stitch (#21, stitch width 0, stitch length 3), the #70 (10) needle, and ecru sewing thread. Trim the seams within 1/16" (1.6mm) of the stitching. Press the seams to the back.

Place the two layers of organza *right sides* together. Pin around the neck and down the back opening. Cut the ribbon into two equal pieces. Reach between the layers and slip the pieces of ribbon into the placket seam at the back neck, raw edges

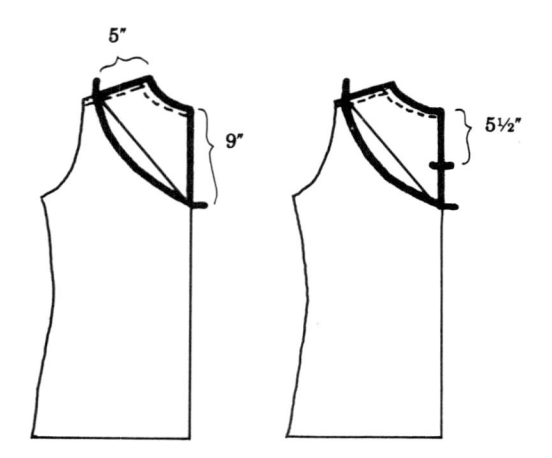

Fig. 11.7 Drafting the collar pattern.

pointing toward the back opening. *Do not slit the opening until you have stitched around the neck and around the back placket.* Use the triple stretch stitch (#21) and stitch ¼" (6.4mm) from either side of the center back opening, tapering to nothing at the point. Take one stitch across the point. Be sure you catch the ribbon into the neck seam. Trim the seam around the neck, leaving about 1/16" (1.6mm) seam allowance. Turn to the right side and press.

Place the lace motifs between the two layers anywhere on the front collar that you choose. Slip the collar over your head and check the placement on your body. You don't want any surprises. Be sure to save at least one or more motifs for the back of the collar (Fig. 11.8). I don't try to match the back placement to the front, but I do want to give a hint or a reprise of what occurs on the front. When you're happy with the arrangement, pin the motifs in place between the layers.

Put the wing needle on the sewing machine and thread with the metallic thread both in the bobbin and on top. Set your machine for triple stretch stitch (#21, stitch width 0) and carefully stitch around the motifs. When stitching, push the needle position button so the machine stops with the needle in the down position. Always be sure you stop after the *second* for-

Fig. 11.8 Back of the organza collar. Note the placement of one of the motifs on the shoulder.

ward stitch before you turn the fabric. Otherwise, the needle will take an eccentric stitch back before it again stitches forward.

When you have finished stitching around all the motifs, try on the collar. You have the contrast of the heavy lace motifs with the organza; the motifs dominate. Now consider how you will relate the motifs to each other. Perhaps you need some lines to bring them into some kind of relationship. I added lines with the double wing needle and a straight stitch. Mine are curvy, watery lines that contrast with the straight edge of the collar and echo the curves of the fish motifs.

If you've used silk flowers or floral motifs, you might want to add some lines suggesting leaves. If you've used heart motifs, perhaps add some curvy lines suggesting ribbon. Some other suggestions include stitching a grid, or straight lines to suggest a trellis, which would contrast with round floral shapes and echo the straight edge of the collar. Then again you might not need additional lines at all. Let the collar lead the way. I used the vanishing marker to mark these lines and studied the placement before I stitched them.

When you have completed all the stitching on the body of the collar, you're ready to finish the edge. Remove the double needle and deactivate the double needle button. Put the wing needle back on the machine. Before you begin, draw a large V on one of the scraps. Practice turning the corner neatly. You can also round off the edge before you start to avoid having to turn any corners. Stitch up to the point or beyond if necessary, so the motif finishes with the left swing of the line (Fig. 11.9). Pivot the fabric and continue stitching.

Now you're ready to stitch around the collar edge, using the edge of the presser foot as a spacing guide. Start at the right shoulder heading down the back, around the back point, up toward the left shoulder, and around the front. This gives you

Fig. 11.9 Stitched sample showing how to turn the corner on the decorative stitching around the edge of the collar.

some practice before you reach the front. Trim the organza from the edge, using sharp pointed scissors and cutting into the holes made by the wing needle.

The decorative stitching creates the edge (structural detail) and highlights it by forming an irregular edge. The triple stretch stitch is a structural detail because it holds the fish motifs in place. The lines of double needle stitching guide the viewer's eye between the motifs and bring them into relationship with each other.

If the edge you want to create or highlight is circular, you need to know how to accomplish this easily on your sewing machine. Any time you need a perfect circle of decorative stitching or lettering, you'll proceed as follows and stitch as much or as little of the circle as you want. You'll find the directions for making circles using tape, a thumbtack, and an eraser or cork in Chapter 1 (see Fig. 1.3).

First, let's consider the parts of a circle. The *diameter* is the measurement from one side to another, and circles are usually described in this manner. Thus, a 3" (7.6cm) circle means one that measures 3" (7.6cm) from side to side. The *radius* of a circle is one-half of the diameter. A 3" (7.6cm) circle has a radius of 1½" (3.8cm). The radius of a circle is what you need to know when you're using either the tape and thumbtack method or a circle maker, in the case of 940/950.

I seldom draw the circles on the fabric directly. I simply put a dot where I want the center of my circle. This would be the spot where the fixed foot of a compass would go—because what you are actually doing is making the machine behave like a compass. Instead of pulling the legs apart to create a larger circle, you simply move the thumbtack away from the needle.

To place the thumbtack accurately, turn the wheel so the needle almost enters the foot plate. Then take a ruler and place the measurement of the radius (1½" [3.8cm]) at the needle. With a vanishing marker, make a dot on the bed of your machine at the exact upper left corner of the ruler. Carefully place the thumbtack so the point falls on this mark.

Try many decorative stitches and lettering in circles (Fig. 11.10). The pictorial

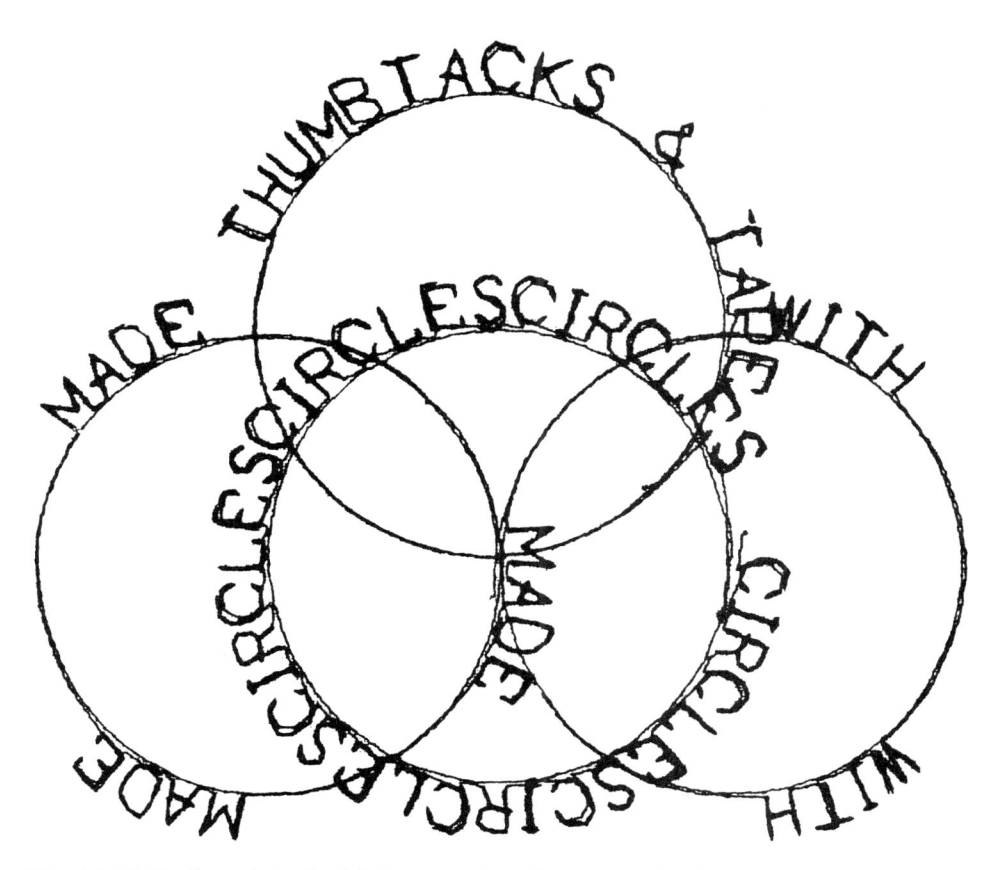

Fig. 11.10 Circles stitched with letters using the tape and tack method.

THUMBTACK CIRCLES

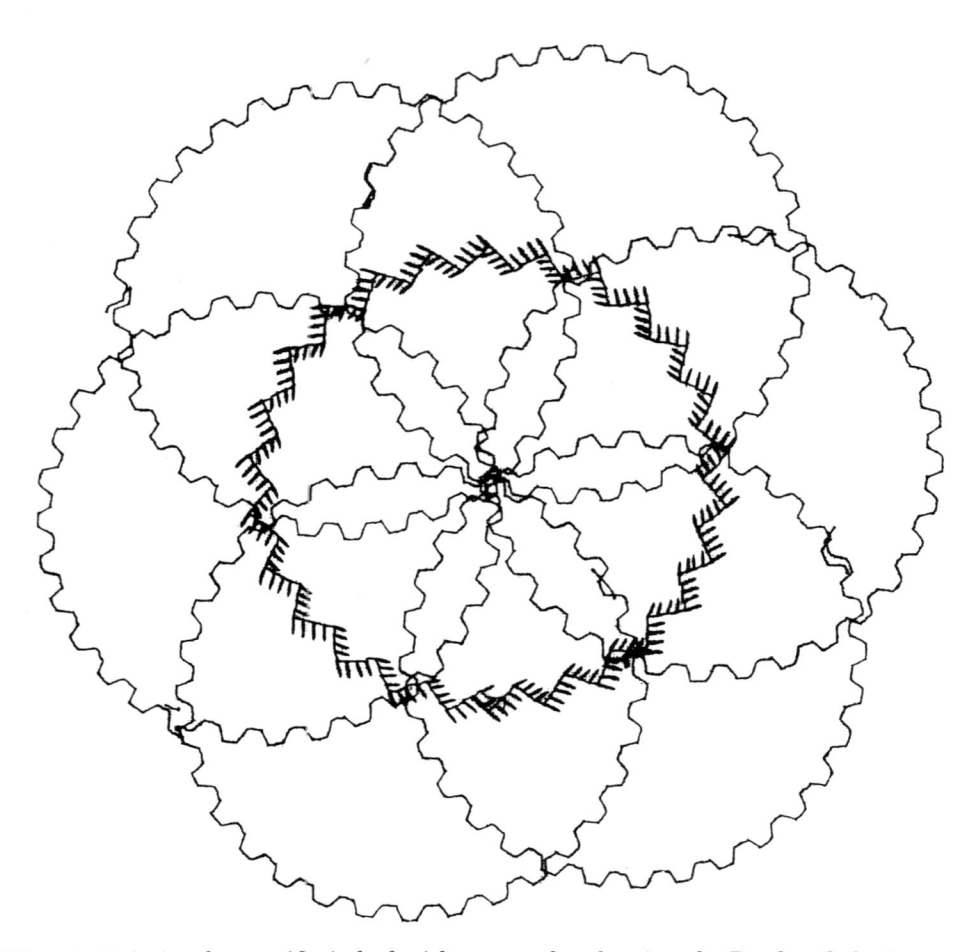

Fig. 11.11 A circular motif stitched with tape and tack using the Brother Galaxie as a compass and decorative stitches as the line.

stitches that are reverse action won't feed smoothly, so the motif becomes badly distorted. No problem. Don't use them. If you use a stabilizer, don't use paper. You want something that the feed dogs can really grab. I like to use a fusible interfacing in the appropriate weight.

Remember when you got your first compass and you made patterns by moving the compass around the edge of the circle? Try the same thing with the thumbtack (Fig. 11.11).

Exercise: In this exercise you will be creating a round edge and highlighting it. Someday when you have absolutely nothing else to do, test all of your stitches in circles. Use 4½" (11.4cm) squares of denim. Use a shiny red thread in the bobbin and a metallic and shiny red threaded together through the needle on top. Using a radius of 1¼" (3.2cm), and placing the center of the square on the thumbtack, stitch a circle of decorative stitches. Sometimes a pattern will work better if you make the stitch longer and/or narrower.

When you've finished stitching lots of circles inside lots of squares, move the thumbtack out ½" (12.7cm), making a radius of 1¾" (4.4cm). Place the circles (one at a time) onto the thumbtack and secure with the eraser, being sure to use the same hole as before. (If you want, you can combine two circles to give a finished back and front to the ornament by placing one square on the thumbtack wrong side up, then placing another square on top, right side up.) Set your machine for a medium to wide close satin stitch and stitch a circle all around the edge.

If you have the Galaxie, you might add a message to the center. You can add a smaller circle, an appliqué, a freely stitched motif, etc.

Trim the excess denim away from your satin stitch circle, being careful not to clip into the stitching. Attach a loop of ribbon or thread to the edge of the circle by straight stitching along the inside edge of

Fig. 11.12 Christmas ornaments stitched with metallic thread on pieces of denim cut from old jeans.

the satin stitching. Hang these on an evergreen tree and have a merry cowboy Christmas (Fig. 11.12).

You don't have to make whole circles as you can see in Fig. 11.13. You can stitch half of a circle and join with other half circles to create big scallops. Turn the partial circles one way and then another to create curving, rhythmic lines. To highlight rounded edges, join half circles with straight lines as I have done on the belt ornament that follows.

The decorative stitching on the following belt ornament is there for several reasons. The stitching follows the edge so the viewer will know the shape of the edge even though part of it is hidden behind the scarf. The stitching is done in the color of the scarf to coordinate it with the ornament. The belt will be worn with my black knit dress, and by stitching the blue/green inside the edge and then finishing the edge with the cross-locked beads, I can lead the viewer's eye around the ornament (and not around my waist). Without the stitching and/or the beads the ornament would be lost on the black dress.

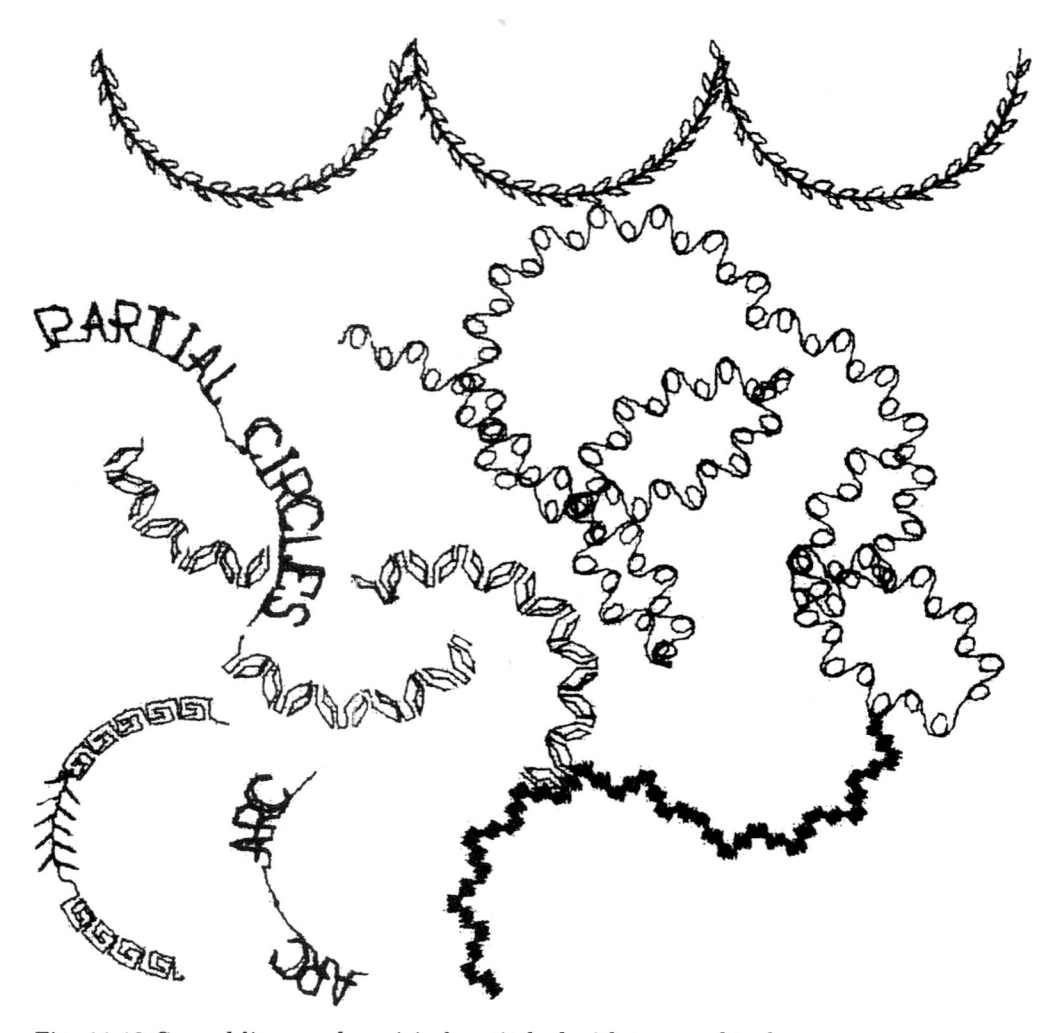

Fig. 11.13 Curved lines and semicircles stitched with tape and tack.

Project
Belt Ornament

In this project (Fig. 11.14), not only will you be stitching two halves of a circle joined with straight lines, but the decorative stitching is enhanced by the two colors of threads I used in a single needle. The colors intentionally do not match because I wanted to give the stitching an iridescent sparkle. To accomplish this I chose colors that lie adjacent on the color wheel (green and blue), which have the same value (degree of light and dark), and the same intensity (purity of color, absence of white or black). I could have chosen orange and yellow, orange and red, blue and purple, red

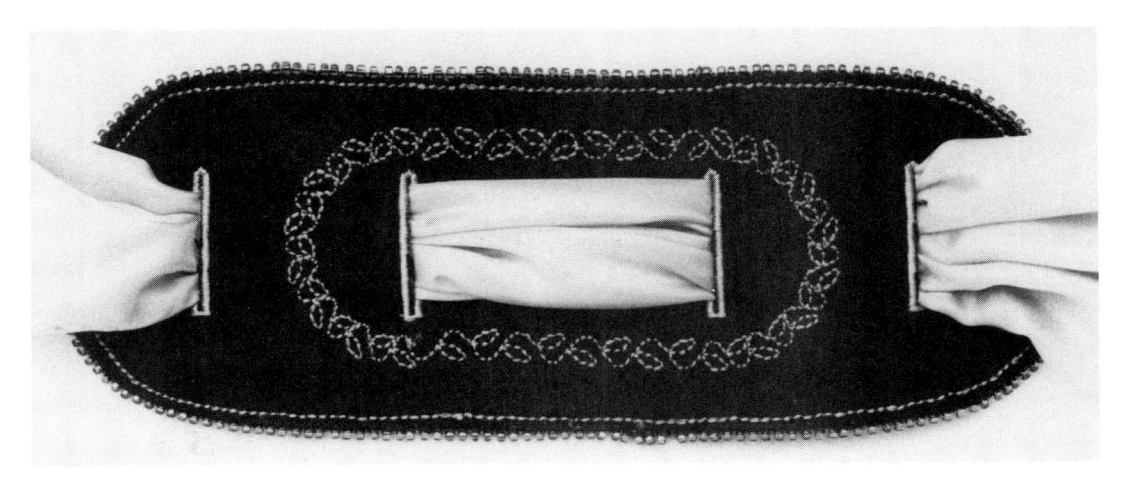

Fig. 11.14 Belt ornament with scarf.

and magenta, etc. Any of these combinations will give an iridescent quality to the stitching when it is stitched on black or a very dark background. There would be some shimmering if these colors were stitched on another color background, but it would not be as strong as when stitched on black.

- Stitch width: auto and medium (3–5); varies
- Stitch length: auto (2–4)
- Needle position: center (left)
- Needle: #90/14
- Feed dogs: up
- Presser feet: transparent zigzag N, buttonhole A, darning spring (optional)
- Fabric suggestions: one piece of fabric 5" (12.7cm) x 10" (25.4cm); two 5" (12.7cm) x 10" (25.4cm) pieces of heavyweight fusibile interfacing; one 5" (12.7cm) x 10" (25.4cm) piece of Wonder-Under; one 5" (12.7cm) x 10" (25.4cm) piece of felt or Ultrasuede; 22" (55.9cm) length of cross-locked beads
- Thread: 2 spools rayon thread as described above to match scarf; one spool sewing thread to match fabric
- Accessories: Oblong scarf 8" (20.3cm) x 54" (1.4m) or ribbon at least 2" (5.1cm) wide x 54" (1.4m); Clo-Chalk or white marking pencil; vanishing marker; thumbtack; masking tape; cork or small eraser

Trace the pattern (Fig. 11.15) onto a piece of paper, transferring all marks. Cut two of heavyweight fusible interfacing and one of Wonder-Under. Transfer marks A, B, C, D, E, and F to one of the pieces of interfacing. Iron this piece of interfacing to the wrong side of your fabric and cut out, adding ½" (12.7cm) seam allowance to the fabric all around the edge. Place pins at the marks and transfer them to the right side, using Clo-Chalk or white marking pencil.

Measure 1" (2.5cm) to the left of the needle and make a mark on the bed of your machine with your vanishing marker. Take a thumbtack and place masking tape over the point and tape the tack so the point matches the mark. Place Point A over the thumbtack and secure with a bit of eraser or a small cork. Move the fabric so the needle enters Point D. Using decorative stitch #98 (#12), stitch half of a circle. Do not raise the presser foot. Slip the eraser off and carefully remove the fabric from

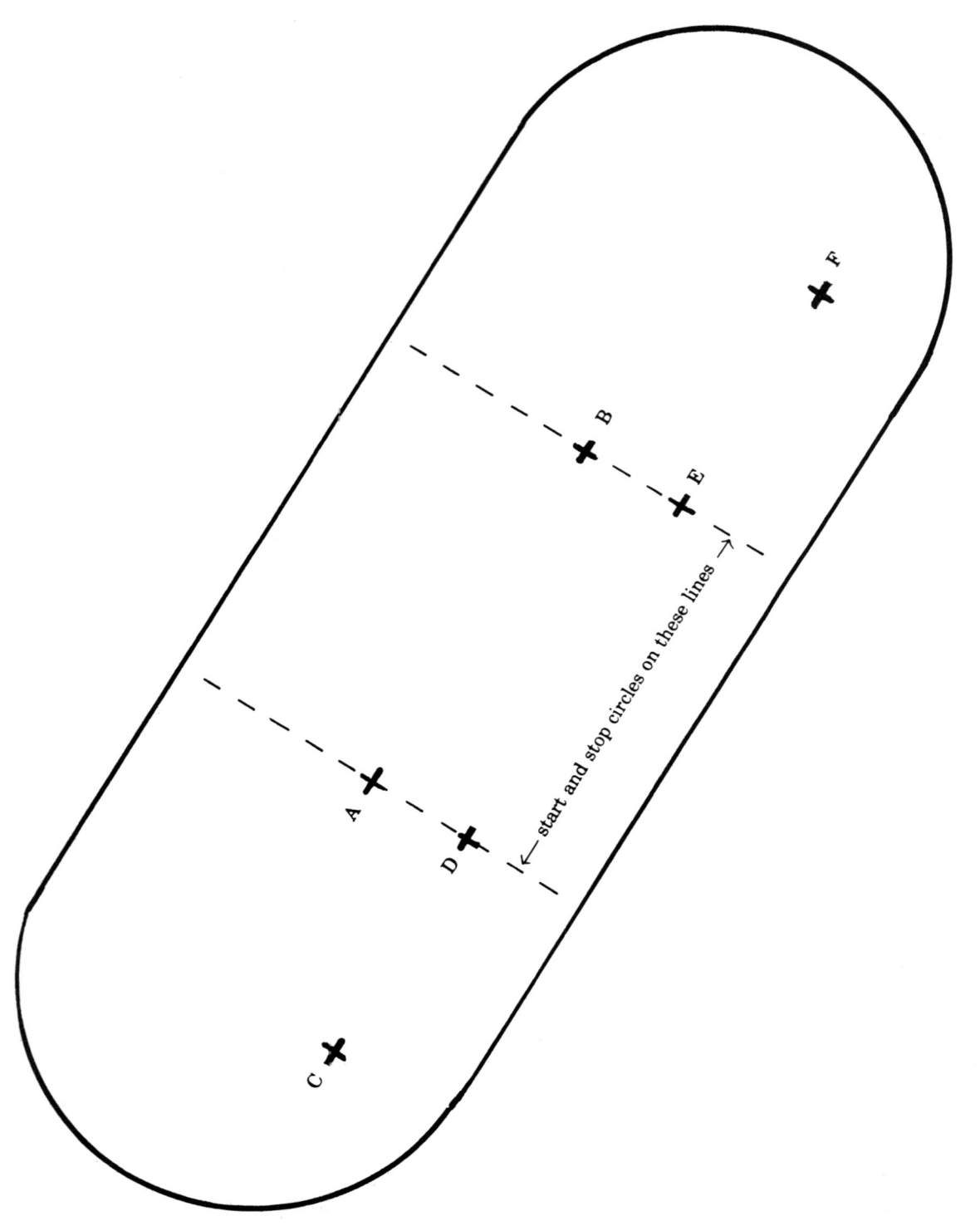

Fig. 11.15 Full-size pattern for belt ornament. Cut along outline shown for interfacing; add seam allowance to fabric only.

the thumbtack. Stitch a straight line until you reach the place that is in line with Point B. Carefully place Point B on the thumbtack. Replace the eraser and stitch another half circle. Again remove the fabric from the thumbtack without raising the presser foot and stitch in a straight line until you reach the starting point.

Remove one spool of thread from the top of the machine. (Or make the buttonholes in the thread to match the fabric if you don't want them to show.) Put on buttonhole foot A and open the back of the foot up as far as possible. It isn't necessary to put a button in the foot. Set the machine for automatic buttonholes. Be sure to pull down the buttonhole lever and position it correctly. Make buttonholes at marks C, D, E, and F. Don't cut them open yet. Remove buttonhole foot A and place transparent zigzag foot N on your machine.

Turn the seam allowance on the fabric to the back and press in place, clipping where necessary on the rounded edges. Thread the machine either with the thread that matches the fabric or the blue and green thread (as I have done) and stitch the edge in place with a straight stitch. Bond the other piece of interfacing to the back of the felt. Cut out the felt, trimming 1/8" (3.2cm) off the interfacing/felt all the way around. Bond a piece of Wonder-Under to the interfacing/felt. Remove the paper and bond to the back of the ornament.

Set the machine for a medium zigzag. Remove the presser foot and slip a darning spring over the needle (or work with a bare needle). Place the cross-locked beads along the edge, beginning in the center of one of the rounded edges (this part will be covered with the scarf). Place the fabric so the left bite of the needle enters the fabric and the right bite stitches in space enclosing the beads. Leave about 1" (2.5cm) of extra beads at the beginning and end in case you have to clean up the area with some hand stitching.

Cut the buttonholes open and thread a scarf or a piece of ribbon through the buttonholes as shown. Tie around your willowy waist.

Lesson 38. Coordinating separate elements

To coordinate the black belt ornament with the blue-green scarf, I used decorative stitching in virtually the same color as the scarf. The completed ornament serves as a transition between the scarf and my black dress. If I simply tied on the scarf without the ornament, I would need to place that color elsewhere on my body (hair or shoe ornament, stitching in a pendant, shoes in the color of the scarf). If you use a strong, contrasting color at least twice in an ensemble (the stitching on the ornament and the color of the scarf), it looks planned; use it once and the accessory appears dubious. The two projects that follow are stitched to coordinate with a certain garment and with each other.

When coordinating separate elements, an important aspect of the stitched line is its scale. Two of the biggest mistakes people make with decorative stitches is sending a weak line and expecting it to make a strong statement and using a strong line when the statement is meant to be subtle.

Become familiar with all of the stitches on your machine. Remember that utility stitches can also be used decoratively. Do lots and lots of samples with different threads, different combinations, different rhythms. Play with the stitches. Make

COMBINATIONS

Fig. 11.16 Combinations of decorative stitches built into "trims."

168

many combinations; then make some more. Keep your mind open and let the lines lead you into other combinations. Work these up on pieces of fabric that are 8″ (20.3cm) x 10″ (25.4cm) and place them in folders in your notebook (Fig. 11.16). Then when you need a stronger statement, you can look through your notebook and find a combination of stitches that will work.

A line, however, doesn't always have to be wider to make a bold statement. Look back at Fig. 11.1, and you'll see that the stitches on the left make a more visible statement than the ones on the right. For one thing you can see them from farther away, and if you want to coordinate two separate elements, the viewer has to be able to see the decoration. For another thing, the scale must be in line with the area it is decorating.

One of my daughters just purchased a classic white shirt on which I stitched one black line of #74 at the top of the pocket (Fig. 11.17) and around the collar. The line decorates the shirt simply, but with a strong statement, and it coordinates the shirt with her black skirt. The scale is appropriate because the line is decorating small areas (the pocket and the collar). The same line would look ridiculous running alone down the length of the sleeve, while a combination of lines doing the same thing could be spectacular.

Black/white is the strongest contrast available, so a single line will read from a great distance. Had she been looking for a shirt to wear with her yellow skirt and found the same one with the line stitched in yellow, it wouldn't have worked. Yellow on white is almost invisible.

Decorative stitched lines have a certain character that is important to consider when you're planning to use them on garments or accessories (Fig. 11.18). The line (#74) used on the blouse makes a sophisticated statement because of the weight of the line and because of the contrast of

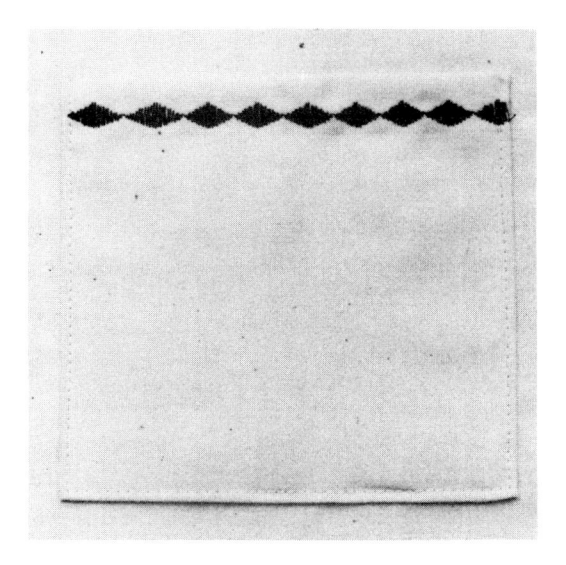

Fig. 11.17 Decorative stitching on a pocket.

Fig. 11.18 Purchased blouse with decorative stitching.

black and white. A line that is the same color as the background is intimate because the viewer must be very close to see it. Stitches that are more open or curved are feminine, while the closer, straight-edged stitches are masculine. The less contrast between the stitching and the background, the more feminine the statement. The pictorial motifs are appropriate for small children's clothing, but they are too cute and too small for anything else.

You will notice that all of the projects in this chapter are small. It's not because I'm lazy, but because I don't like decorative stitches on large areas. If I'm planning to fill a large area, I like to work with appliqué and free-machine embroidery. Then I might add decorative stitches to serve as transition between bits of appliqué, much as Jackie has used single lines to blur an edge (Chapter 4, Lesson 11).

Project
Scarf

I wanted a scarf to wear with my bone-colored Units outfit that would bring one of my better colors next to my face (Fig. 11.19). Then I could wear it when I was tired and everyone would (I hope) com-

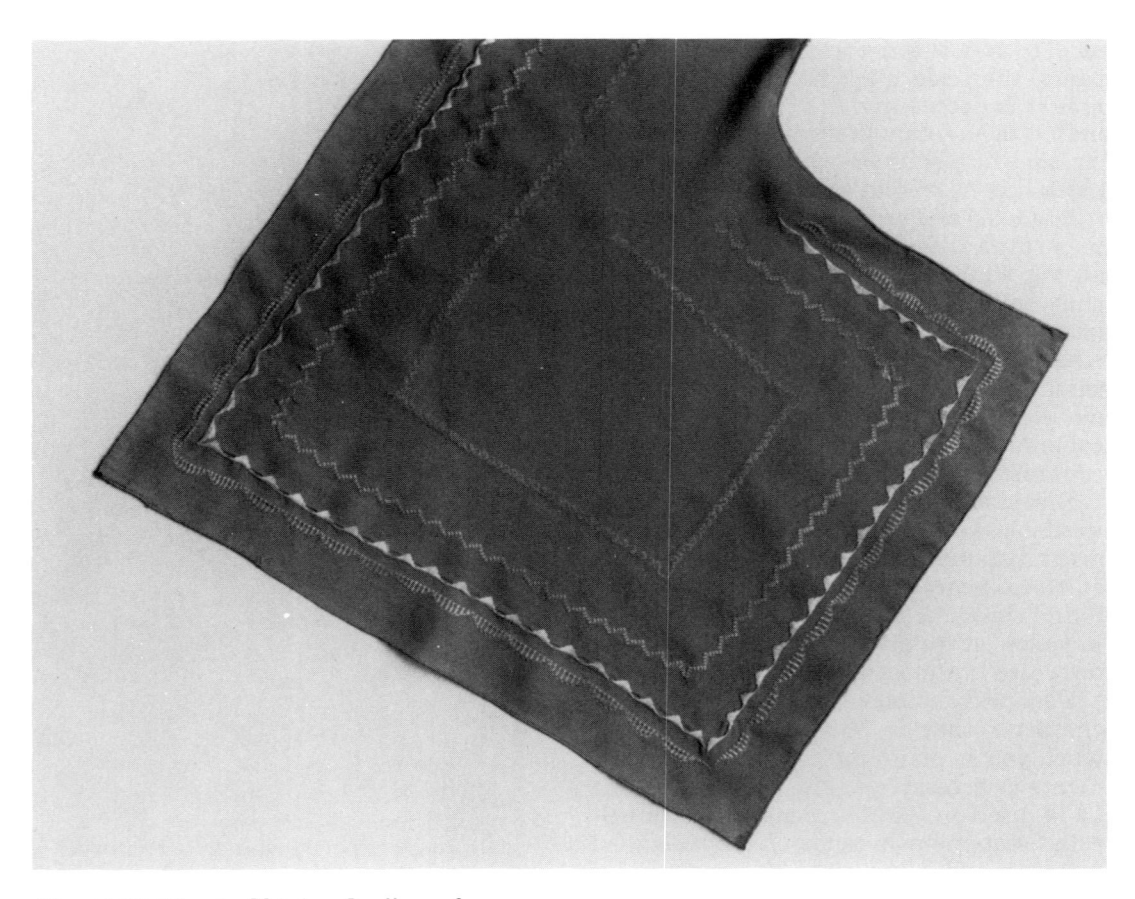

Fig. 11.19 "Sea to Shining Sea" scarf.

ment on how great I looked, instead of how worn-out I appeared. The decoration would bring the color of the dress into the scarf so they would coordinate. I decided to stitch simple lines around the edge of the square part to create a border, a classic use of decorative stitching. I also wanted a line that would echo the edge and highlight the soft folds of the scarf. A complicated design would simply be lost.

Have you ever bought a scarf because it had a beautiful flower on it, and no matter how you tied the scarf, the flower always ended up hiding in the folds? With the decoration along the edge, I eliminated that problem.

I have always had a terrible time keeping scarves tied and where I wanted them to be. When I discovered this one, I was really excited. It is a square with a long rectangle along one end that ends in a loop. You pull one of the corners through the loop and the scarf stays where you put it (Fig. 11.20).

I bought my scarf at the outdoor market in the French Quarter in New Orleans. On a trip to California, a friend told me about a woman in Carmel who was making the same scarf. Later Jackie in Illinois said, "Oh, you mean the Oklahoma scarf." It seems, like dandelions, to have sprung up everywhere. So I decided to be fair and dub it the "Sea to Shining Sea" scarf.

The purchased scarf is two layers with a fold along the long edge (see Fig. 11.21). This eliminates the need for any hems. You simply sew along the edges, leaving the little end open. Turn the scarf through this open end and press. Make a loop 2" (5.1cm) wide by folding this end over and stitching down. But because the silk I chose for this scarf is fairly crisp, I decided to use only one layer and to roll the edges as explained in Chapter 8, Lesson 23.

Stitch width: 4–7 (3–5)
Stitch length: automatic (1/2–5)
Needle position: automatic (center)
Needle: #70/10
Feed dogs: up
Presser foot: transparent zigzag foot N
Decorative stitches: #72, #84, #88, #98
Tension: *top*, 3; *bobbin*, slightly loosened
Fabric suggestion: ½ yd. (45.7cm) China silk or silk broadcloth
Thread: Natesh color #511 or Sulky color #942-2202
Accessories: ruler; vanishing marker

Draft a full-size pattern following the diagram in Fig. 11.21. Place the pattern on your fabric and cut out. Mark the stitching lines with a vanishing marker.

I first did the rows of decorative stitching. I don't normally worry what the underside of my stitching looks like because it seldom shows. In this case, however, it does, so I was careful to balance the stitching as much as possible. To do this I first loosened the bobbin tension screw by a quarter turn, then experimented with the upper tension until I had the best looking stitch on each side. I didn't want to use a paper or tear-away stabilizer because I didn't want to spend hours picking out bits of residue. I tried water-soluble stabilizer which didn't make much difference in the stitching; and no matter how much I rinsed, the silk was still spotted. So I stitched without any stabilizer and pressed the stitched area flat on my superior wool pressing pad (see Chapter 1).

I wanted lines of different visual weights, so I experimented with various

Fig. 11.20 Two ways to wear the "Sea to Shining Sea" scarf.

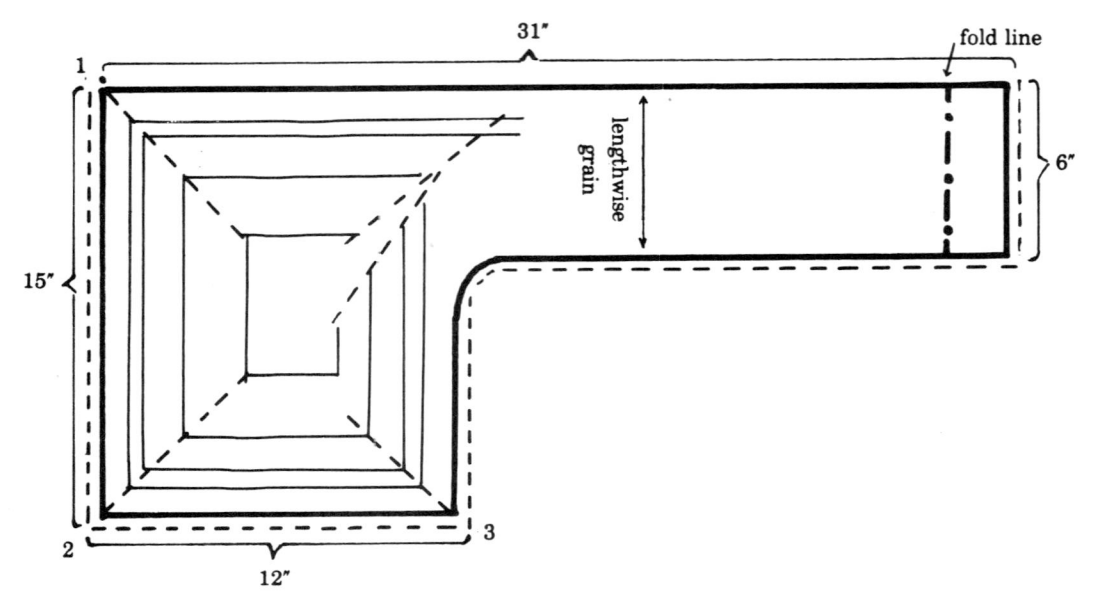

Fig. 11.21 Cutting and stitching diagram for the scarf. Cut it on a fold if you do not want to do a rolled hem.

stitches until I found ones that worked. I also tried several threads and decided on the pastel variegated Natesh thread. It looks like Spring to me and has more interest than the plain, bone-colored thread.

I tired different widths of lines and varying intervals until I made my final choices. I stitched the scarf on the Galaxie, so I chose #88 (open, large scallops), placed #72 close beside it (closed and pointed for contrast). Then I moved further into the middle and stitched #84 (feathery and visually smaller, though it's worked full width). I finished with #98 because I love the curvy, sensuous line and because it reduces nicely in both length and width.

Since this isn't a square scarf, I decided where to start and stop the stitching. My solution is shown on Fig. 11.21. Now the only problem was turning the corners. I used the vanishing marker to draw a straight line from the center of each corner to the middle. As I neared the line each time, I slowed down to see if the motif would end at the turning point. If so, I simply stitched to the line and pivoted.

If, however, it is obvious the motif will not cooperate, finish as near the line as possible. Set the machine for straight stitching and stitch to the marked diagonal line, counting the number of stitches. When you reach the line, pivot the fabric, stitch the same number of straight stitches, and then resume the decorative stitching (Fig. 11.22).

After you complete the decorative stitching, change the thread to one that matches the silk. Be sure to return the bobbin tension to normal, by turning the screw one quarter turn to the right. Set the upper tension to 5. Set your machine for zigzag with a stitch length of 4 (3), width automatic (3). Trim the edge carefully to be sure there are no stray threads before you start. Begin stitching with the right side up. Hold the fabric in front and behind the

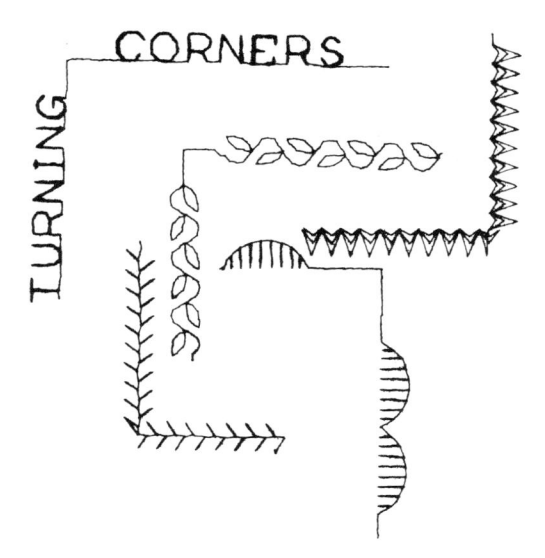

Fig. 11.22 Turning the corner with the decorative stitches on the scarf. Your motif probably will not fall at this exact same spot. Just be sure to count the straight stitches to the turning point and stitch the same number before resuming the decorative stitching.

presser foot, pulling just the slightest bit from behind while holding the fabric taut in front.

When you reach a corner, remove the fabric from the presser foot and pull out about 4" (7.2cm) of thread. Hold this thread *behind* the presser foot. Lower the presser foot and begin stitching in space over the thread in your hand before you reach the corner. Stitch around a second time if necessary. Don't worry too much about how the corners look because when you're all through, you'll trim any excess fabric if necessary. Dab a drop of No-Fray right on the corner and roll gently between your fingers.

Press a narrow hem at the short end. Turn this end over to form a 2" (5.1cm) loop and stitch in place.

Now put the scarf around your neck so the loop is on your right side. Pull corner #2 (Fig. 11.21) through until it's where you want it (about 5" [12.7cm]). You can pull it through even further to make it look like a bow.

A few pages back I said you need to wear an accent color on at least two places on the body to make it look planned. So far, I have my bone Units outfit and a blue-green scarf. I decided to complete the look by making a shoe ornament for my bone pumps that would repeat the color of the scarf. I could have made a bow from the silk scraps and attached it to the shoe, but I was looking for a more subtle statement, one that would be more sophisticated.

Project
Shoe Ornament

I have this mad passion for Italian shoes, but, to put it bluntly, I can't afford to buy them. I dislike absolutely plain shoes. A girl in my elementary school used to design the most exciting spike-heeled shoes. She'd take a notebook and some crayons and draw one shoe to a page, each one more beautiful than the one before. She taught me how to draw the arched foot so I could draw shoes too, but my vision never approached hers. Every time I look at high-heeled shoes with flowers and ribbons and cutouts and stitching, I think of her.

Now I can make my own embellishments with the blank shoe clips I found in my local fabric store. I can look through magazines and shamelessly copy a style if I want (Fig. 11.23), or I can put my own imagination to work and create one of my own.

I had tried Jackie's method for making fringe with one piece of fabric (Chapter 9, Lesson 32), and I was intrigued with the results. The shoe ornament is exactly the right scale for the tiny fringe and for a single line of open decorative stitching, and

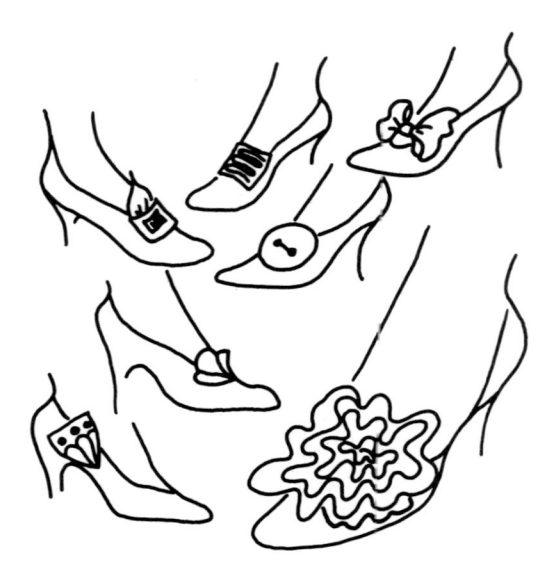

Fig. 11.23 Some ideas for shoe ornaments.

my treasure box had exactly the right button to place in the center (Fig. 11.24).

 Stitch width: varies
 Stitch length: varies
 Needle position: auto (left)
 Needle: #80/12
 Feed dogs: up
 Presser foot: fringe foot, transparent zigzag foot N
 Fabric suggestions: small scrap of silk shantung 3" (7.6cm) x 20" (50.8cm)
 Thread: sewing thread to match shantung; rayon thread in color to match scarf for fringe and decorative stitching; #3 pearl cotton to match fringe; cordonnet
 Accessories: 2 shoe clips; 2 buttons; ruler; scissors; handsewing needle

Cut two pieces of silk shantung 3" (7.6cm) x 10" (25.4cm). Press each piece down the center along the 10" (25.4cm) edge. Grasp one short end at the fold, press your finger against the fold, and tuck into the middle. Press. Repeat at the other end.

This presses a triangular shape into each end.

Look at Chapter 9, Lesson 32 to refresh your memory on the method for making the fringe. Now open the shantung out flat and stitch a row of fringe along the fold line on the right side, beginning and ending 1/4" (6.4cm) inside the pressed triangles at the ends. Carefully refold on the line, smoothing the fringe in place and press, being careful not to disturb the fringe.

Stitch one row of #91 (#13) within a hair of the folded edge to set the fringe. Take a piece of #3 pearl cotton in the same color as the decorative stitching and couch it down with a plain zigzag 3/8" (9.5mm) be-

Fig. 11.24 Shoe ornament. This ornament may be placed on the side and at the heel, as well as at the front of the shoe.

low the stitching. Thread the machine with the sewing thread. Finish the raw edges with a close zigzag and gather by zigzag stitching over cordonnet ¼" (6.4mm) from the edge (Chapter 3, Lesson 7). Pull these gathers very tight, forming a circle.

Tie off the cordonnet and hand stitch this area together, finishing with the button in the center. Stitch the ornament onto a shoe clip. Clip to the shoe wherever you want—in front, to the side, or at the top of the heel.

Lesson 39. Guiding the eye

In addition to highlighting structural details and coordinating separate elements, each of the preceding projects has been designed to guide the viewer's eye to what I want it to see. By connecting the scarf (Fig. 11.19) and the shoe ornament (Fig. 11.24) with the bright colors, I want the viewer to shift his vision between the feet and the face and to skip the body altogether. In creating the belt ornament (Fig. 11.14), I want to draw attention to the center of the waist rather than the circumference. (I also wear a matching black jacket, open at the front, which lets the viewer see only a small part of the scarf at the center front.) I tie a ribbon in my hair that matches the scarf and keeps the viewer's attention between the waist and the top of my head. The shadow appliqué collar (Fig. 11.6) is the same color as the dress, as are the stockings and shoes I wear. Since there is no other ornamentation, the viewer's attention is held at the upper body and face.

Now you understand. Want the viewer to look at your face? Decorate the yoke, collar or neckline. Want him to look at your legs? Decorate the hem or your shoes. Want her to look at your hands? Wear long sleeves and decorate the cuffs. Have a small waist you want the viewer to admire? Wear an elaborate belt. Want to hide a portly neck? Wear a scarf. Want to show off your bust? Wear a pendant. Want to camouflage an ample body? Create a narrow line or a V (right side up or upside down) down the front.

That's taking the big picture. Let's focus down a bit and see how you can guide the eye within a small area, within a design itself. For the next project I've chosen one of Jackie's tote bag square designs—the quilted square from Chapter 7, Lesson 19—to demonstrate that the designs in this book can be used in other applications.

I particularly like the division of space (strong diagonals with areas in which to place both vertical and horizontal lines) within this square because it gives me a chance to discuss another aspect of line, and that is its direction (Fig. 11.25). Vertical and horizontal lines create stability and give a sense of gravity and balance, while diagonal lines suggest imbalance, movement, and vitality.

In terms of covering the body, horizontal lines lead the eye around and make the figure appear shorter and heavier. Vertical lines lead the eye up and down, making the figure appear taller and thinner. Diagonals that intersect into V- shaped lines create an illusion of narrowing or contracting. These lines are the most active, as the eye is drawn up and down.

Project
Purse

I chose black and white for the body of the purse because it affords the strongest contrast and because it shows how the

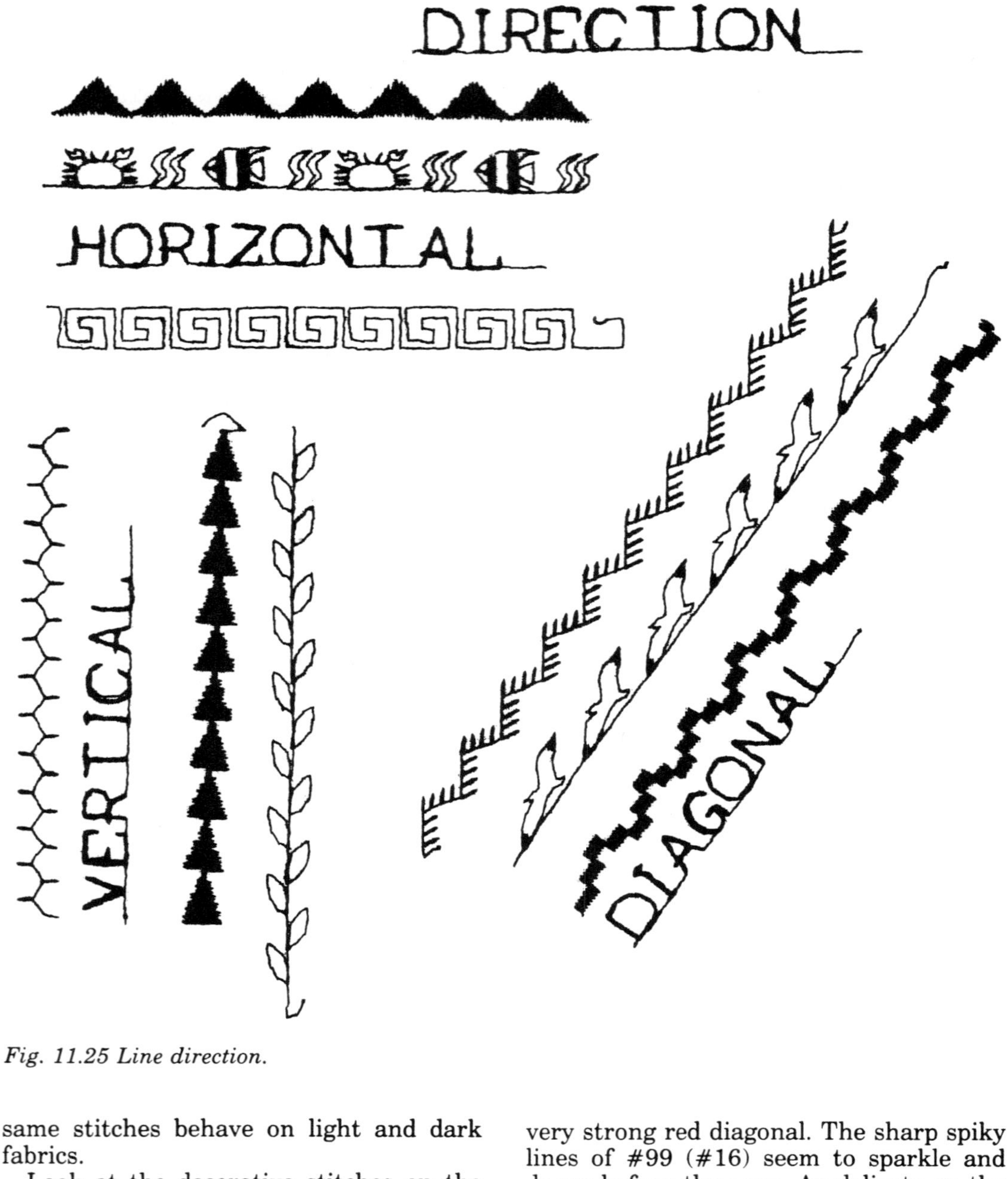

Fig. 11.25 Line direction.

same stitches behave on light and dark fabrics.

Look at the decorative stitches on the purse (Fig. 11.26). The stitches are the same on the black and the white. Thus a continuous line leads the eye across the very strong red diagonal. The sharp spiky lines of #99 (#16) seem to sparkle and dance before the eyes. As delicate as the motifs are, they still enclose the area that contains #69 (#8) — a heavier, more stable line — and create a checkerboard effect.

Fig. 11.26 Purse.

Notice, too, that although the lines are exactly the same distance apart on the black and the white, they appear closer on the black side. You can see that the black lines seem to contract on the white background, while the white lines appear to expand on the black background.

The horizontal lines are placed in the top area for two reasons: Horizontal lines are the least active, so a lot of them can fill a large area without that area overwhelming the rest of the design. And looking from top to bottom, these horizontal lines halt the eye and keep it from running right out the top of the design. Note that there is a slight vertical and diagonal thrust to #99 (#16) which echoes the direction of the other lines.

The vertical lines of #77 (#20) carry the eye up and down. Triple stretch stitch is stitched on either side of #77 (#19) to further emphasize the vertical direction of the lines. If the lines of #77 were placed closer together and the triple stretch stitch removed, you would create an optical illusion called the herringbone effect. The lines would appear to move and shift from larger at the top to smaller at the bottom and vice versa.

The narrow diagonal running from the bottom left to mid-right is left plain and stitched with the heaviest weight lines in the design. This serves as an opposition to the strong red Ultrasuede line. In the lower right-hand corner you can see just two diagonal lines, also heavy with a lot of white space. These reinforce the other diagonal line, contain the vertical lines, and keep your eye moving within the area. The black stitching on the red Ultrasuede is there to soften the edge and integrate it into the square.

Stitch width: varies
Stitch length: varies
Needle position: auto (left)
Needle: #80/12, 2.0mm double needle
Feed dogs: up
Presser foot: transparent zigzag foot N, zipper foot
Decorative stitches: #69, #72, #76, #77, #99, triple stretch stitch (#8, #9, #16, #19, #20, #21)
Tension: *top*, 3 and 5; *bobbin*, normal
Fabric suggestions: 9" (22.9cm) square of white fabric; 12" (30.5cm) x 45" (1.1m) black fabric; a scrap of Ultrasuede and a scrap of felt at least 2" (5.1cm) x 9" (22.9cm); ¼ yd. (22.9cm) heavyweight fusible interfacing; three 9" (22.9cm) squares of fleece; three 9" (22.9cm) squares of tulle; two 9" (22.9cm) squares of cotton for lining
Thread: black cotton #200; white cotton #100; black sewing thread
Accessories: 9" (22.9cm) zipper to match Ultrasuede; vanishing marker; Clo-Chalk or a white marking pencil; ruler

Trace the design in Fig. 11.27 and cut out the pattern. Place the pattern on the fusible interfacing with the adhesive surface up and cut out without adding any

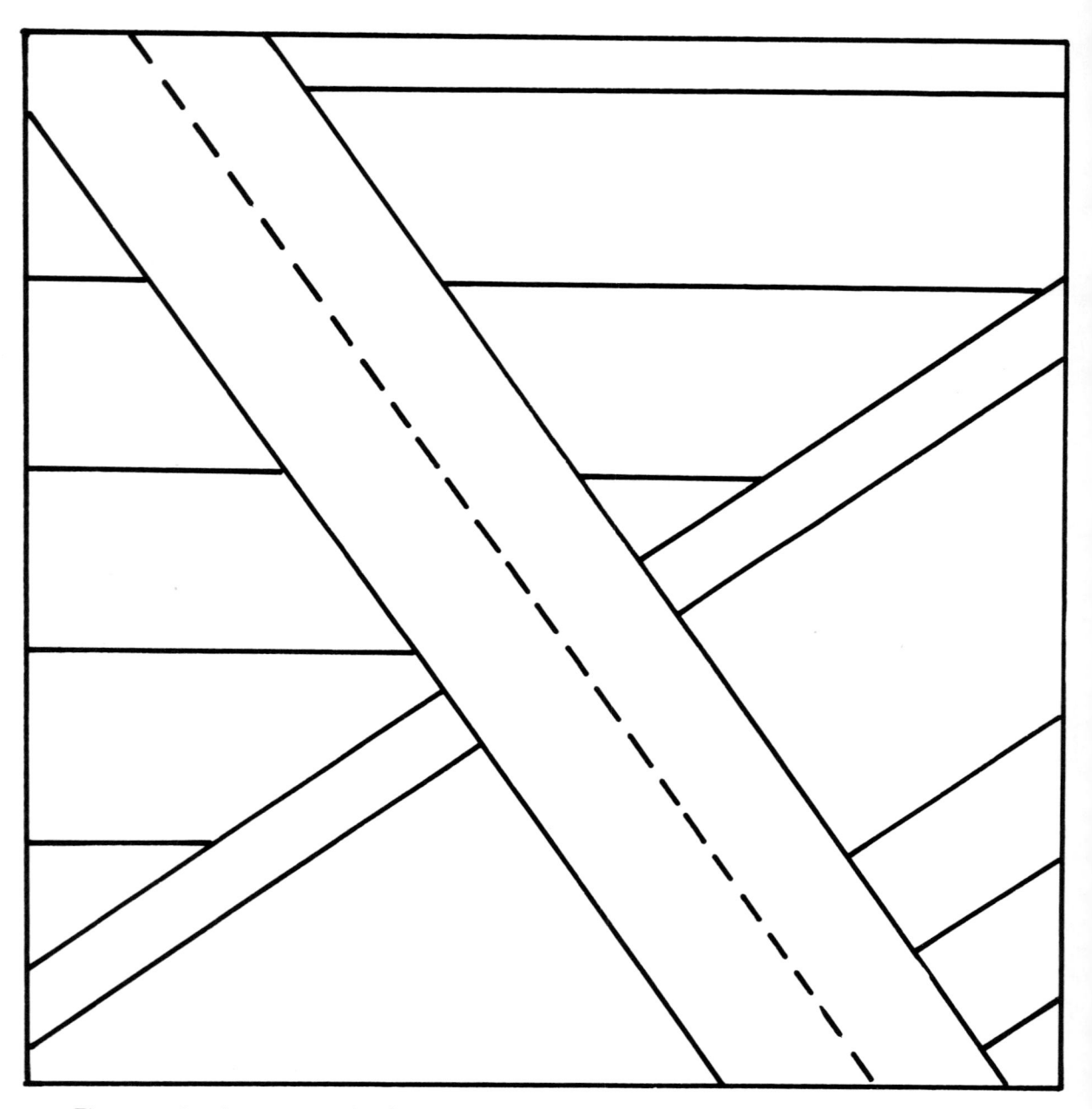

Fig. 11.27 Stitching pattern for the purse.

seam allowances. Cut apart on the middle dotted line. Bond the right piece to white fabric and the left piece to black. Cut out the two pieces, adding about 1" (2.5cm) all the way around each piece.

Join the two pieces in the center and press the seam open. Now mark the stitching lines on the front of the fabric using Clo-Chalk or white marking pencil on the black and a vanishing marker on the white.

You will stitch with white thread on the black and black thread on the white. Stitch vertical rows of #77 (#20) starting in the lower left corner with white thread on the black fabric. Work up and down, stopping on the first marked diagonal line, and using the outside edge of the transparent zig-zag foot N as a spacing guide. Finish up the stitching with a triple stretch stitch (#21, stitch width 0) on either side of #77 (#20). Clip all your threads on the front and remove any stitches which have strayed into the diagonal area.

Now work the horizontal pattern by stitching #99 (#16) on the marked lines. Stitch slightly into but not across the center diagonal area where the red Ultrasuede will eventually go. Cut off the thread ends. Next stitch a row of #69 (#8) right beneath this row and finish with another row of #99 (#16) in the opposite direction from the first row. Stitch four rows of this combination. Work a close satin stitch on the diagonal lines that run from lower left to upper right. Stitch slightly over the rows of vertical stitching to lock the thread ends.

When you finish stitching the black side, thread the machine with black #100 thread and stitch the same patterns in the white area. Stitch the heavy diagonal pattern #72 (#8) on the lower right diagonal lines. Add a line of triple stretch stitch (#21, stitch width 0) just above #72 (#8). Cut off all thread ends on the right side, but do not cut the thread ends on the wrong side.

Cut the piece of Ultrasuede to fit the center line and cut a piece of felt that is just slightly narrower to pad the area. Place the felt and Ultrasuede in position and stitch the edges down using two strands of black thread on the top and pattern #76 (#29). Trim the square to allow ½" (1.2cm) seam allowance all around.

Cut out one 9" (22.9cm) square of black fabric. To quilt the back side of the purse, make a sandwich of the solid black square right side up, one piece of fleece in the middle, and a piece of tulle behind. Put the 2.0mm double needle on the machine, activate the double needle button, and thread the machine with black thread. Mark vertical stitching lines every 1¼" (3.2cm) with Clo-Chalk or white marking pencil. Stitch along the marked lines with a straight stitch.

Take the pattern and mark the seam lines on the front. Trim to within ½" (12.7cm) of the line. Repeat this procedure (sandwich of lining, fleece, and tulle; double line quilting; and trimming) for the two lining pieces.

Remove the presser foot and the double needle from the machine. Turn off the double needle light. Put on the #80/12 needle and the zipper foot. Right sides together, place the zipper's woven-in stitching line along the seam line on the front piece with the top tab-end of the zipper tape in line with the side seam allowance. The other end of the zipper will extend beyond the seam allowance. *Stitch with a large stitch to baste the zipper in place and to create a line along which you will stitch the next step. Place the lining on top of the zipper and purse front, right sides together, and make a zipper sandwich — the outer piece, the zipper, and the lining. Stitch along the previous stitching line.** Open out and repeat from * to ** for the back side of the purse.

Cut a piece of black fabric 1¼" (3.2cm) x 45" (1.1cm) for the shoulder strap and holders. Bring the two long sides together and press. Open out, bring each side edge to the middle, and press. Again press the center fold and stitch carefully along both sides about 1/16" (1.6mm) from the edge.

Cut off two 4" (7.2cm) pieces for the strap holders. Bring the two cut ends of these holders together. Open the purse out flat and place the strap holders on top of the zipper at each end with the loops pointing toward each other. Stitch on the holders, sewing right through the zipper at the bottom end.

Replace the zipper foot with the transparent zigzag foot N. Open the zipper (or you won't be able to turn the purse right side out). With right sides together, match the back and front. Treating the bag and lining as one fabric, stitch each side from the top down. Stitch the bottom seam.

Trim the seam allowances to ¼" (6.4mm) and overcast the edges with a close zigzag. Clip corners. Turn the bag through the zipper to the right side. Take the strap and slip each end through a holder. Adjust the length and stitch the end to the strap, being careful that it does not twist. (Optional: Make a zipper pull by slipping a ⅛"-wide strip of Ultrasuede through the hole in the zipper tab. Sew a doubled square of Ultrasuede at the end of the strip to secure the ends).

That completes the accessories for your wardrobe. Now it's your turn to be the designer. Remember: never put a line somewhere merely for the sake of making a mark. Ask yourself if you have created a unified whole. Does the line look stuck on, or is there a real reason for it? If you don't know why you're stitching a line, don't do it.

Ask yourself what it is you want of the line. Do you merely wish to introduce a color into a plain area so that two pieces relate—as in the shoe ornaments and the scarf or the black and white areas of the purse? Do you wish to attract the eye to a more desirable part of your figure and away from less attractive areas? Do you need this line to reinforce or create an edge, to highlight a structural detail? The whole purpose is to captivate the viewer's eye and to direct it along the visual path you have chosen. You can visually "sculpt" your figure. Now aren't you glad you own a Brother sewing machine?

CHAPTER **12**

Making the Tote Bag

The year I became program chairman for an embroiderer's guild, I began to assess previous programs: Why was one a success, another a failure? I remembered the many needlework workshops I had taken, the many projects I had started in those classes and never finished because they were too big or demanded too much of my time. And I knew I wasn't the only one who felt this way, as other members also had boxes of half-finished needlework.

That's when I came up with the idea of the tote bag. I asked the teachers that year to gear their workshops toward making samples small enough to fit in a 6" (15.2cm) square frame. The fabric squares could then fit into the frames made by the handles on a tote bag I designed. Each new square could easily slip in and out. Not only were the class projects small enough to complete easily, but they were useful and decorative as well.

I'm using the same tote bag for this book (Fig. 12.1). After you've made the tote bag, it can be used to show off the sample squares found in the lessons.

First, I'll explain how to finish the squares you made throughout the lessons in this book. Then I'll explain the tote bag.

Finishing the squares

Specific instructions for each square are included in the lessons. A brief recap: Start with a piece of fabric large enough to fit in a 7" (17.8cm) hoop, if you will be working with one. I suggest starting with a 9" (22.9cm) square, as it is better to have extra fabric than not enough. The finished square will be 6¾" (17.1cm). The area that will show in the frame will be 6" (15.2cm) square. Cut a piece of acetate or cardboard 6¾" (17.1cm) square to use as a template.

After completing the embroidery, quilting, appliqué—whatever the lesson calls for—center the acetate pattern over the

Fig. 12.1 The tote bag, with one of the squares in position on the pocket.

181

square. Draw a line at the edge of the acetate all the way around with a vanishing marker or the Clo-chalk.

Back the square with stiff fabric, fleece, or iron-on interfacing if it is not stiff enough for the pocket. Stitch along the line you've drawn and cut off the extra fabric to that line.

Slip typing paper or heavy tear-away stabilizer under the square. Finish by satin stitching at the widest setting around the edge. Dab the corners with No-Fray or Fray-Check to keep them from raveling.

Glue or stitch Velcro dots under the corner of each square to correspond to the ones in the pocket frame. (If the square is stiff enough, this will not be necessary.) An alternative to Velcro is an idea from Marilyn Tisol of Hinsdale, Illinois. She backs each square she makes by first cutting a piece of plastic canvas the size of the square; then she attaches the fabric square to it by whipping the edges together. The plastic is rigid enough to keep the square in the frame.

Tote bag construction

My tote bag is made of canvas, but it can be made of any heavy-duty fabric. I used canvas because I wanted a bag that would stand by itself. If the fabric you've chosen is not heavy enough, press a layer of fusible webbing between two layers of material. Whatever you choose, pre-wash and press all fabrics before you cut.

Supplies:
1½ yards (1.4m) of 36" (0.9m) canvas (includes body of bag, handles, pockets, and bottom of bag)
3⅛ yards (3m) of 1" (2.5cm) wide fusible webbing
Teflon pressing sheet
Four Velcro dots
Sewing thread to match canvas, or monofilament
Rotary cutter and mat are timesavers
24" × 6" (60.9 × 15.2cm) plastic ruler
Vanishing marker, pencil or sliver of soap
Transparent zigzag foot N
Jeans needle

My tote (see color insert) is made up of many colors and looks as if Dr. Seuss invented it. It includes royal blue for the bottom, yellow pockets, green handles, and red for the body of the bag.

I chose those colors because the striped lining fabric included them all. I backed the lining with Pellon fleece and quilted down each stripe to give my bag even more body. I added pockets to the lining, too.

Lining is optional, but if you choose to include one, you will need another piece of fabric at least 34" × 20" (86.4cm × 50.8cm). Add 20" × 20" (50.8cm × 50.8cm) to this if you wish to make pockets for your lining.

The layout of the bag is provided in Fig. 12.2; note that the layout is predicated on cutting all pieces from a single length of cloth, rather than several different colors.

Body of bag:
34" × 20" (0.85m × 50.8cm)

1. Cut out fabric. Fold in half and notch bottom on both sides, 17" (43.2cm) from top. Draw a line between the notches on the inside (Fig. 12.3).

2. Place a 1" (2.5cm) strip of fusible webbing along both 20" (50.8cm) edges on the right side of the bag and fuse in place using the Teflon pressing sheet. Fold at the top of the webbing to the backside. Press the fold, using the Teflon pressing sheet on top to protect your iron. Then fold over 1" (2.5cm) again, using the pressing sheet *between* the fusible webbing and the body of the bag.

3. Mark a line down the length of this piece 6¼" (15.8cm) from each side, as shown in Fig. 12.4 to use later as guidelines for construction of the bag.

Pockets: 10" × 20"
(25.4cm × 50.8cm); cut 2

1. Use the ruler and marking pen to indicate stitching lines from top to bottom—

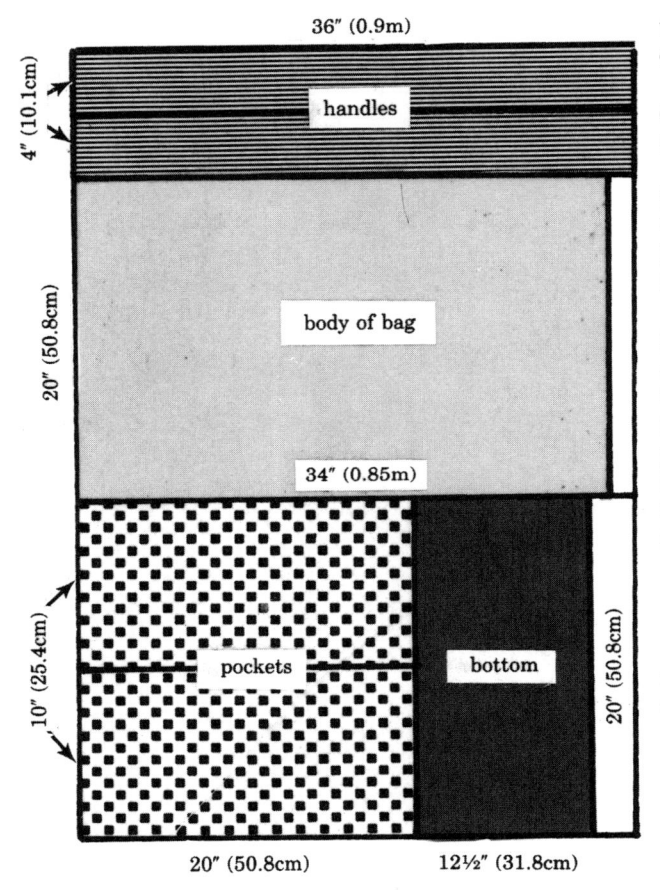

Fig. 12.2 Layout for the tote bag.

the fabric. This middle flap creates the top of the frame.

3. Stitch across the top of all three pockets ⅛" (3.2mm) from the top edge. Do this on both pocket pieces.

4. Then stitch across side pocket sections through all three layers of fabric at ⅛" (3.2mm) from each bottom fold. Finish both side pockets on both pocket pieces this way (Fig. 12.5B).

5. Open out the top of the middle sections on both pocket pieces to enable you to stitch across the folds without stitching them to the pockets. Stitch across the 7½" (19.1cm) middle sections on both pocket pieces at ⅛" (3.2mm) from each bottom fold. This flap will create the top of the frames in which you'll slip the 6" (15.2mm) squares.

Handles: 4" × 36" (10.2cm × 0.9m); cut 2

1. Stitch down one long side 1" (2.5cm) from edge. Fold. Do the same with the other side. (This stitching is used as a guide to

6¼" (15.8cm) from each side. Center area will be 7½" (19.1cm).

2. Cut slits 1½" (3.8cm) down from the top on these lines. Make a mark ¾" (19.0mm) from the top and another ¾" (19.0mm) down from the first. Draw lines through those marks across the top of the pockets (Fig. 12.5A). It is easier if you mark the middle section on the *back* of the fabric, so you'll be able to see the lines as you fold. Fold on the lines as follows: Each side should be folded twice toward the inside of the bag. The middle 7½" (19.1cm) should be folded twice toward the front of

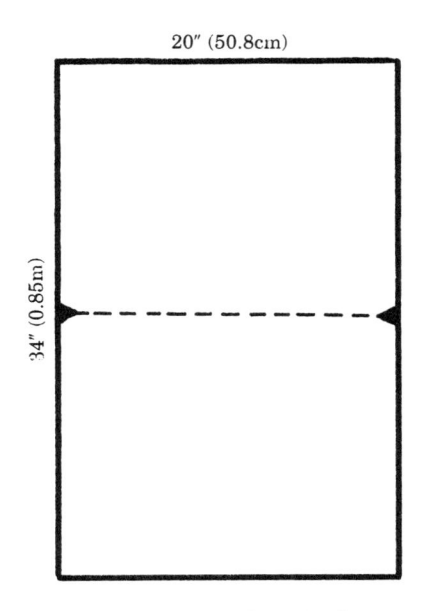

Fig. 12.3 Notch and mark the inside of the bag.

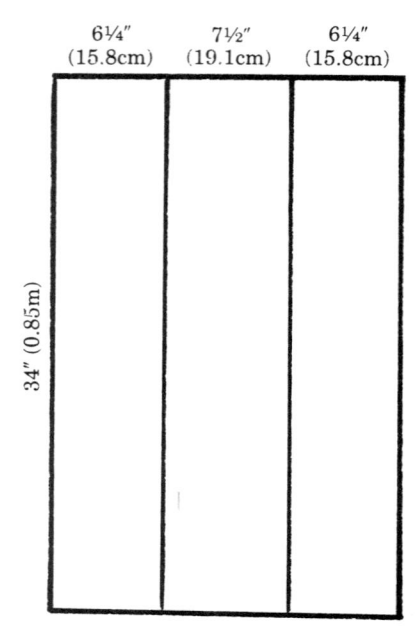

Fig. 12.4 Mark the outside of the bag.

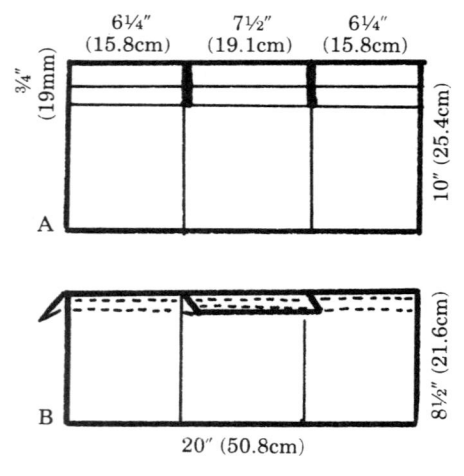

Fig. 12.5 Pocket construction. A. Mark lines to indicate the pockets. Then mark lines across the pockets, ¾" (19.0mm) and 1½" (3.8cm) from the top. Cut down 1½" (3.8cm) between the pockets. B. Fold the tops of the side pockets to the back, the top of the middle pocket to the front.

make folding the handles easier and more accurate.) Bring folded edges together and fold again, creating the 1" (2.5cm) wide handles. Place strips of 1" (2.5cm) fusible webbing inside the length of the handles and press to fuse. The handle is four layers (plus fusible webbing) thick (Fig. 12.6).

2. Topstitch both sides ⅛" (3.2mm) from edge. Use the edging foot with needle position at far left. Then sew ¼" (6.3mm) in from those lines of stitches on both sides.

Bottom: 12½" × 20" (31.8cm × 50.8cm)

1. Fold over 1" (2.5cm) top and bottom along the 20" (50.8cm) edges and topstitch across ⅛" (3.2mm) from the fold. Draw a line ¾" (19.0mm) from each fold.

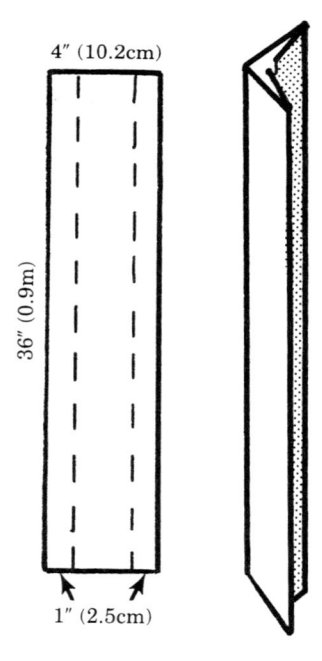

Fig. 12.6 Stitch down the length of the handles 1" (2.5cm) from each side. Fold down 1" (2.5cm) at each side, the length of the handle. Then fold the handle in half. Place strip of fusible webbing inside and press in place. Stitch the handles together.

2. Fold the bottom in half the long way and notch on the fold on both sides, 6¼" (15.8cm) from top and bottom (Fig. 12.7).

Assembly

1. First sew pockets to the bag. The pockets will be 3" (7.5cm) from the top. (Remember that the bag has been folded over 2" (5.1cm) at the top. Measure from the top of the last fold. Line up the markings, 6¼" (15.9cm) from each side on bag and pockets and pin in place. Stitch on the lines you've drawn to create pockets and, using a ¼" (6.3mm) seam allowance, stitch down each side and across the bottoms of the pocket pieces.

2. Sew handles next. Find the center of the bag by folding it double the long way. Measure 3" (7.6cm) from the center to each side of the bag and make a mark with the water-erasable pen; 6" (15.2cm) will be open in center. Using the 24" × 6" (60.9cm × 15.2cm) ruler, draw guidelines through these marks the length of the bag. Pin handles in place outside those lines. Stitch across the bottom of the handles and up, ⅛" (3.2mm) from the edge, on the existing outside stitching. Extend your stitching all the way to the top of the bag. Do this on the next outside lines as well (you will often stitch on top of other lines of stitching). The top edge of the bag will not be sewn down until later, but sew through the folds as you attach the handles.

3. To make the open frame, stitch only the top of the handles above the pockets on both sides. Leave ¾" (19.0mm) around the frame to insert workshop squares (Fig. 12.8).

4. Attach bottom next. Match notches with those of the bag and pin the bottom in place. Stitch over the ⅛" (3.2mm) stitching line to ¾" (19.0mm) from each side of the center pocket (see Fig. 12.8). *Do not* stitch across the center pocket. Then stitch all across the bottom piece on the ¾" (19.0mm) mark. This will create the bottom of the frame. Double check. Is the frame done correctly? Be sure you can slip a fabric square inside.

5. Finish the side edges of the bag with a zigzag stitch (Fig. 12.9). Then put it all together. Fold at center bottom notches with right sides together. Check to see that pockets and bottom meet at each side. Stitch in a ⅝" (15.9mm) seam line from top to bottom. Now refold the top edge of the bag and press in place to fuse. Topstitch in place at the top edge and bottom fold.

6. Bag corners should be finished this way: On the inside, pinch the bottom by matching the side seam with the line drawn across the inside of the bottom of the bag (Fig. 12.10). Measure, on the seam line, 2" (5.1cm) from the point. Draw a line across. Be sure it is exact on each side so stitching is perpendicular to the side seams. Stitch on drawn line for corners. This forms the bottom of the bag. If you wish to cut a piece of ⅛" (3.2mm) Masonite or linoleum tile to fit the bottom, do so now before you line your bag.

7. Press one side of four adhesive-backed Velcro dots into the four corners of the frame.

Lining

If you line your bag, create the lining as if making another bag. Do not include bottom, pockets or handles. However, if you wish to add pockets to the lining, then cut out two pieces of 10" × 20" (25.4cm × 50.8cm) fabric, the same size as the bag pockets. At the top of each pocket piece, turn over 1" (2.5cm) two times and sew

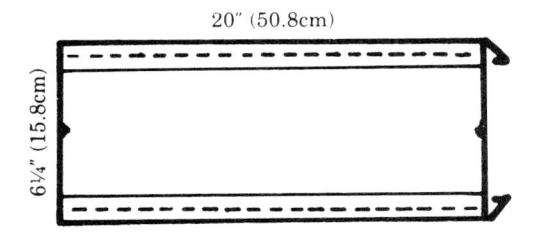

Fig. 12.7 Follow this diagram to fold, mark and stitch the bottom piece of the bag.

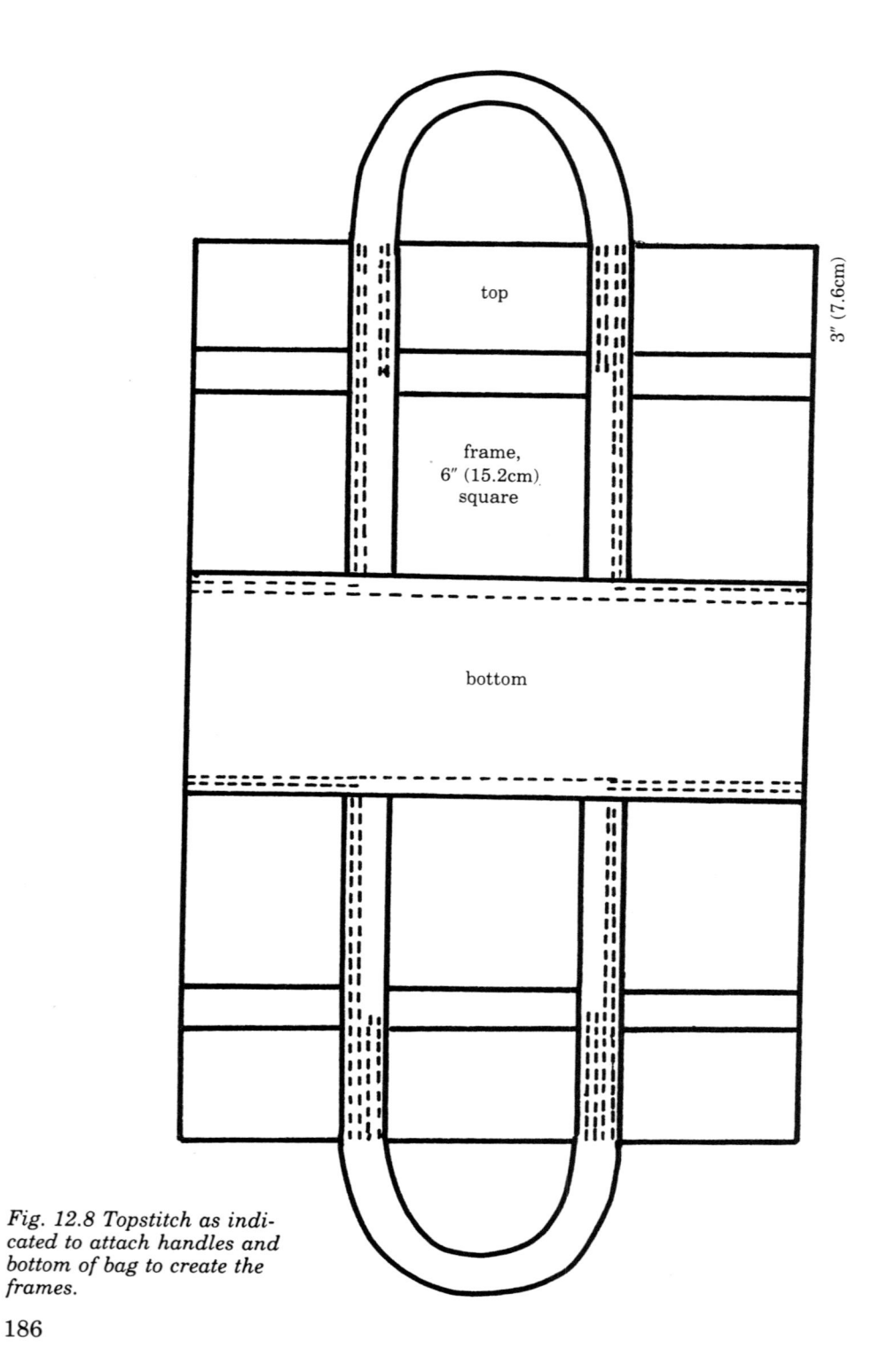

Fig. 12.8 Topstitch as indicated to attach handles and bottom of bag to create the frames.

Fig. 12.9 Finish the edges with zigzag stitches. With right sides together, stitch each side of the tote bag.

Fig. 12.10 Make the tote bag corners by stitching lines perpendicular to the side seams, 2" (5.1cm) up from the points.

down at the top and at the fold. Press up 1" (2.5cm) at the bottom. Place the pocket pieces 3" (7.6cm) from the top of the lining and pin in place. Sew across the bottom of the pocket at the fold and ¾" (19.0mm) from the first stitching line. (The double line of stitching will add strength to the pockets.) Then attach the pockets to the sides of the lining by stitching down on each side with a ¼" (6.3mm) seam allowance. With a ruler and water-erasable marker, draw lines down the pocket pieces to indicate where you will divide the fabric for pockets. Stitch those in place.

Sew up the sides of the lining, using a ⅝" (15.9mm) seam allowance) and create the bottom corner. Fold over the top as you did for the bag. I use the double fold for stability.

Whip stitch invisibly by hand around the top to keep the lining and bag together. With heavy canvas, you may prefer to make the lining and then place wrong sides together (bag and lining) and machine stitch around the top.

AFTERWORD

Know Your Brother could go on forever, as there is no way to include, in one book, everything that can be accomplished by your machine.

I hope you're inspired to experiment, to fill your notebook with samples, and to take those long-cuts, choosing decorative over mundane.

A Brief History of Brother International

Brother International Corporation began in Japan in 1908 as a sewing machine repair and parts production business known as the Yasui Sewing Machine Company. The name *Brother* was chosen in 1928 upon production of the first sewing machine, an industrial model. But it wasn't until the 1930s that Brother was officially incorporated and entered the home sewing market.

Brother International expanded into the knitting machine market in the 50s and into the business world with typewriters in the 60s. When the first high-speed Brother printer was developed in 1971, the 10,000,000th sewing machine moved off the production line. The 80s have seen the production of the 10,000,000th typewriter and the 10,000,000th knitting machine.

Today, Brother manufactures electronic typewriters in the United States through a subsidiary, BIUS, in Bartlett, Tennessee. Production of knitting and sewing machines, electrical home appliances, printers, and word processors continues in Japan and the United Kingdom. United States operations are supervised from corporate headquarters in Piscataway, New Jersey.

Brother Presser Feet and Attachments

Standard Feet and Accessories Available for Brother Models 940 and 950

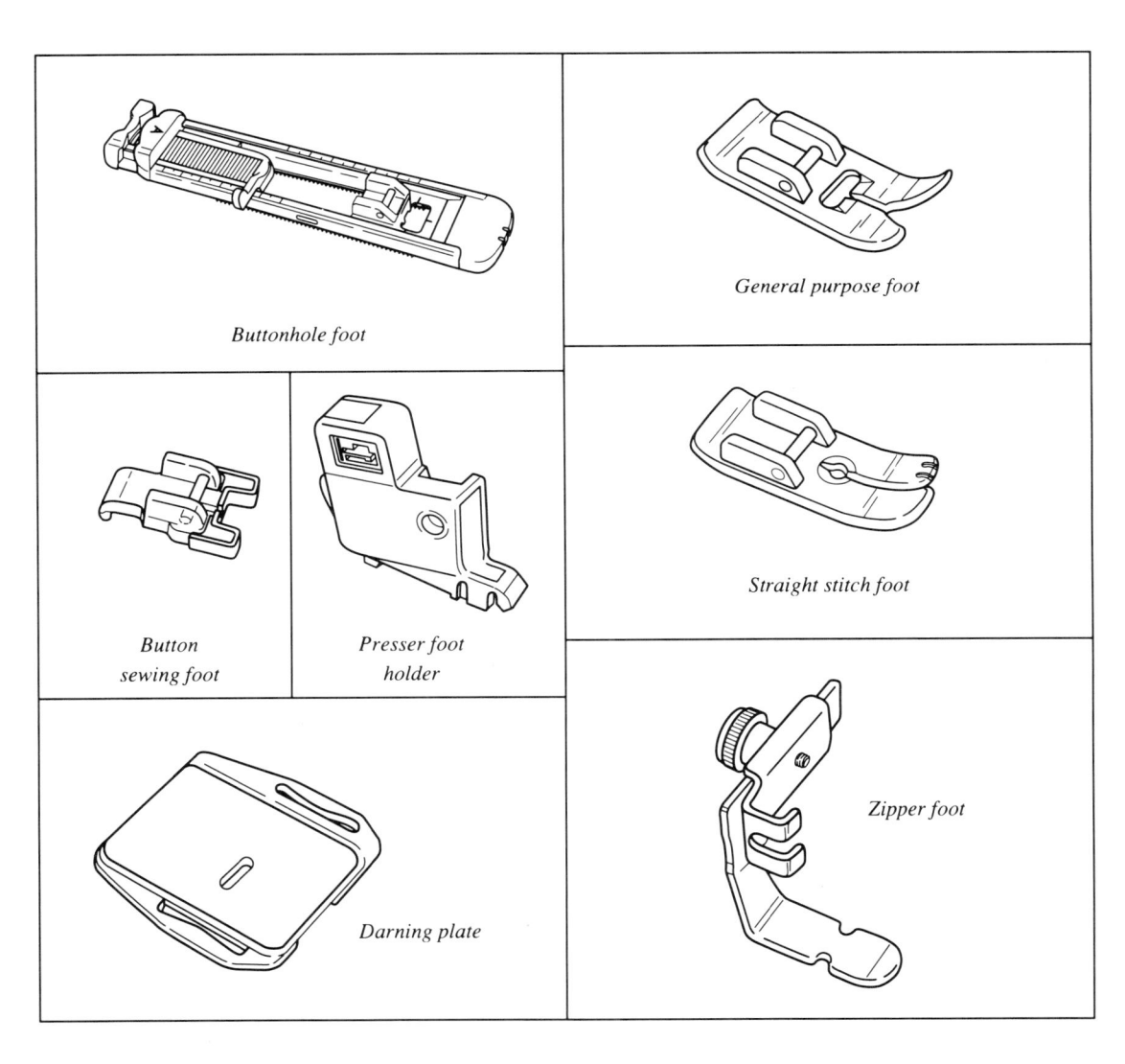

Buttonhole foot

General purpose foot

Button sewing foot

Presser foot holder

Straight stitch foot

Darning plate

Zipper foot

Sources of Supply

Sewing Machine Company
Brother International Corporation
8 Corporate Place
Piscataway, NJ 08855

(**Note**: The following listings were adapted with permission from *The Complete Book of Machine Embroidery* by Robbie and Tony Fanning [Chilton, 1986].)

Threads
Note: Ask your local retailer or send a pre-addressed stamped envelope to the companies below to find out where to buy their threads.

Extra-fine
Assorted threads
    Robison-Anton Textile Co.
    175 Bergen Blvd.
    Fairview, NJ 07022

DMC 100% cotton, Sizes 30 and 50
    The DMC Corporation
    107 Trumbull Street
    Elizabeth, NJ 07206

Dual-Duty Plus Extra-fine, cotton-wrapped polyester
    J&PCoats/Coats & Clark
    30 Patewood Dr., Suite 351
    Greenville, SC 29615

Madeira threads
    Madeira Co.
    56 Primrose Drive
    O'Shea Industrial Park
    Laconia, NH 03246

Mettler Metrosene Fine Machine Embroidery cotton, Size 60/2
    Swiss-Metrosene, Inc.
    Wm. E. Wright Co.
    South Street
    West Warren, MA 01092

Natesh 100% rayon, lightweight
    Aardvark Adventures
    PO Box 2449
    Livermore, CA 94550

Paradise 100% rayon
    D&E Distributing
    199 N. El Camino Real #F-242
    Encinitas, CA 92024

Sulky 100% rayon, Sizes 30 and 40
    Speed Stitch, Inc.
    PO Box 3472
    Port Charlotte, FL 33949

Zwicky 100% cotton, Size 30/2
    White Sewing Machine Co.
    11750 Berea Rd.
    Cleveland, OH 44111

Ordinary
Dual Duty Plus, cotton-wrapped polyester—see Dual Duty Plus Extra-fine

Also Natesh heavyweight, Zwicky in cotton and polyester, Mettler Metrosene in 30/2, 40/3, 50/3, and 30/3, and Metrosene Plus

Metallic
    Madeira Co. (see address above)

Troy Thread & Textile Corp.
2300 W. Diversey Ave.
Chicago, IL 60647
    Free catalog

YLI Corporation
45 West 300 North
Provo, UT 84601

Machine-Embroidery Supplies
(hoops, threads, patterns, books, etc.)

    Aardvark Adventures
    PO Box 2449
    Livermore, CA 94550
        Also publishes "Aardvark Territorial Enterprise"

Clotilde Inc.
1909 SW First Ave.
Ft. Lauderdale, FL 33315

Craft Gallery Ltd.
PO Box 8319
Salem, MA 01971

D&E Distributing
199 N. El Camino Real #F-242
Encinitas, CA 92024

Verna Holt's Machine Stitchery
PO Box 236
Hurricane, UT 84734

Lacis
2982 Adeline St.
Berkeley, CA 94703

Nancy's Notions
PO Box 683
Beaver Dam, WI 53916
    Catalog $.60 in stamps

Patty Lou Creations
Rt 2, Box 90-A
Elgin, OR 97827

Sew-Art International
PO Box 550
Bountiful, UT 84010
    Catalog $2

Speed Stitch, Inc.
PO Box 3472
Port Charlotte, FL 33952
    Catalog $2

SewCraft
Box 1869
Warsaw, IN 46580
    Also publishes newsletter/catalog

Treadleart
25834 Narbonne Ave.
Lomita, CA 90717

Sewing Machine Supplies

The Button Shop
PO Box 1065
Oak Park, IL 60304
    Presser feet

Sewing Emporium
1087 Third Avenue
Chula Vista, CA 92010
    Presser feet, accessories

Miscellaneous

Applications
871 Fourth Ave.
Sacramento, CA 95818
    Release Paper for appliqué

Berman Leathercraft
145 South St.
Boston, MA 02111
    Leather

Cabin Fever Calicoes
PO Box 54
Center Sandwich, NH 03227

Clearbrook Woolen Shop
PO Box 8
Clearbrook, VA 22624
    Ultrasuede scraps

The Fabric Carr
170 State St.
Los Altos, CA 94022
    Sewing gadgets

The Green Pepper Inc.
941 Olive Street
Eugene, OR 97401
    Outdoor fabrics, patterns—$1 catalog

Home-Sew
Bethlehem, PA 18018
    Lace—$.25 catalog

Libby's Creations
PO Box 16800 Ste. 180
Mesa, AZ 85202
    Horizontal spool holder

LJ Originals, Inc.
516 Sumac Pl.
DeSoto, TX 75115
    TransGraph

Lore Lingerie
3745 Overland Ave.
Los Angeles, CA 90034
    1 lb. of silk remnants, $9.45

Newark Dressmaker Supply
PO Box 2448
Lehigh Valley, PA 18001

Osage Country Quilt Factory
400 Walnut
Overbrook, KS 66524
    Washable fabric spray glue

The Pellon Company
119 West 40th St.
New York, NY 10018
    Machine appliqué supplies

The Perfect Notion
115 Maple St.
Toms River, NJ 08753
    Sewing supplies

Salem Industries, Inc.
PO Box 43027
Atlanta, GA 30336
    Olfa cutters, rulers

Solar-Kist Corp.
PO Box 273
LaGrange, IL 60525
    Teflon pressing sheet

Summa Design
Box 24404
Dayton, OH 45424
    Charted designs for knitting needle machine sewing

Susan of Newport
Box 3107
Newport Beach, CA 92663
    Ribbons and laces

Tandy Leather Co.
PO Box 791
Ft. Worth, TX 76101
    Leather

Theta's School of Sewing
2508 N.W. 39th Street
Oklahoma City, OK 73112
    Charted designs for knitting needle machine sewing, smocking directions and supplies for the machine

Magazines
(write for rates)

Aardvark Territorial Enterprise
PO Box 2449
Livermore, CA 94550
    Newspaper jammed with all kinds of information about all kinds of embroidery, design, and things to order. I ordered the gold rings from them.

Creative Needle
Box 99
Lookout Mtn, TN 37350
    Smocking, handsewing, machine heirloom sewing, embroidery, and other needle arts.

disPatch
1042 E. Baseline
Tempe, AZ 85283
    Newspaper about quilting and machine arts

Fiberarts
50 College St.
Asheville, NC 28801
    Gallery of the best fiber artists, including those who work in machine stitchery.

Sew Beautiful
518 Madison St.
Huntsville, AL 35801
    "A magazine for those who love elegant sewing"

SewCraft
Box 1869
Warsaw, IN 46580
    Newspaper and catalog combination containing machine embroidery articles, designs and supplies.

Sew It Seams
PO Box 2698
Kirkland, WA 98083
    Bi-monthly contemporary sewing magazine.

Sew News
PO Box 1790
Peoria, IL 61656
    Monthly tabloid, mostly about garment sewing

Threads
Box 355
Newton, CT 06470
    Magazine on all fiber crafts

Treadleart
25834 Narbonne Ave., Ste. 1
Lomita, CA 90717
    Bimonthly about machine embroidery

Groups

American International Quilting
  Association
14520 Memorial Dr., #54
Houston, TX 77079

American Sewing Guild (ASG)
PO Box 50936
Indianapolis, IN 46250

Smocking Arts Guild of America (SAGA)
PO Box 795
Sterling, VA 22170-0795

Bibliography

Alexander, Eugenie, *Fabric Pictures*, Mills and Boon Ltd., London, 1967.

Ashley, Clifford W., *The Ashley Book of Knots*, Doubleday & Co., 1944.

Beaney, Jan, *The Art of the Needle,* Pantheon Books, 1988.

Bennet, dj, *Machine Embroidery with Style*, Madrona Publishers, 1980.

Butler, Anne, *Machine Stitches*, BT Batsford, Ltd., 1976.

Clucas, Joy, *Your Machine for Embroidery*, G. Bell & Sons, 1975.

———, *The New Machine Embroidery,* David & Charles, 1987.

Coleman, Anne, *The Creative Sewing Machine*, BT Batsford, 1979.

Ericson, Lois, *Fabrics. . .Reconstructed* (Lois Ericson, Box 1680, Tahoe City, CA 95730), 1985.

———, *Belts. . .Waisted Sculpture,* 1984.

Fanning, Robbie and Tony, *The Complete Book of Machine Quilting*, Chilton Book Co., 1980.

———, *The Complete Book of Machine Embroidery*, Chilton Book Co., 1986.

Gray, Jennifer, *Machine Embroidery*, Van Nostrand Reinhold, 1973.

Hall, Carolyn, *The Sewing Machine Craft Book*, Van Nostrand Reinhold, 1980.

Harding, Valerie, *Textures in Embroidery*, Watson-Guptill, New York, 1977.

Hazen, Gale Grigg, *Sew Sane* (The Sewing Place, 100 W. Rincon Ave., Ste. 105, Campbell, CA 95008; $14.95 postpaid), 1985.

Hogue, Refa D., *Machine Edgings* (c/o Treadleart, 25834 Narbonne Avenue, Lomita, CA 90717).

Hoover, Doris and Nancy Welch, *Tassels* (Apple Tree Lane, 3505 Evergreen Drive, Palo Alto, CA 94303), 1978.

Hubbard, Liz, *Thread Painting,* David & Charles, 1988.

James, Irene, *Sewing Specialties,* I. M. James Enterprises, 1982.

Lawrence and Clotilde, *Sew Smart,* IBC Publishing Co., 1984.

———, Supplement, IBC Publishing Co., 1984.

Macor, Alida, *And Sew On*, Alida Macor, 1985.

McNeill, Moyra, *Machine Embroidery—Lace and See-Through Techniques*, BT Batsford, 1985.

Nall, Mary Lou, *Mary Lou's Sewing Tchniques* (c/o Treadleart, 25834 Narbonne Avenue, Lomita, CA 90717).

Nicholas, Annwen, *Embroidery in Fashion*, Watson-Guptill, 1975.

Ota, Kimi, *Sashiko Quilting* (Kimi Ota, 10300 61st Ave. So., Seattle, Washington 98178), 1981.

Pullen, Martha, *French Hand Sewing by Machine* (518 Madison St., Huntsville, AL 35801), 1985.

Shaeffer, Claire B., *The Complete Book of Sewing Short Cuts*, Sterling Publishing Co., Inc., 1984.

Short, Eirian, *Quilting*, BT Batsford, London, 1983.

Skjerseth, Douglas Neil, *Stitchology*, Seth Publications (PO Box 1606, Novato, CA 94947), 1979.

Tecla, *Greeting Cards by the Dozen,* 1986; c/o Treadleart.

Thompson, Sue, *Decorative Dressmaking*, Rodale Press, 1985.

Turner, Mildred, *Mimi's Machine Heirloom Sewing*, (Mimi's Smock Shoppe, Inc., 130 Elizabeth Chapel, Waynesville, N.C. 28786, $12.95), 1988.

Warren, Virena, *Landscape in Embroidery*, BT Batsford, 1986.

Wiechec, Philomena, *Celtic Quilt Designs,* Celtic Design Co., 1980.

Zieman, Nancy, *The Busy Woman's Sewing Book*, Nancy's Notions Ltd., 1984.

Index

accessories, 6–8
  for knits, 150
adding-machine tape, as stabilizer, 12
Alençon lace, 100–101
American International Quilting Association, 193
American Sewing Guild, 193
appliqué, 59–80
  bubbles in, 79
  collar project with shadow appliqué, 157–163
  cording edges of, 67
  with feed dogs up, 62
  with free machining, 69
  methods of applying, 59–61
  thread, 79
  three-dimensional, 78–79
  tote bag square with, 108–110
  tote bag square with edge-stitch, 65
  tote bag square with reverse, 63
appliqué paper, 12, 60
appliqué pressing sheet, 12
attachments, 189

ball point needles, 11
bangles, 48–49
bar-tacks, 5
basting thread, wash-away, 91
Battenberg lace, 90–93
batting, 12
baubles, attaching, 44–47
beads, attaching, 44–47
belt loops, 144
belt ornament project, 164–167
bias binder, 6
bias tape, 135–136
bird collage project, 49–53

blind hemming, 16, 131–132
  for appliqué, 61, 63, 65
blind hemming foot L, 5, 31, 108, 141
blurring, 69, 78
bobbin
  tension of, 4, 36
  thick thread on, 35–38
bobbin case, 9, 36
bonnet for infant, 94–98
bridal veil, edging for, 138
bridal veiling, to hold appliqué, 70
"brides," 82
Brother 950 machine, 4
Brother Galaxie machine, 3
  settings for, 17–18
Brother International Corporation, 188
Brother Pacesetter, model XL5001, 3
bubbles, in appliqué, 79
built-in stitches, 14–16
  hemming with, 130
  for seams, 127
button foot M, 5
button loops, 144
button project, 21–25
button sewing foot, 189
button shank, 44
buttonhole foot, 5, 84, 189
buttonholes, 3
buttons, attaching, 44

cable stitching, 35–38
  tote bag square with, 38–40
canvas-type fabrics, hemming, 130
Carrickmacross, 73
  doily project with, 73–75
chain stitch, 3
chalk pencils, 8

195

changing needles, 11, 12
children's clothing, piped edges for, 141
Christmas ornament project, 99–100
circle maker, 6–7, 32, 34
circles, of decorative stitching, 160–163
Clo-Chalk, 8
closed stitches, 14
collar project, for tassels, 144–146
collars
    edging for, 138, 139
    project with shadow appliqué, 157–163
contrast, of decorative stitching, 169–170
coordinating separate elements, 167–170
cord, 142–144
    couching in Carrickmacross, 75
    covering, 137–138
    for gathering, 55–56
cording foot, 55
    attaching cord with, 35
    for thick thread couching, 31
cording
    appliqué edges, 67
    on corners, 113
    edges, 137–139
    Italian, 111–113
cordonnet
    for gathering, 56
    smocking with, 53–54
    for texture stitch, 31
corners, 34, 160
    with cording, 113
    with decorative stitching, 172, 173
    of lace, 122–123
    on narrow hems, 134
cotton thread, 9
couching
    cord in Carrickmacross, 75
    thread, 31
covered wire, tassel project with, 146–147
crocheted cotton, for texture stitch, 31
crocheted edges, 139
curves, smooth filling of, 84
cutting wheel, 9
cutwork, 81–82, 84
    needlecase project of, 82–84

darning foot, 8, 34–35, 51, 110
darning plate, 5, 189
darning stitch, 18
darning thread, 10
decorative stitches, 150–180
    circles of, 160–163
    combinations of, 168

    for coordinating separate elements, 167–170
    scarf project with, 170–173
    tote bag square of, 154–156
denim rug project, fringed, 41–43
diameter, 161
diamonds, piecing, 126
doily, of Carrickmacross, 73–75
doll tassel project, 147
double needles, 11
    for hemming sheers, 130
    on knits, 129–130
dressmaker's carbon, 8
Dritz Trace-B-Gone Tracing paper, 8

earrings project, 86–90
edge-stitch appliqué, tote bag square with, 65
edges
    bias tape for, 135–136
    cording, 137–139
    crocheted, 139
    narrow, zigzag stitch for, 136
    piping, 141
    rolled and whipped, 115–117
    shaped, covered wire for, 136–137
    shell, 134
    as structural detail, 156–157
elastic
    for gathering, 56
    reshaping knits with, 139
    smocking with, 55
embroidery, pressing pad for, 9
encroaching zigzag stitch, 28, 30
English piecing by machine, 126–127
Entredeux, 115, 118–119
    attaching to lace insertion, 119–120
even-feed foot, 8, 107
eyelet maker, 7
eyelets, 73, 74, 84

fabric. *See also* transparent fabric
    fringing, 40–41
fagoting, 120–121
fake lapped hem, 124–125
feather stitch, 21
    for seams, 127
feed dogs, covering, 18
fiberfill, 12
Fine Fuse, 12
fishing line, for shaped edges, 137
flannel, 12
fleece, 12
florist's wire, for shaped edges, 137

196

flowers, 28–29
   centers of, 27
   project with sheers and overlays, 69–71
   of ribbon, 98, 124
foot controller, 3
four-ply yarn, on bobbin, 36
Fray-Check, 102, 156
free-machine embroidery, 16–21
   for appliqué, 69
   cabling with, 37–38
   quilting with, 110
   for seams, 127–128
freezer wrap, 13, 108
French handsewing, 114
French seams, 115, 116
   side cutter for, 7
fringe
   thread, 139–141
   denim rug project with, 41–43
   yarn and fabric, 40–41
fringing fork, 40–41
fusibles, 12
   for appliqué, 60

gathering, 55–56
   lace edging, 119
   rolled and whipped edges, 117
   with smocking, 53
gathering foot, 7, 56
general purpose foot, 189
gimp, for gathering, 56
glacé finished quilting thread, 10
glass beads, pre-strung, 47
gluestick, 72, 91
greeting card project, 32–35
Greist circle maker, 6
groups, 193
guiding the eye, 175

Halloween costumes, 137
handkerchief project, wedding, 121–122
handles, of tote bag, 183–184
handpieced quilts, imitating, 126
heirloom sewing by machine, 114–124
hemming presser feet, 132
hems
   blind, 131–132
   with built-in stitches, 130
   with double needle on sheers, 130
   fake lapped, 124–125
   narrow, 132–135
   quilting of, 130

roll and shell, 134–135
   turning once, 129–130
hemstitching, 94
hemstitching needles, 11–12
herringbone effect, 177
hexagons, piecing, 126
hoop, 8
   for free-machining, 16
   free-machining without, 18
   working with, 70
horizontal lines, 177
   in clothing, 175
hotline telephone number, 4

infant's bonnet, 94–98
insertion (lace), 117, 119–120
interfacing, 13
iridescent sparkle, 164–165
Irish lace, 73
Italian cording, 111–113

Japanese Sashiko, 37
Jiffy Fuse, 12

knits
   accessories for, 150
   double needles on, 129–130
   reshaping with elastic, 139
   stitching over thread on, 125–126

lace, 57
   Alençon, 100–101
   attaching to lace, 120
   attaching to rolled and whipped edges, 119
   Battenberg, 90–93
   gathering edging of, 119
   sewing on, 133–134
lace insertion, 117
   attaching entredeux to, 119–120
lacy spiderwebs, 84
layers
   of net, moiré look from, 79
   of transparent fabric, 75
leather needles, 12
lettering, circles of, 160–163
lines, 151–154
   in clothing, 175
   purpose of, 180
lingerie, edging for, 134
lining of tote bag, 182, 185, 187
long-cuts, xi

loops, for belts and buttons, 144
lubricant, silicone, 8

machine-embroidery, supply sources for, 190–191
machine-embroidery cotton, 9
magazines
  ideas from, 3
  sources of, 192
Magic Polyweb, 12
maintenance of machine, 13
metallic thread, 10, 86
  sources of, 190
milliner's wire, 146
  for shaped edges, 137
mirror images, 15–16
moiré look, from net layers, 79
monk's cord, 4, 25, 142–144
monofilament, 10
  for attaching cord, 35
  for couching, 65
  for quilting, 107
motifs, 157

narrow edge, zigzag stitch for, 136
narrow hemmer, 67, 134
needle plate, 3
needle threader, 3
needlecase project, of cutwork, 82–84
needlelace
  to attach beads, 45–46
  free-machined, 84–86
needles, 11–12
  selecting, 10, 62
  for special threads, 10
  thick thread through, 31
needleweaving, 104–106
New Home gathering foot, 7
New Home presser feet, 4
new machines, breaking in, 16–17
No-Fray, 102, 156
notebook, 1–3, 5, 21, 81
  built-in stitches in, 14–16
  cabling sample for, 36–37
  fabric for samples in, 9
  thread samples in, 9
nylon filament, 137
nylon stocking, for collage project, 50–51
nylon thread, 9

oiling, 13
open-space stitching, 81–103
  Battenberg lace as, 90–93
  hemstitching as, 94–98
  needlelace as, 84–86
  in rings, 99–100
open stitches, 14
openwork, 84
  sleeve project, 104–106
overlock stitch foot G, 5

patch pockets, 65
patterns, for collar, 158
pearl cotton, 138
  for texture stitch, 31
pendant project, 21–25
pierce point needles, 11
  vs. universal point needles, 62
pincushion project, of Alençon lace, 101–103
pintucking, 96
piping edges, 141
plaid matcher, 8
plastic sandwich bags, as fusible, 12, 61
pockets, in tote bag, 182–183
presser feet, 4–6, 189
presser foot holder, 189
pressing pad, 9
projects
  Alençon pincushion, 101–103
  belt ornament, 164–167
  bird collage, 49–53
  bird-shaped Battenberg lace, 90–93
  buttons and pendants, 21–25
  Carrickmacross doily, 73–75
  Christmas ornaments, 99–100
  covered wire tassel, 146–147
  cutwork needlecase, 82–84
  doll tassel, 147
  earrings, 86–90
  flower of sheers and overlays, 69–71
  fringed denim rug, 41–43
  greeting card, 32–35
  infant's bonnet, 94–98
  openwork on sleeves, 104–106
  purse, 175–180
  scarf, 170–173
  shadow-appliqué collar, 157–163
  shadow work picture, 75–78
  shoe ornament, 173–175
  tassel collar, 144–146
  tassel tops by machine, 147–149
  three-dimensional appliqué, 78–79
  wedding handkerchief, 121–124
puckers
  in appliqué, 61, 79
  in quilts, 107

pulling threads together, 57–58
purse project, 175–180

quilting, 37, 107–113
    with free-machining, 110
    hand-pieced, imitating, 126
    of hems, 130
    tote bag square with, 108–110
quilting thread, 10

radius, 161
rayon thread, 9
reverse appliqué, 62
    tote bag square of, 63
ribbed bands, side cutter for, 7
ribbon
    cabling with, 37
    roses from, 98
    rosettes of, 124
ribbon thread, 10
rickrack stitch, 22
rings, stitching in, 81, 99–100
roll and shell hemming, 134–135
rolled and whipped edges, 115–117
    attaching lace to, 119
    gathering, 117
roses, from ribbon, 98
rosettes, of ribbon, 124
ruffler, 7
ruffles, gathering, 103
rug project, with fringed denim, 41–43

safety pins, 107
samples, fabric for, 9
Saral, 8
Sashiko (Japan), 37
satin stitch, 22, 27, 152
    for appliqué, 62
scallop stitch, joining veiling with, 127
scalloped lace
    attaching to fabric, 134
    as insertion, 117
    joining, 117–118
scarf project, with decorative stitching, 170–173
scissors, 8
scribbling, 71–73
seam guide, 5
seams, 114–128
    built-in stitches for, 127
    free-machining for, 127–128
    French, 115, 116

    on knits, 125–126
    with side-cutter, 125
    as structural detail, 156–157
seed beads, attaching, 45
sewing machines
    breaking in new, 16–17
    maintenance of, 13
    settings for, 13, 16
    starting and stopping, 4
sewing thread, 9
shadow-appliqué collar project, 157–163
shaped edges, covered wire for, 136–137
shapes, filling in, 29–30
shell edging, 134
shirring, 7
shisha mirrors, 47–49
shoe ornament project, 173–175
side-cutter, 7, 115
    seams with, 125
silicone lubricant, 8
silk thread, 10
single-hole needle plate, 3
sleeves, openwork project on, 104–106
smocking, 53–55
Smocking Arts Guild of America, 193
snap-on presser foot holder, 4
soap, 8
soutache, 34
stabilizers, 12–13
    using with hoop, 16
stained-glass method of appliqué, 62
stair-step zigzag method, 29–30
stay-stitching, side cutter for, 7
Stitch Witchery, 12
stitches, programming, 4
stitch-in-a-ditch, 108
straight stitch appliqué, tote bag square with, 65, 67
straight stitch foot, 5, 189
stretch, adding to fabric, 55
stretch stitch, 22
structural details, 156–157
supplies, 8–13
    sources of, 190–193

T-square, 8
tailor tacking foot, 120, 139
tassels, 144
    collar project, 144–146
    covered wire for, 146–147
tear-away stabilizer, 76
Teflon pressing sheet, 12, 60
telephone number, hotline, 4

tension
  adjustment of, 14–15
  of bobbin, 4, 36
  for gathering, 56
texture of lines, 153–154
texture stitches, 26–58
  with thick threads, 31
  zigzag as, 29–30
thick thread, 31
thick thread on bobbin, 35–38
  embroidery on smocking with, 54–55
thread, 9–10
  couching, 65
  for heirlooms, 115
  metallic, 86
  pulling together, 57–58
  selection of, 10
  sources of, 190
thread appliqué, 79
thread bars, 82
thread fringe, 139–141
three-dimensional appliqué, 78–79
topstitching, 141
  presser foot for, 5
topstitching needles, 10, 11
  for thick thread, 31
tote bag, 181–187
  construction of, 182–187
tote bag squares
  with appliqué and quilting, 108–110
  with cabling, 38–40
  of decorative stitches, 154–156
  with edge-stitch appliqué, 65
  finishing, 181–182
  with Italian cording, 111–113
  modified reverse appliqué, 63
  with straight-stitch appliqué, 65, 67
transparent fabric, 69
  hemming with double needle on, 130
  layers of, 75
transparent zigzag foot, 5, 31, 111
trapunto, 79, 111
Tri-Flow lubricant, 8

triple needle, 11
tulle, 108
twill tape, 16
typing paper, as stabilizer, 12

universal-point needle, 11
  vs. pierce-point needle, 62
upholstery, cord for, 141

V-shaped lines, in clothing, 175
veiling, joining with scallop stitch, 127
vertical lines, 177
  in clothing, 175
Viking button reed, 44

walking foot, 8, 107
water-erasable markers, 8
water-soluble stabilizer, 13, 57, 75, 81
waxed quilting thread, 10
wedding gowns, 137
wedding handkerchief project, 121–122
wedge needles, 12
weed-trimmer line, for shaped edges, 137
weight, of decorative stitching, 169–170
whipped edges. *See* rolled and whipped edges
whipping, 19–20
width of lines, 152
wing needles, 11–12
wire, covering for shaped edges, 136–137
Wonder-Under Transfer Fusing Web, 12
woolly overlock, 9

yarn, fringing, 40–41
Yasui Sewing Machine Company, 188

zigzag presser foot, 111
  transparent, 5
zigzag stitch
  encroaching, 28, 30
  for filling in shapes, 29–30
  for narrow edge, 136
zipper foot, 108, 189